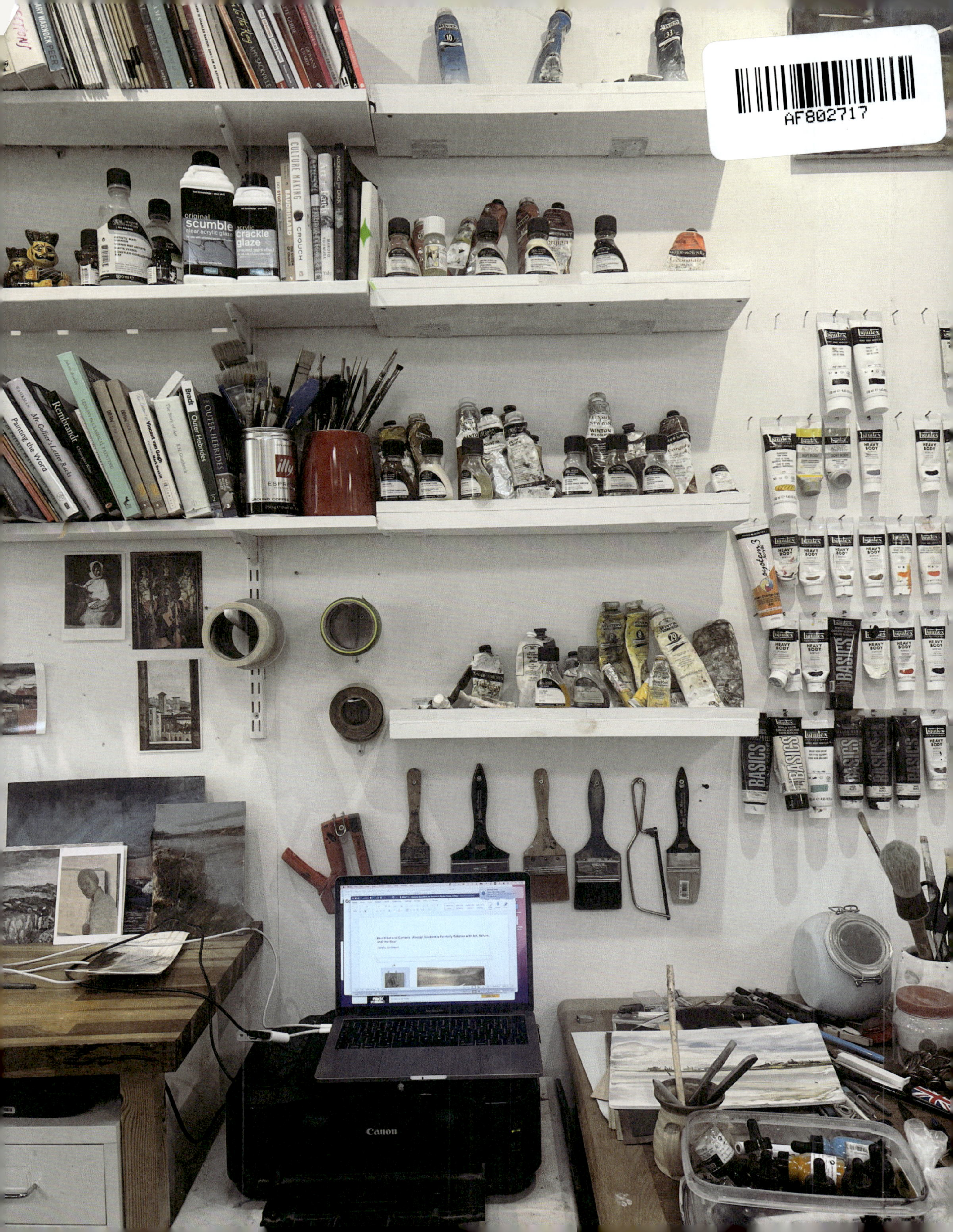

original
scumble
clear acrylic glaze
acrylic
crackle
glaze
CULTURE MAKING
CROUCH
Rembrandt
Painting the Word
Bradt
Outer Hebrides
OUTER HEBRIDES
Vincent van Gogh
illy
liquitex
HEAVY BODY
BASICS
system3
Canon

Quod libet

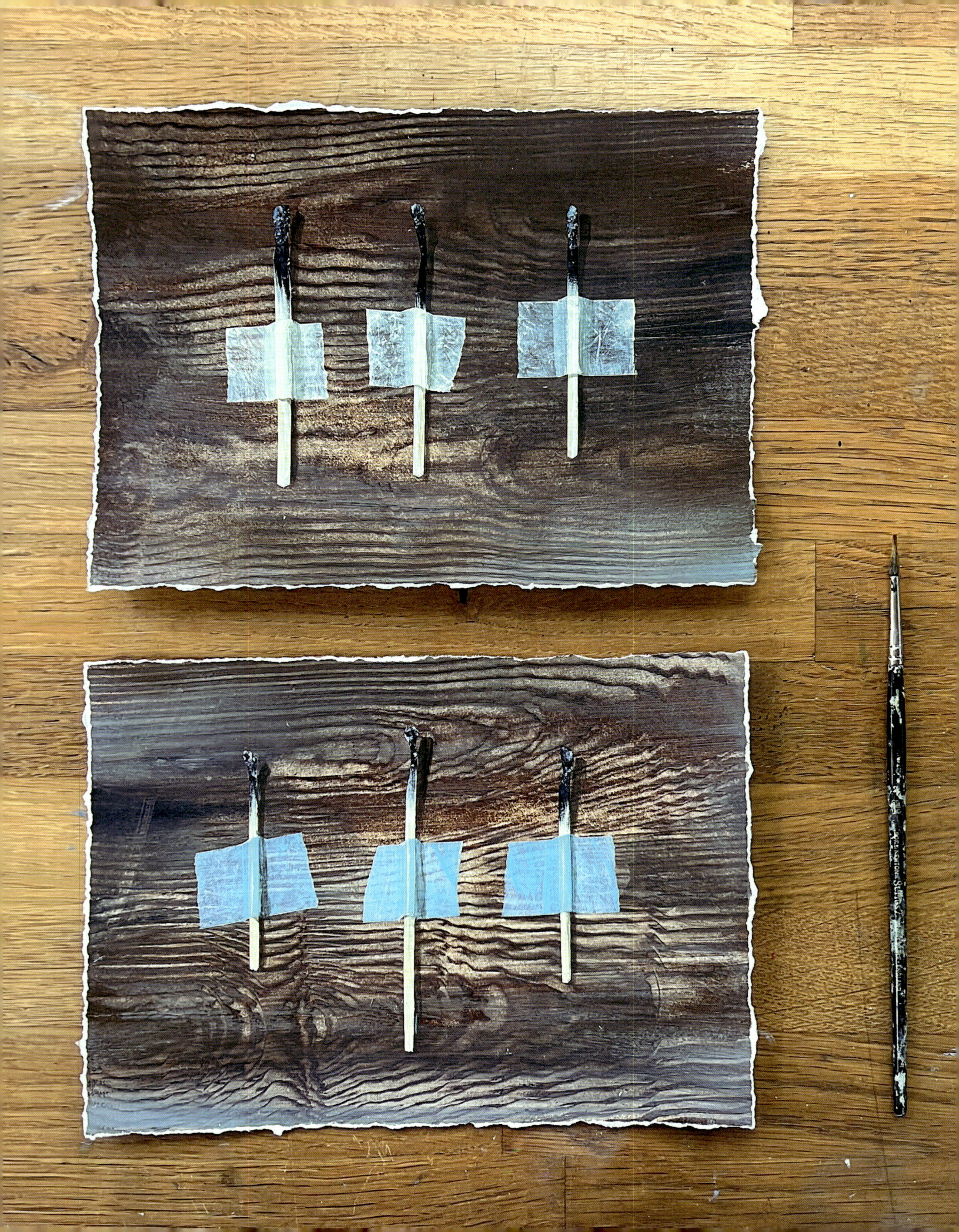

Alastair Gordon

Quodlibet

Anomie Publishing

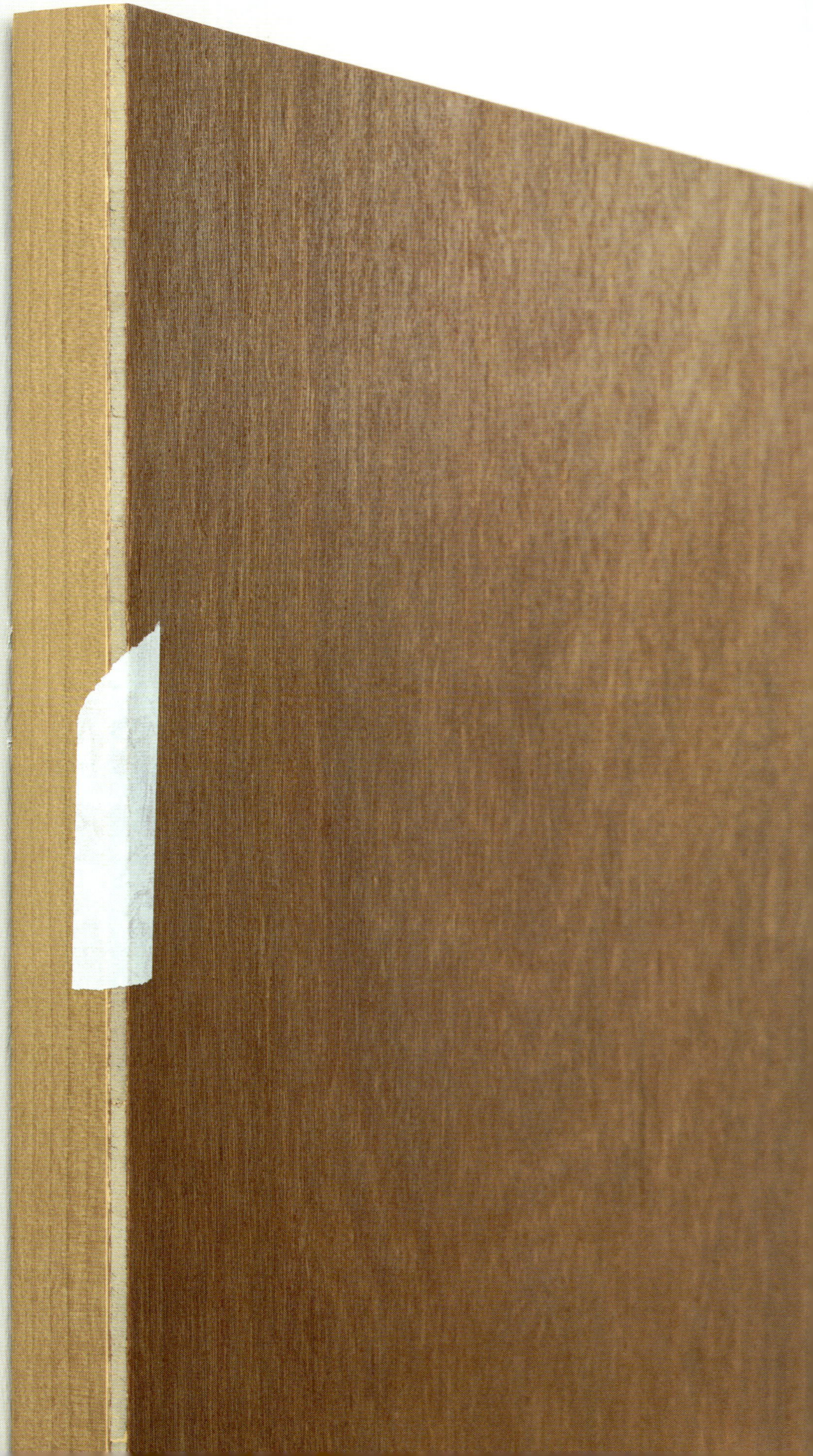

Contents

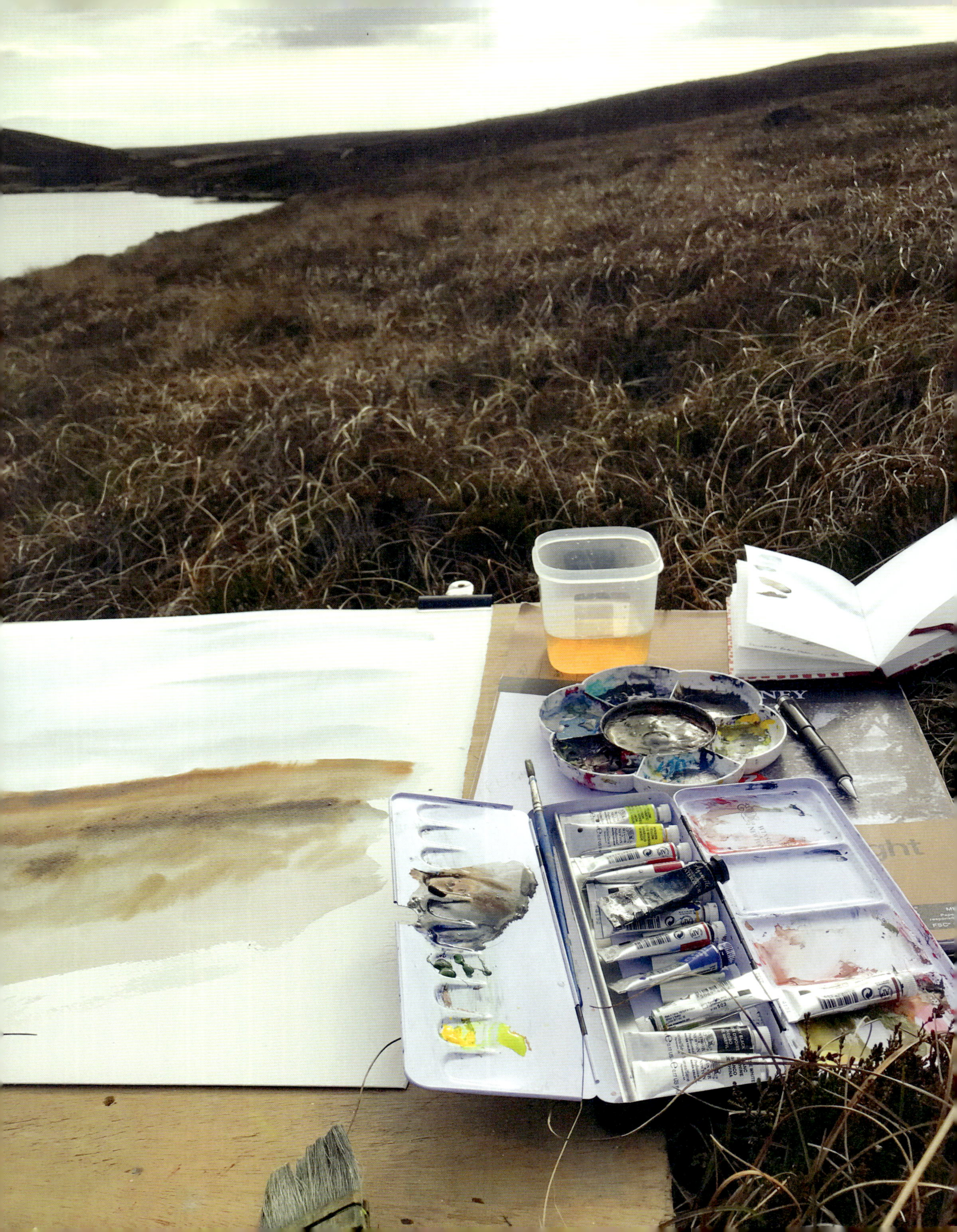

Introduction

Julia Lucero

Sitting on a grassy mound in a Scottish bog on a clear summer's day, Alastair Gordon meditates with his eyes wide open. He looks to the horizon and considers the variations of colours rising from the earth through to the sky. The waters mirror the firmament, the tall grasses move to the rhythm of the wind. The ground is wet and cold. Attentive, his gaze stretches across the sky until it meets the open sea. Silent meditation in nature is an important part of the artist's practice of coming forth into the light of things.[1] Gordon chooses to contemplate the beauty and wonder of the natural world, informed by the concept of the *axis mundi*, that metaphysical and mystical connecting point where heaven meets Earth.

Although Gordon has found a relentless source of inspiration in the outdoors, and sketches abundantly on his Scottish wanderings, the transcendent is often rendered unassumingly in his work. Turning the attention away from the landscape, he introduces glimpses of the artist's presence with his characteristic yellow masking tape, or the charcoal crayon he has used. He sketches what he sees, and then paints to expound on what was seen. Informed by seventeenth-century quodlibet, a singular *trompe-l'oeil* painting technique, Gordon's invisible brush mark and collection of letters, postcards, photographs and texts, collated together on a wood-grain background, offer a rare opportunity to the viewer. The gift of a second look. Another glance at what is seen, before the illusion is revealed. And, once the veil of artifice has been lifted, something mystical happens: an ordinary item, a snapshot of everyday life, has been instilled with profound value. Something as simple as a matchstick becomes sacred. The object represents the universe it comprises: the wood that used to be a robust tree, full of energy, in the middle of a luxuriant forest by some high mountains. The hands it passed through before it became the commonplace item one can hold. The anticipation of striking it, the candle it lit, or the stove it turned on, to feed, to keep warm, to give light or to pray. The scent and smoke a simple flick of the wrist created while using it. In Gordon's work, everything shares life and has its importance. Even the short lifespan of a matchstick carries the power of divine creation within it.

For Gordon, painting is simultaneously a prayer, a sacrament and an act of devotion. His visual repertoire of everyday objects highlights the sacramental qualities of a painting. More than a mere suggestion, the sacrament is the bread and wine during Holy Communion, or the wedding rings exchanged by two beings to symbolise their union. A painting is then the embodiment of something holy, and eternal. The blank canvas becomes a vessel that upholds the dignity of the mundane, while, at the same time, to paint is to partake in something of the divine.

Through the act of painting, Gordon interprets what he has seen and sketched while experiencing nature or life indoors. He squeezes the gap between himself and the work, only allowing for an honest exploration of what might manifest when accessing the *axis mundi*. Treating all subjects with open curiosity, he considers the wood-grain of a beautiful slat of oak as he might the paper aeroplanes lovingly folded with his daughter. Rendering the worn-out shoes of missionaries. Every chip, crease and stain, representing the life of its carrier and their vocation of care for the world, is as valuable to him as the portrait of their owner. To Gordon, a glowing sunrise evokes and encapsulates the divine as much as a feather held in place by yellow masking tape.

Gordon's snapshots of life and everyday items become a vehicle to address his concerns regarding truth, beauty, death and the value of life. His work is as much about the act of painting itself as it is about finding the extraordinary in the simplest of forms.[2] With reverence to the world in which he lives, he is an artist who sets his own pace, with quiet contemplation at the centre of his practice.

Julia Lucero is Associate Director of Nahmad Projects, London

1 'Come forth into the light of things, Let nature be your teacher' is from the William Wordsworth poem, 'The Tables Turned', in William Wordsworth and Samuel Taylor Coleridge, *Lyrical Ballads: with a Few Other Poems* (London: J & A Arch, 1798).

2 David Trigg, interview with Alastair Gordon, *Studio International*, 20 September 2021, accessed 26 January 2023, https://www.studiointernational.com/index.php/alastair-gordon-interview-quodlibet-aleph-contemporary-christianity.

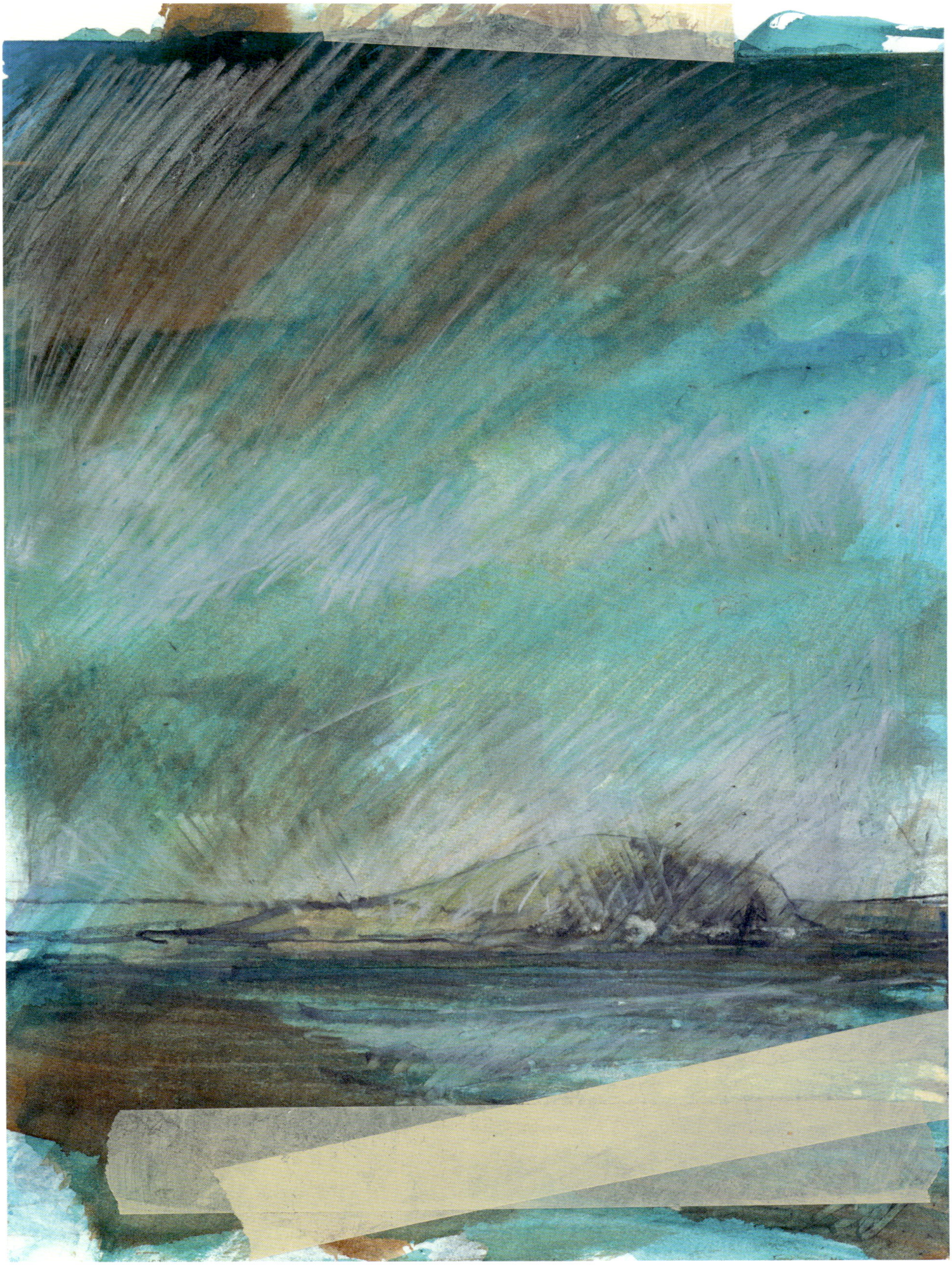

Where Once a Hermitage (North Berwick) 2021 Watercolour, ink, graphite and coloured pencil on paper 30 × 23 cm

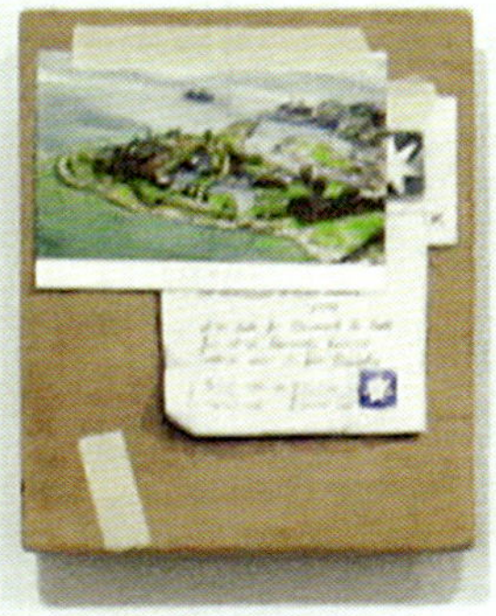

Installation view of **Danish Departed** exhibition at Husk Gallery, London, 2013

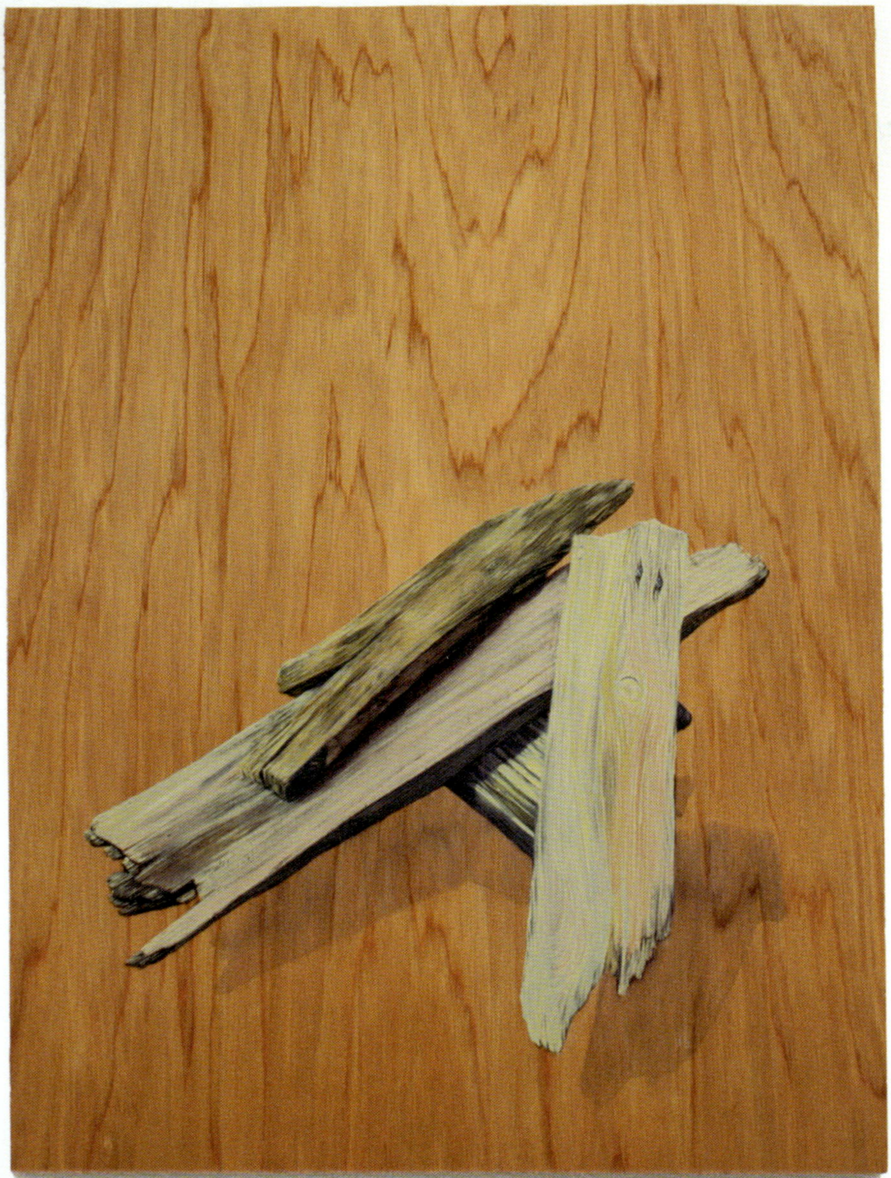

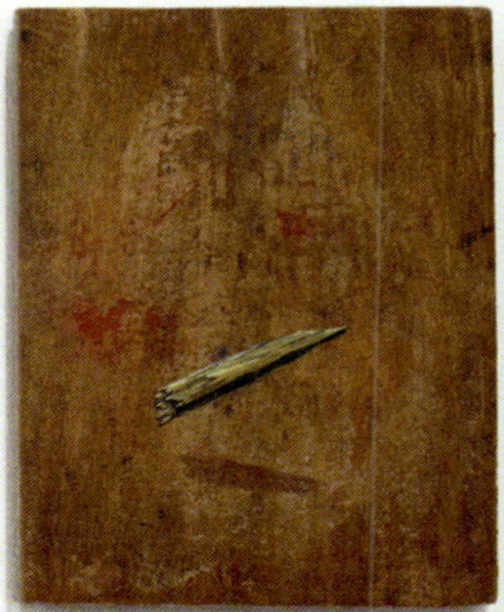

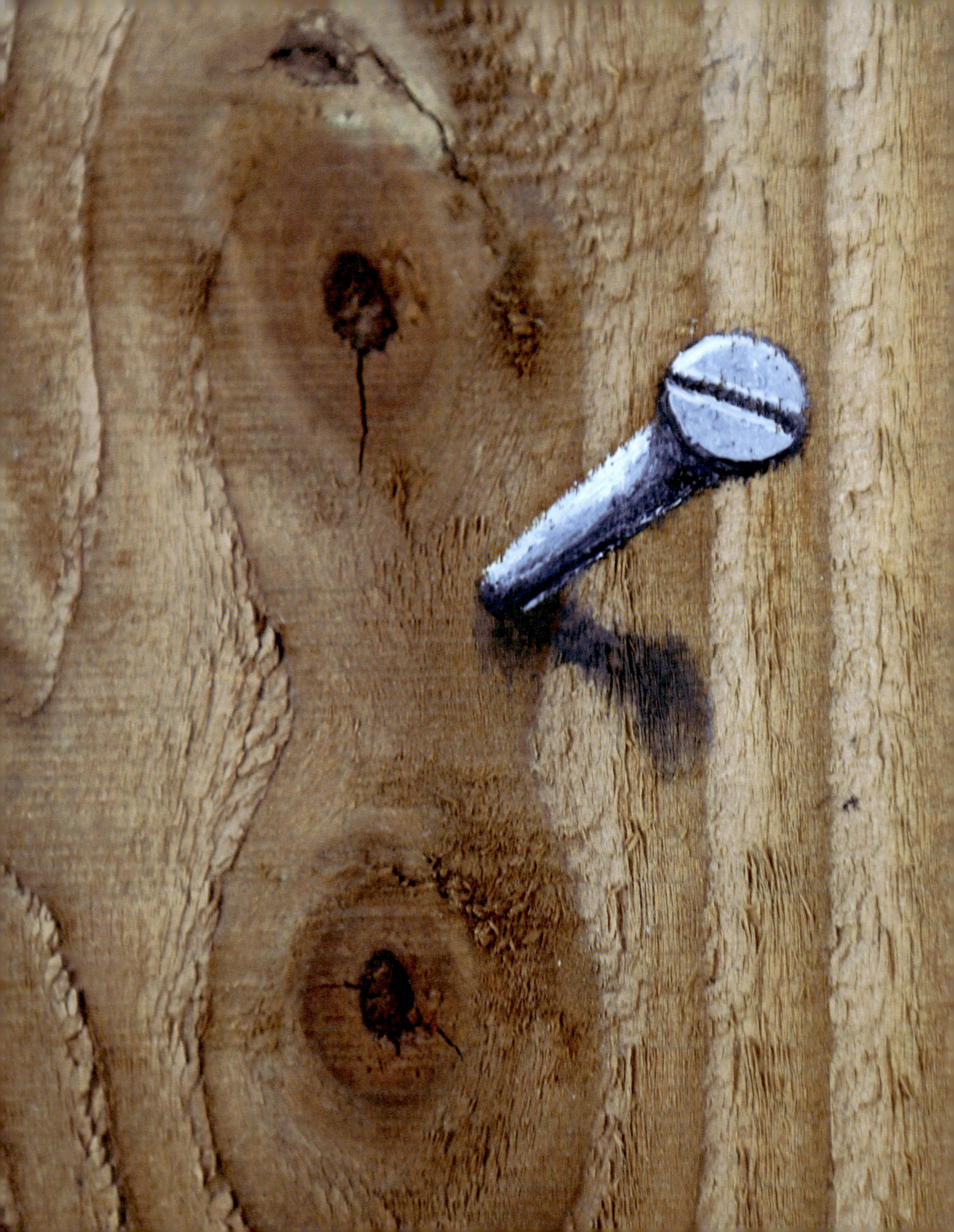

Quodlibet and Cortesia: Alastair Gordon's Painterly Debates with Art, Nature and 'the Real'

Jorella Andrews

1

Stretching up and over the drawing table in his studio, Alastair Gordon lifts down a small wooden plank, somewhat splintered at the edges, and shows it to me. This is *Nail*, from 2012 (fig. 1 (detail) and p. 35), named for the small *trompe-l'oeil* iron nail, which appears to jut out of it, into our space. It was painted, during a research residency in the studio of Paul Cézanne at Les Lauves on the outskirts of Aix-en-Provence, on a piece of wood his hosts had gifted to him. Speculatively, it was a floorboard from Cézanne's studio. The painted nail references the actual nail hammered into one of the studio walls, on which, reputedly, Cézanne would hang his jacket. Gordon describes *Nail* as a 'happy accident' and a 'genesis piece', which pivoted his work in a new direction.[1]

Crucially, *Nail* marks the beginning of a more conscious artistic commitment to two intertwining factors. One – and this is how Gordon's practice is most consistently positioned – is a commitment to the ancient painterly technique of *trompe-l'oeil* (French for 'deceives the eye') with its reality-bending provocations and, more specifically, to a sub-genre of *trompe-l'oeil* known as *quodlibet* (Latin for 'what you will', 'what you please' or 'whatever you want'). The other commitment, just as significant as his immersion in quodlibet and inseparable from it, I will describe as an ever-deepening induction into the agencies of wood.

2

Painted quodlibets rose to prominence in Europe in the seventeenth century. They are often referred to as 'letter-rack paintings', in which everyday items, mostly associated with communication and correspondence (accumulations of the affairs and cares of humankind?), are depicted realistically, to scale, and in an apparently un-staged and improvised manner.[2] Quodlibets succeed by convincing viewers that what they are looking at – or rather overlooking – is an ordinary, already anticipated, and thus unremarkable physical component of the environment, a portion of actuality as opposed to a painted figure on a painted ground. As such, they follow in the ancient tradition of the artist Parrhasius, whose

Fig. 1 **Nail** detail 2012 Oil on found wood 22.5 × 9 cm

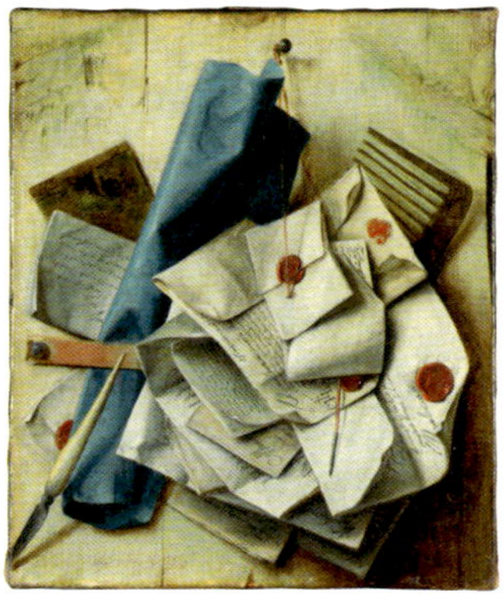

Fig. 2
Cornelis Gijsbrechts
Quodlibet or 'Vanitas-Stillleben' 1675
Oil on canvas 41 × 34.5 cm
Wallraf-Richartz-Museum & Fondation Corboud, Cologne
© Rheinisches Bildarchiv Köln, Wolfgang Meier, rba_d013160

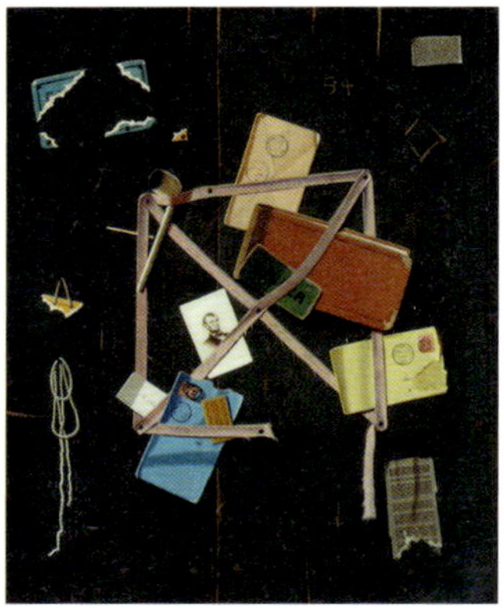

Fig. 3
John Frederick Peto
Old Time Letter Rack 1894
Oil on canvas 76.5 × 64.1 cm
Museum of Fine Arts, Boston. Bequest of Maxim Karolik/ Bridgeman Images

painted curtain, Pliny the Elder tells us,[3] tricked even his most discerning critics into thinking that the work of art they had been invited to judge lay behind it. In quodlibets, this tricky space is intensified. As Manuel van der Veen has put it, *trompe-l'oeil* painting 'occupies a classical support [a piece of canvas or wood], but only to be its alienation, because the procedure stacks other depicted supports onto the image support (e.g. planks of wood, papers, canvases, etc). With each depiction, the physical support is pushed forward piece by piece [see fig. 2]. Therefore ... the carrier is suppressed by both its multiplication and by its disappearance.'[4]

The visual misdirection on which quodlibet (and *trompe-l'oeil* painting more broadly) depends requires from artists the most exquisite visual acuity. Paradoxically, they also cultivate this acuity in their viewers. For as viewers become visually enthralled and intrigued, they are also increasingly undeceived – which is part of the fun. In other words, these works begin to present as also having a more serious, even pedagogic character. Close looking is followed by still closer looking, and questions inevitably arise, both speculative and personal, about the nature, content, workings and intentions of perception and communication. Key, of course, are queries about the transitions these paintings orchestrate between prosaic, preconditioned or non-seeing sight and the rigour, surprise and openness of purposeful visual investigation where nothing is taken for granted. Viewers discover they have been tutored by *trompe-l'oeil*. A door has suddenly opened (or a curtain been pulled aside) into new domains of visual awareness and insight.

In his 1989 book *Real Presences* (which has the reality-querying subtitle *Is there anything in what we say?*), the literary critic, writer and educator George Steiner applied the concept of *cortesia* to hospitable, artistic invitations into learning of this kind. Cortesia, which he described as unfolding 'out of Christian

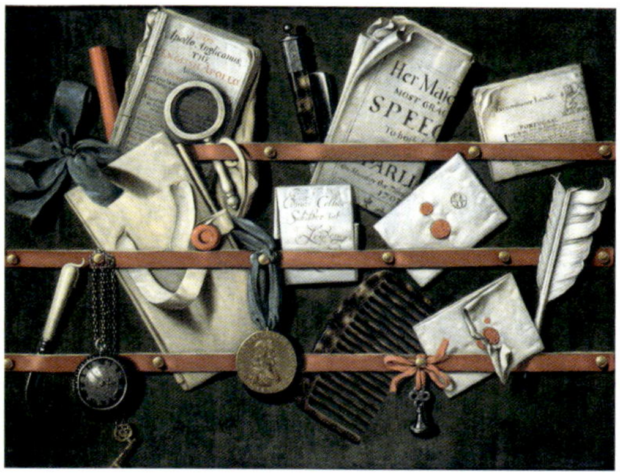

Fig. 4
Edwaert Collier
Trompe l'Oeil Letter Rack with Watch and Seal 1702–03
Oil on canvas 49.5 × 65.4 cm
Museum De Lakenhal, Leiden

romance and the western formulations of "courtly" love,'[5] may be described as the gracious intellectual welcome and elemental trust between artists and beholders, writers and readers, composers and audiences, without which apprenticeship into the novelties of art cannot occur.[6] In Steiner's words: 'Where freedoms meet, where the integral liberty of donation or withholding of the work of art encounters our own liberty of reception or refusal, *cortesia*, what I have called tact of heart, is of the essence.'[7] In their reflections on *Real Presences*, the physicists Wilson Poon and Tom McLeish have emphasised the radical hospitality of cortesia. 'According to Steiner,' they write, 'the "discipline of courtesy" consists of seeking to hear the language of the stranger accurately, "lexical *cortesia*" and being sensitive to "syntax, to the grammars which are the sinew of articulate forms". When we do that, we discover that "we have met before".'[8]

Steiner was writing about relations between persons within artistic contexts. But I would like also to include, indeed foreground, certain works of art as unassuming visual material carriers and communicators of cortesia – including, as described, initially 'deceptive' works of *trompe-l'oeil* and quodlibet with their inbuilt dynamics of hiding and revealing; their open-handed modes of holding back, proffering and impressing.

During the seventeenth century – particularly in the Dutch Republic, then the global centre for technological advancement in optics and Europe's most literate nation – burning questions were raised about perception and communication. Quodlibets were important painterly sites for reflection and visual commentary on such matters. Well-known examples from the period include *Trompe l'Oeil Letter Rack* (1658) by Wallerant Vaillant, *Trompe l'Oeil of a Letter Rack with a Proclamation* (1672) by Cornelis Gijsbrechts, and the work of Edwaert Collier, a Dutch artist of Scottish heritage, who moved from the Dutch

Republic to London in the 1690s (while the Dutch-born William III was King of England, Scotland and Ireland). Here, as was the case with Gijsbrechts and others, his large output of quodlibet paintings – including *Trompe l'Oeil Letter Rack with Watch and Seal* (1702-03, fig. 4) – intermix depictions of personal correspondence with mass-media material: broadsheets, newspapers, pamphlets and proclamations, often referencing political events. However, Collier sometimes slightly altered (or tampered with) the documents he was depicting.[9] As the American critic Caryn James reports, in *Trompe l'Oeil of Newspapers, Letters, and Writing Implements on a Wooden Board* (1699) (which was included in the 2022–23 exhibition *Cubism and the Trompe l'Oeil Tradition* at the Metropolitan Museum of Art in New York), he reproduces *The London Gazette* and a pamphlet commenting on the Glorious Revolution but 'tweaks the spelling and words in the texts they are based on'.[10] By such means, his works raised questions: about the persuasiveness of illusionism with its 'rhetorics' of veracity and about the problematics of discernment in the burgeoning realms of seventeenth-century public and mass communication. How do we know whether a communication is real or true if its original form of expression is unavailable? In Gordon's words: 'It's fascinating how a seemingly innocent painting, whimsical, all that stuff thrown onto a board, could actually be a tool for political subversion, even for political revolution.'

Gordon describes quodlibet as a 'secret corner of western painting history', having remained unaware of the genre until he himself had been painting in this vein for some time. As with those seventeenth-century forerunners, many of his quodlibets have also depicted correspondence. Postcards first became core motifs in 2013, during a year-long residency at Departure, a former seamen's mission in east London. While there, Gordon came across old postcards and letters the sailors had variously written or received. He started to paint them as if they'd been stuck or pinned onto wooden boards (fig. 5). In his words: 'They'd appear almost as though they were some sort of museum artefact, and there was this play between the real and the fake, and between something that's an artefact and something that's an artifice. And then, looking at the wood-grain in the background, you'd be left asking whether this was a painted ground or not, and does it matter.'[11]

Numerous iterations of works featuring postcards followed, including records of postcards received by the artist. *All the Postcards Sent to My Studio (01.12.14 to 25.12.14)* (2015, p. 55) is just one example. Many of the postcards referenced here were received from friends and were reproductions of works of art. Painted postcards were also at the heart of Gordon's 2017 solo exhibition,

Fig. 5 **Postcards and Letters** detail 2013 Oil on wood approx 17 × 12 cm

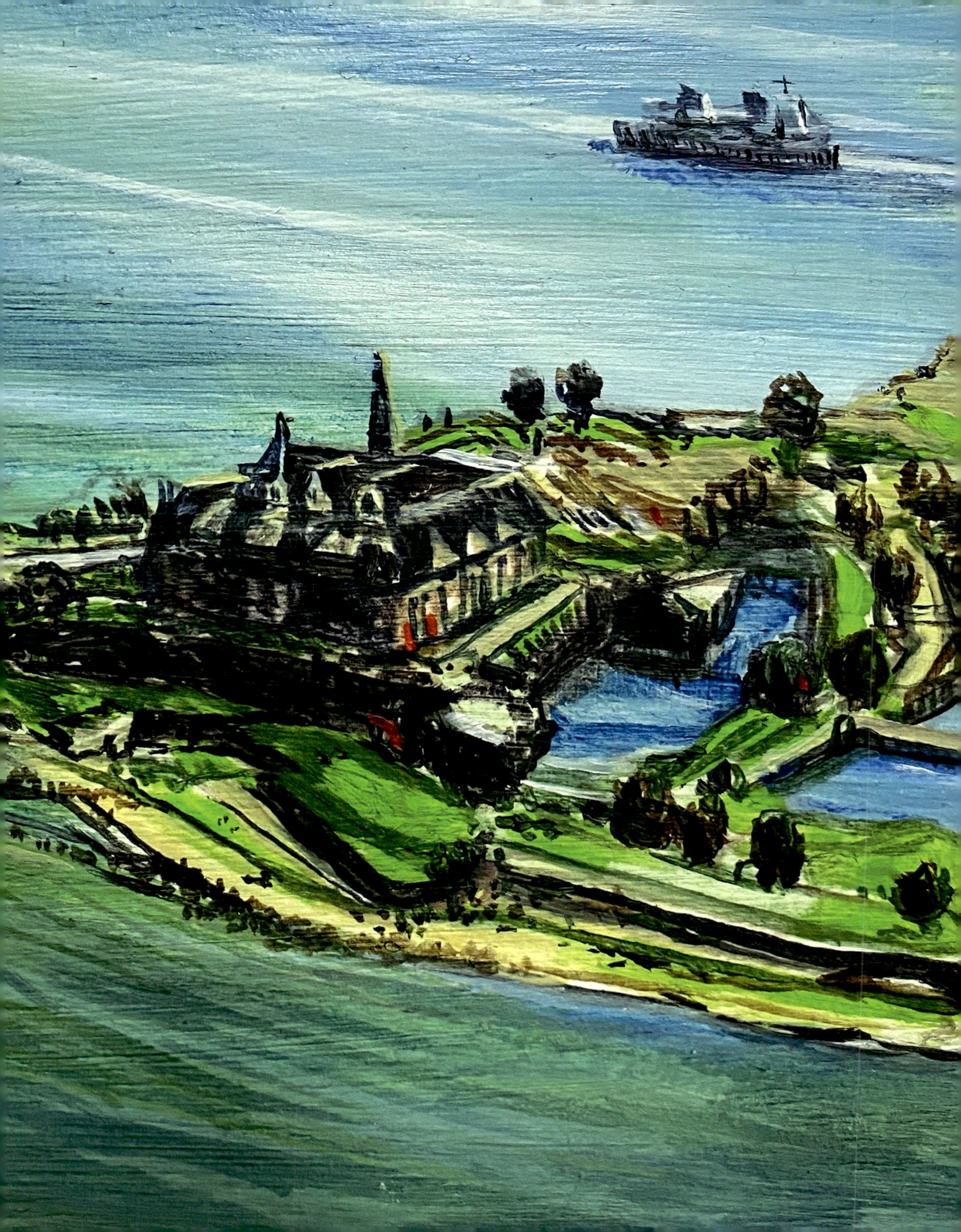

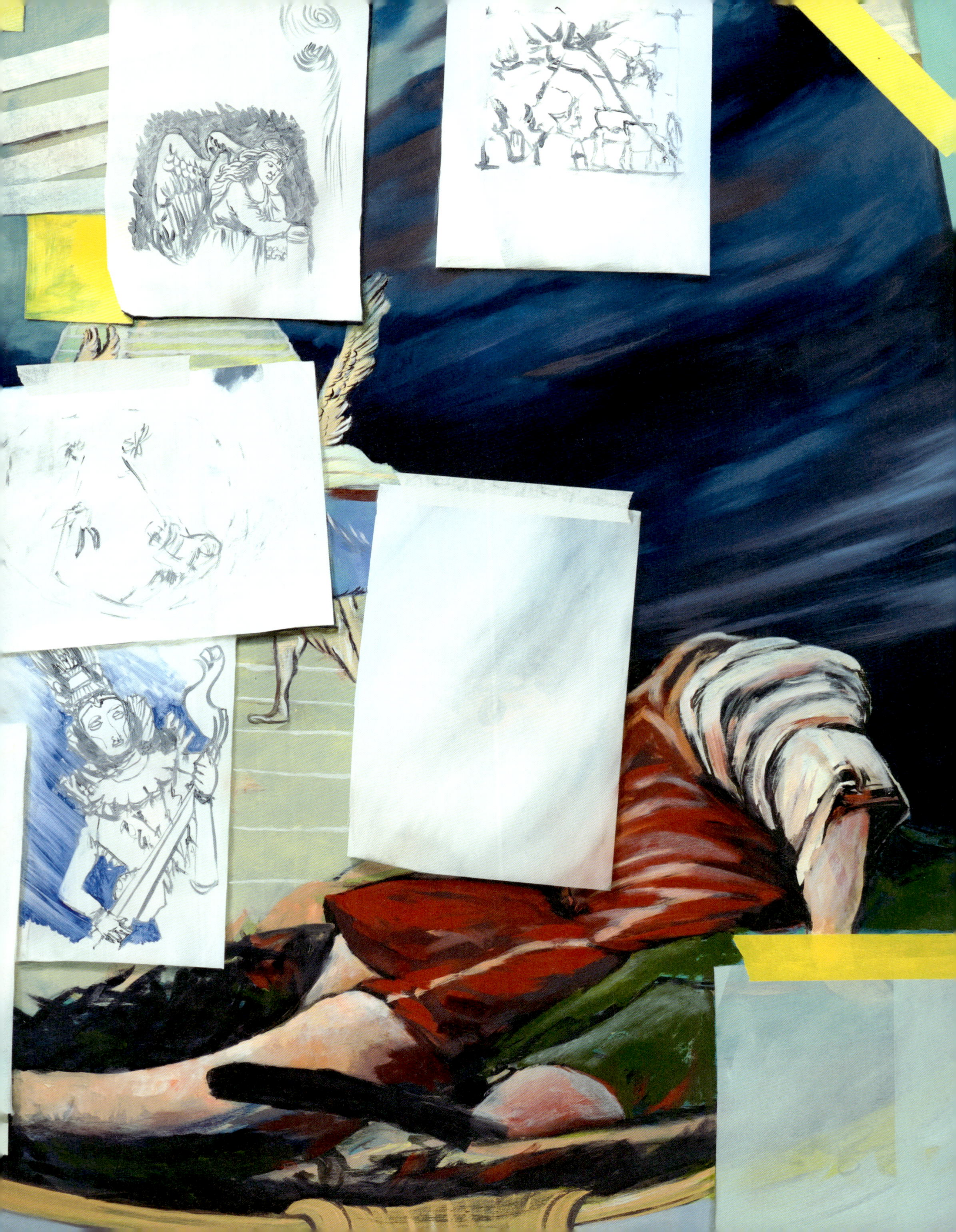

Souvenirs from the Waste Land, at the Ahmanson Gallery, Irvine, California.[12] This time, they were sourced from the Ahmanson's extraordinary catalogued archive of more than 18,000 postcards in which Gordon had been invited to immerse himself a year earlier.

Returning to historical matters, the output of quodlibets appears to have lessened in the art world of the eighteenth and early-nineteenth centuries. But in the later nineteenth century, such painters as the Americans William M Harnett and John Frederick Peto returned to the genre. As in *Old Time Letter Rack* (1894, (fig. 3), there is an elegiac sensibility to Peto's approach with which several quodlibets by Gordon have affinities. In the words of the contemporary master woodcarver David Esterly, who made an in-depth study of painted quodlibets: 'The melancholic Peto offers up a tattered world of dangling straps, half-finished cameo portraits, and disintegrating remnants of tickets and newspaper clippings.'[13] Gordon, too, has made pieces that convey a sense of loss and aftermath. Speaking of works such as *Perimete*r (2014), or the later *All the Tape Left Over from my Last Painting (Diagonal Assembly)* (2019, p. 63): 'They're all the leftovers; it's all about the remnants ... For a season, I made a series of paintings of old masking tape, and they were the leftovers from the previous painting. And as I completed the painting, those traces would be the subject of the next one. Or it might be remnants of postcards and letters, or paper aeroplanes, or things that are normally thrown out or disregarded or overlooked. Perhaps, better, things that just aren't perceived. Things that are in the periphery of our vision.'

This focus on things that have passed away of course positions these paintings within the *vanitas* tradition, which is rich in the idea of lament and remembering death. The paper planes, taped onto board (as in *Paper Planes*, and *Three Paper Planes*, both 2014, p. 124, and *Fifteen Paper Planes*, 2016, p. 127) are personal memorials. But they also hold on to the possibility of flight: 'There's the idea that painting isn't this static thing but holds suspension enough for you to have the belief that you are looking at something that is about to move.'

A sense of the elegiac, as well as the apprehension that fragmented remainders of the past are reactivating, also characterises Gordon's paintings with biblical themes: *Into the Laquearia* (2017, p. 98),[14] for instance, and its 2021 reworking, *Jacob's Dream* (fig. 6 (detail) and p. 99). Both are responses to an instance of eighteenth-century (rococo) *trompe-l'oeil* painting in an architectural setting: Giovanni Battista Tiepolo's *Jacob's Dream*, a ceiling fresco – known as a *quadratura* – painted around 1726–29 in the Palazzo Patriarcale (Patriarchal

Fig. 6 **Jacob's Dream** detail 2021 Oil and acrylic on birch 120 × 180 cm

Palace), Udine, Italy. It is a remarkable work because, as with other such ceiling frescoes, it required the application of linear perspective to a concave surface in order to create an effect of uninterrupted flow from the realms of human (in this case religious/political) space into the realms of infinity and the divine. To this end, Tiepolo depended on the skills of a specialist, the painter Gerolamo Mengozzi Colonna, with whom he had often collaborated since 1719.

In this piece by Tiepolo, we see the figure of the sleeping Jacob from Genesis 28:12. In this portion of the biblical account, Jacob (who is the son of Isaac and grandson of Abraham and is destined to be the third of the great patriarchs of the then-still-emergent people of Israel) has left his father's house. He is journeying across rough terrain to the home of Laban, his mother's brother, where he intends to find a wife and fulfil that promised destiny physically. But night has fallen, so he stops to rest. While he sleeps, he has a dream 'in which he saw a stairway resting on the Earth, with its top reaching to heaven, and the angels of God were ascending and descending on it.' The dream ends with a vision of God, who reaffirms the patriarchal promise and the fact of God's enduring favour on him and on his descendants for the blessing of all humanity.

In Tiepolo's context, in a public culture that validated itself politically as well as religiously according to a Judeo-Christian belief system, both the theme of this painting (the indisputably divine identification of the biblical patriarchs) and its style (*trompe-l'oeil*) were used strategically within the Patriarchal Palace's broader visual programme to assert a political claim to power. But times change. In Gordon's painterly engagements with this theme, the transcription of Tiepolo's painting has been pushed to the background. The strong and straight spiritual ladder, central to Tiepolo's rendering, has been all but obscured, as have his decisive, hurrying angels. Indeed, in each of Gordon's paintings, and particularly so in *Jacob's Dream*, the illusionism of quadratura has been replaced by that of quodlibet and our eyes are overwhelmed not with a vision of divine access and approval but by a swirl of reference materials, including postcards, which appear to be taped onto a work-in-progress canvas. Most have religious connotations, and several are of angelic beings. In *Jacob's Dream*, we find references to Paul Gauguin's *Vision of the Sermon (Jacob Wrestling with the Angel)* (1888), Rembrandt's cartoon of *Jacob Wrestling with the Angel* (1659), and Eric Gill's treatment of the same subject, as well as to angelic symbols from Judaism, Islam and Zoroastrianism. Also referenced (left of centre) is a depiction of Aruna, the charioteer to the sun god Surya, who is described in the Hindu tradition as a super-spiritual being who incarnates the rising sun. Gordon's reference is to the Indonesian tradition that describes Aruna as an angel, a being of light and fire.

Here, then, we are faced with a flurry of religious sources from diverse cultures, among which are also remnants of the Christian belief system that was once so formative to western culture and western art. For, although visual references to Christian art are still endlessly reduplicated – as they are in these postcards – and disseminated globally in the contemporary west in particular, the belief system itself has lost its overt centrality to public life. Contemporary secular minds are configured to exclude matters of human-divine interaction and faith. But, in these paintings, a space of lively and hospitable visual provocation opens up that is grounded in studious artistry, although not in an imposing or hierarchical manner from above. Metaphorically, Gordon's images, and by implication the scenarios they display, may be picked up and studied more closely – or not. They may be reshuffled to generate sequences of differently nuanced or accented wordless conversations. Here, again, the possibilities of Steiner's cortesia are at issue. As, indeed, is his assertion, also in *Real Presences*, that 'the best readings of art are art'.[15] *Jacob's Dream* was included in Gordon's aptly titled 2021 exhibition, *Quodlibet*, at Aleph Contemporary, London.[16]

3

Earlier, I described Gordon's long immersion in quodlibet as inextricable from 'an ever-deepening induction into the agencies of wood.' Returning to *Nail*, its wooden substrate, for Gordon, was 'a really important part ... I started to read the wood-grain as a sort of painterly mark in itself'. And, indeed, when I was confronted with the piece, it immediately seemed that two generators of the aesthetic were actively encountering each other. One was expressed in the configurations of *Nail*'s grain – in Gordon's words, 'marks that were made by the creation itself, and pigment that is the stuff of sap and carbon.' Particularly evocative was that knotted figure of eight in its upper portion – like a naturally occurring infinity symbol if seen on its side or, more fancifully, some sort of homunculus – which had been pierced by that small, domesticated spike.

This sensitivity to wood, stuff, matter, as having a language of its own, points us in two directions conceptually. First to the communications of what, in pre-modern and early-modern times, was called the 'book of nature', where nature was understood to carry and express divine presence and revelation. Among these expressions are so-called 'natural images', some of which exist deep within wood or stone, invisible to human eyes until the wood or stone in question has been sliced open. Astonishingly, these images often appear to mirror aspects of the 'real' world, like landscapes and cityscapes.[17] Secondly, we are directed towards areas of contemporary scholarship, such as new materialism and object-oriented ontology, where attending to the agencies of matter has returned to the philosophical and ethical agenda.[18]

The other generators of the aesthetic in *Nail* are human creativity, mark-making and intention in relation to those material prompts. In this early work, and in Gordon's work more broadly, the interactions that emerge seem to me to be antiphonal. That is, spaces of aesthetic call and response, and of disputation, come into play. Significantly, this is also the defining space of quodlibet in its inaugural (pre-seventeenth-century and pre-painterly) theologico-philosophical and musical expressions. As explained by the theologian Lydia Schumacher, quodlibet was originally the 'name of an academic exercise in medieval universities, chiefly Paris. Twice a year, before Christmas and Easter, a disputation was held in which the master undertook to deal with any questions (*disputatio de quolibet*) raised by any of the participants (*a quolibet*). The subjects ranged from abstruse questions of theology to the smallest details of daily life. The answers of the masters were afterwards drawn up in writing and published.'[19] Where the quodlibet in music is concerned, we read in *The Oxford Companion to Music* that it is a formation 'in which well-known tunes or texts (or both) are quoted, either simultaneously or in succession, generally for humorous effect.'[20] In Gordon's words: 'A group of musicians would all lay down a line of music, and then respond to one another, and create an improvised piece, which would give the appearance of being spontaneous, but was actually very considered.' Thus, returning a third time to that inaugural work, *Nail*, and as Gordon has observed: 'The majority of this piece is the wood, and my intervention is very minimal.' But, he continued: 'It's a plank of wood, and it's different from painting on a tree, for example, or painting on a piece of MDF, or a piece of plywood. I think I was reading Jean Baudrillard at the time who, in *The System of Objects* [1968], describes a certain romance with wood-grain, since it participates in the natural order, and therefore its communications differ from those of chipboard and other engineered wood-derived products … For me, because this is an old piece of wood, and because the feet of Paul Cézanne may have walked on it, it is almost a secular relic. This is all speculative, of course, because his feet may not have touched it, and it may not even have been a floorboard. My hosts at Les Lauves didn't know for sure. And so, this time following Umberto Eco on the subject of hyperreality, we can also think of this floorboard as a kind of "authentic fake". For me, this also connects with and comments on the nature of *trompe-l'oeil*.'

In any case, during 2013, wood became central to Gordon's way of working. Other early works on found wood from this year include *Splinter, Descending* (p. 46); *Splinter, Falling*; *Splinter, Ascending* (p. 38); *Book, Bound* (p. 40); and *Block* (p. 39). He also began to paint on wooden panels, sometimes manufactured and sometimes, as with *Nail*, found pieces carrying a sense of history – perhaps as part of a building's fabric or furniture. Significantly, this development occurred during another residency – residencies being such exceptional opportunities for artists to re-situate themselves physically, perceptually, intellectually and technically, and, in so doing, to reconsider and relearn. This time, it was at the aforementioned Departure (the former seamen's mission in east London): 'In the archive of this rather beautiful old mission hall, there were these pieces of wood, which may have been part of the original architecture of the building. I started painting on those.'

Then, in 2019, Gordon's approach shifted again, and he started experimenting with the creation of faux-wood surfaces, using painters' and decorators' techniques in a fine-art context. Once again, this change came about on a residency, this time at the City & Guilds of London Art School, where he was working with students focusing on the decorative arts [see pp. 130–35].

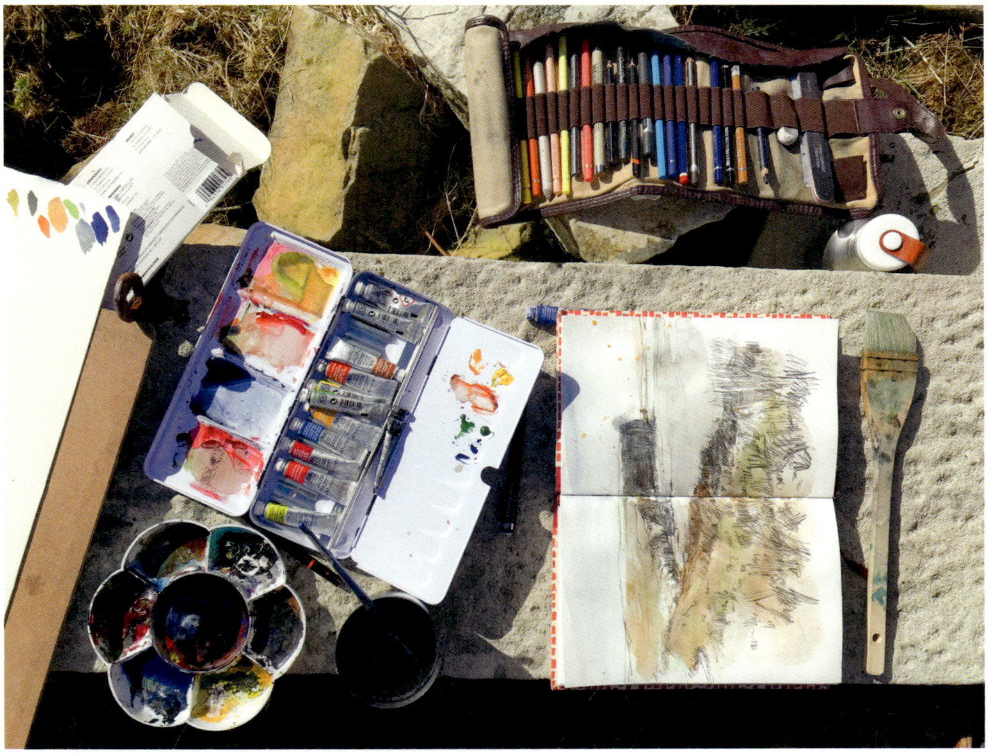

Fig. 7 Preparatory studies made on location in Caithness, 2022

In works such as *Thirty Feathers and a Mouse* (2019, p. 121), Gordon developed these varied techniques to create hyperrealistic wood-grain effects; in *The Beauty of the Parochial* (2022), he painted the sides of the canvas to emulate MDF, which then seemingly makes contact with the apparently natural wood ground of the painting's surface.

Another development in Gordon's relationship with wood came alongside this one, and it can be seen in his works on MDF board, such as *Improvisation* (fig. 8 (detail) and p. 149); *A New Beginning* (p. 151), *Harmony* (p. 154), and *B Flat* (all 2021); and *Nocturne* (2022, p. 155) and *Duet* (2022, p. 148).

Here, wood also appears in its natural setting, in or as landscape, and, as in *Improvisation*, as quivering *trompe-l'oeil* twigs, apparently stuck to the painting's surface with Blu Tack. As Gordon put it, he was now 'trying to juxtapose that sharp, decorative illusionism with this more gestural, intuitive approach'. This reflects the fact that Gordon was also more intentionally attempting to bring his studio practice into conversation with another crucial part of his artistic life: his sustained habit of painting in the landscape, responsively (fig. 7). Again, Gordon reaches up over his drawing table and brings down a much-handled sketchbook. He leafs through its pages. 'I make very different paintings when I'm out there. I draw every day, and I'm out painting as much as I can be. But this language of paint, this kind of observational but intuitive drawing and painting, is very different from what happens in the studio, when things become much tighter and hyperrealistic. In the paintings I'm making now, I want to bring these things together. That is where I'm heading.'

4

Gordon's explorations of wood continue to evolve and diversify. As they do so – quietly and unassumingly, even in the case of his large-scale pieces – they present ever-varied challenges to sight and thought. Perhaps, then, there is no better place to draw these reflections to a close than by turning to a final set of thematically related works: his depictions of *trompe-l'oeil* matches, begun in 2013 and continuing into the present.

Matches can be used to illuminate, to be inflammatory, and even to destroy, to burn down. *Match* (2013, fig. 9), and *Match, Levitating* (2014, p. 43), were made as part of the artist's residency and subsequent exhibition at the Nunnery Gallery, London, located just around the corner from where the Bryant and May match factory was once located. Both were painted on found wood from stools, which had been discovered, years ago, on the factory site.

Fig. 8 **Improvisation** detail 2021 Oil and acrylic on MDF board 100 × 120 cm

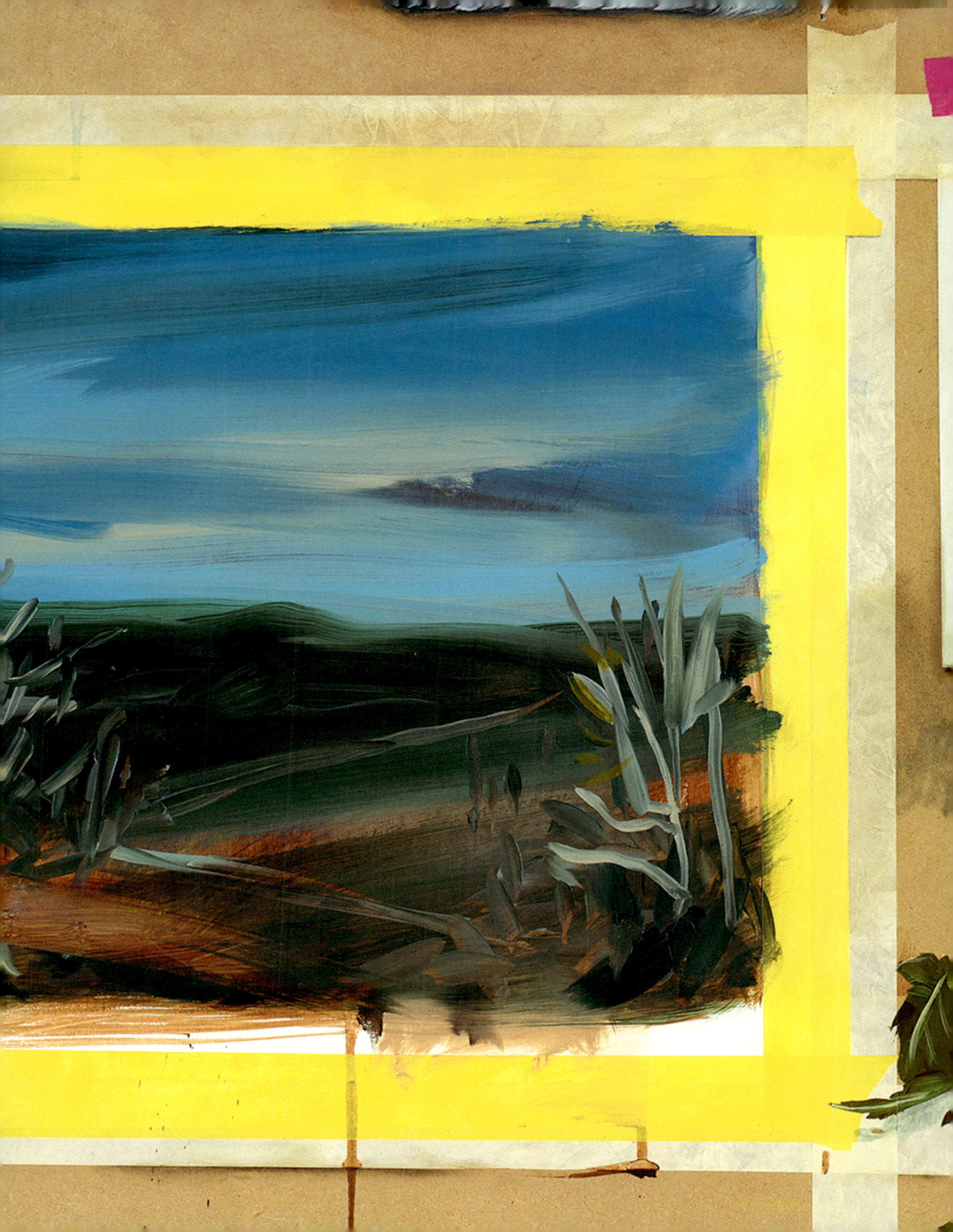

The tiny incendiary device in *Match* appears as if suspended in pictorial space. On the one hand, its quivering flame could so easily be snuffed out. As such, it recalls the iconography of the western *vanitas* tradition in still-life painting – again, often highly illusionistic – where everyday objects, such as candles, lamps and hourglasses, invited viewers to reflect on the brevity of life. On the other hand, this match looks as though it could do foundational damage, incinerate the very ground on which it depends. This is apt. Gordon recalls that during this residency he became interested in the socio-political history of the nearby factory, which had been redeveloped in the 1980s to create Bow Quarter, a gated community of residential housing. In his words: 'The match factory became synonymous with Annie Besant and the match girls' strike of 1888, when the all-woman workforce took industrial action against horrendous working conditions and low pay. The strike was significant for the evolution of the Trade Union Act (first established in 1871) and for the formation of the suffragettes in 1903. Apparently, too, the young Mahatma Gandhi (newly arrived in London to study law) was acquainted with the strike action in that he befriended Besant during a visit to east London two months after the strike. This encounter, in turn, is said to have encouraged Besant in her understanding of and engagement with theosophy. In any case, a simple picture of a floating match painted onto a wooden stool from the factory opens several possibilities.'[21]

A different kind of attention to matches and their representations resulted in Gordon's *Prayer Matches* series of 2020, painted (this time on Fabriano paper) during that year's extended periods of Covid-19 lockdown in the UK. Take, for instance, *Prayer Matches, Day 114* (p. 139), where three spent matches are apparently held in place by that other recurrent motif in Gordon's paintings, masking tape. Appropriately, in their spent-ness, they seem to form three cross-like entities, reminiscent of the three crosses that are so often depicted in traditional paintings of the crucifixion of Christ. At the time of creating these works, Gordon described their emergence as follows:

> Like many, lockdown has afforded me both time and limitation. I have been home-schooling my daughter which has been a real privilege, but I've missed the long days in the studio. So, I've been painting at night, working through the evenings when all the emails have stopped and you can focus just on the painting. It's been both exhausting and wonderful. The prayer matches began at the start of lockdown. I've been meeting with a group of friends on Zoom to pray every morning. We light a candle, and the match is the memory of that prayer. I've made a painting every

Fig. 9 **Match** detail 2013 Oil on found wood 31 × 22 × 3 cm

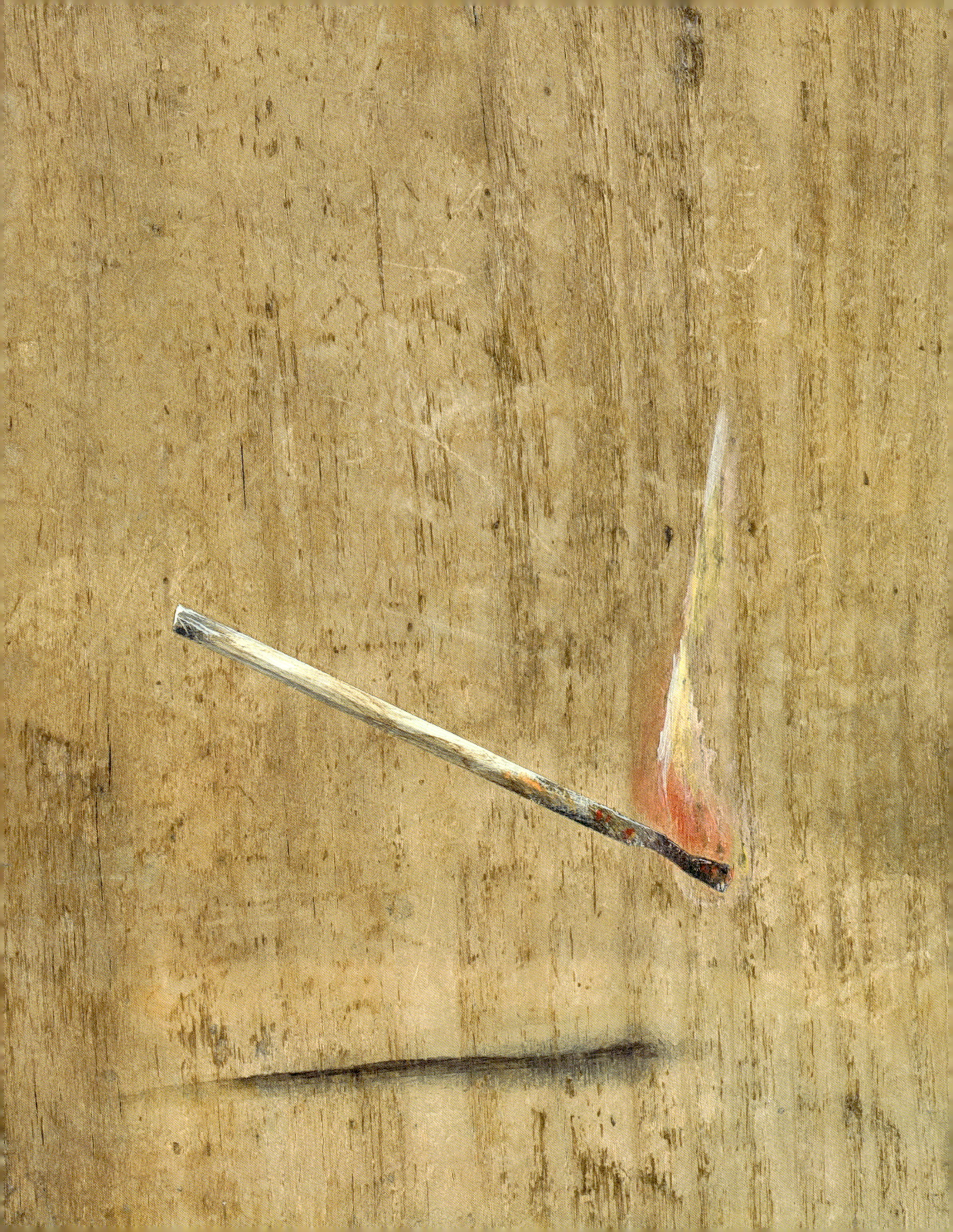

day since the beginning of lockdown of the matches for that day. Like a memory or record of prayer. As the days went on, my prayers became more agitated and restless. With all the protests, anger, death and struggle we've seen in recent months, I couldn't make painting that was ordered or tightly controlled. As I have felt myself unravel, so the paintings have become more agitated and restless.[22]

5

Gordon is not the only contemporary artist to have used the language of quodlibet to interact with issues of concern to us today. He recalls how, having discovered this genre for himself, he soon came across other painters working in the idiom, most famously Lucy McKenzie, 'who works on canvas and paints what look like pinboards with items stuck on top. But she uses it as a device to explore political questions, and early forms of feminism, and fascism.' Then there is Esterly, the master woodcarver referenced earlier, who has described the technical challenges of transposing seventeenth-century painted letter racks into three dimensions as uppermost.[23] Also taking a three-dimensional approach to quodlibet is Jim Cheatle, who was the curator of the group exhibition *Subradar: The Deceptive Image in the Screen Environment* at the Laure Genillard Gallery, London, in 2022. Featuring artworks by Susan Collis, Neil Gall, Andrew Grassie and Gavin Turk, alongside his own, the show 'considered how illusion is used today, when screens are almost overtaking reality'.[24] By contrast, Gordon insists that, for him, quodlibet painting 'is more about how paintings are constructed and the process of painting itself'.

But this is not an insular, art-for-art's-sake concern. We live in a world that is at once increasingly visual *and* increasingly invisible, and algorithmically driven, where so much is evident only indirectly, from its traces and effects. Alongside this, there is that other invisible-yet-visible realm of incarnated divinity and revelation, to which Gordon's works often return, and which is less willingly engaged with in technologically developed contexts. Given all of this, it is vital that we learn to pay greater attention to the mechanics of sight and re-sensitise and diversify our visual and communicative capacities. Paintings release insight which transcends their medium. As materiality and content contend with one another in Gordon's work, fresh insight and expressive possibilities are made available. Indeed, *Nail*, in its simplicity, is also like a rudimentary visual-material prayer.

Jorella Andrews is Professor of Visual Cultures at Goldsmiths, University of London

1 This, and further quotations below, unless otherwise referenced, are from my conversation with the artist during a studio visit, London, 25 March 2022.

2 On inspection, they are very carefully composed.

3 See Book 35 of Pliny the Elder's *Natural History* (AD 77). Available online at http://www.attalus.org/translate/pliny_hn35a.html. Accessed 9 May 2022.

4 Manuel van der Veen, 'Crossroads of Seeing: About Layers in Painting and Superimposition in Augmented Reality', *AI and Society* 36 (2021): 1191, accessed 6 May 2022, https://doi.org/10.1007/s00146-020-01.

5 George Steiner, *Real Presences* (London: Faber and Faber, 1989), 147–48.

6 The wording here is drawn from Bruce Herman, 'Cortesia: Bruce Herman, Artist in Residence', *Transpositions: Theology, Imagination and the Arts*, 25 September 2013, accessed 25 April 2022, http://www.transpositions.co.uk/courtesia/.

7 Steiner, 155.

8 'Two Scientists' Response to George Steiner', *Theology* 102 (1999), accessed 6 May 2022, https://www2.ph.ed.ac.uk/~wckp/Steiner_Theology.pdf.

9 See the entry on this painting in the online 'Exhibition Objects' guide, Met Museum, New York, 2022, accessed 23 January 2023, https://www.metmuseum.org/exhibitions/listings/2022/cubism-trompe-loeil/exhibition-objects.

10 Caryn James, 'Trompe l'Oeil and the Images that Fool the Mind', *BBC Culture* website, 17 November 2022, accessed 8 January 2023, https://www.bbc.com/culture/article/20221116-trompe-loeil-and-the-paintings-that-deceive-our-eye.

11 The residency culminated in an exhibition at the centre with paintings relating to the Danish sailors who had been supported at the mission. Gordon's activities also involved art workshops for the local homeless community and working in the café. A year later, his role evolved into that of gallery manager as the centre was rebranded as Husk. Gordon set up a gallery showing a combined programme of work by recent graduates and local artists.

12 *Alastair Gordon: Souvenirs from the Waste Land*, Ahmanson Gallery, Irvine, California, 17 March–22 September 2017, accessed 6 May 2022, https://www.ahmansongallery.com/sourvenirs-from-the-waste-land.

13 David Esterly, 'Lost (and Found) Illusions', *The Magazine Antiques* 181: 5 (2014), 100, https://www.themagazineantiques.com/article/esterly-illusions/.

14 Laquearia refers here to a panelled ceiling (it can also refer to a genus of fungi) and, specifically, a line in TS Eliot's *The Waste Land*.

15 Steiner, 17.

16 *Alastair Gordon: Quodlibet*, Aleph Contemporary, London, 3–29 September 2021, accessed 25 April 2022, https://alephcontemporary.com/viewing-room/28-alastair-gordon-quodlibet/.

17 Interestingly, whereas the book-of-nature metaphor (which has been employed within a wide range of cultural, philosophical and theological contexts for very different purposes) was seen to be in harmony with the sacred scriptures in patristic and medieval literature, 'from the early-modern era onwards it was presented also as an autonomous book, other than biblical Revelation'. Giuseppe Tanzella-Nitti, 'Book of Nature, Origin and Development of the Metaphor', *Interdisciplinary Encyclopaedia of Religion and Science*, 2019, accessed 30 April 2022, https://inters.org/book-of-nature.

18 During 2020, Gordon facilitated the online 'Make Good' lecture series through his arts organisation, Morphē Arts, to engage with such topics.

19 See the entry on quodlibet by Lydia Schumacher in *The Oxford Dictionary of the Christian Church* (4th ed) (Oxford University Press, 2022). Where the quodlibet in music is concerned, see the entry on quodlibet in *The Oxford Companion to Music* (Oxford University Press, 2011). Developed in the first quarter of the thirteenth century by Thomas Aquinas and Gerard of Abbeville, by the end of the century and the start of the next, quodlibet had become one of the preferred modes of teaching and must have been thrilling, and often enjoyable, to witness. While many quodlibets presented a master's thought at its most advanced and refined, expertly articulated, others had a more humorous intent.

20 See Alison Latham (ed), *The Oxford Companion to Music* (Oxford University Press, 2011).

21 The residency culminated in an exhibition, *Strike*, at the Nunnery Gallery, London, 1 February–31 March 2013.

22 Hannah Payne, 'THE ART FIVE, Issue 8, with Artist, Alastair Gordon', *THE ART FIVE*, 16 July 2020, accessed 7 January 2023, https://www.theartfive.com/post/the-art-five-with-artist-alastair-gordon.

23 David Esterly, 'Lost (and Found) Illusions', *The Magazine Antiques* 181: 5 (2014), 97.

24 *Subradar: The Deceptive Image in the Screen Environment*, Laure Genillard Gallery, London, 2022, accessed 8 January 2022, http://lglondon.org/index.php/project/subradar--febapr-2022/.

overleaf Fig. 10 **River Wasteland** detail 2019 Oil and acrylic on wood with found objects 180 × 240 cm

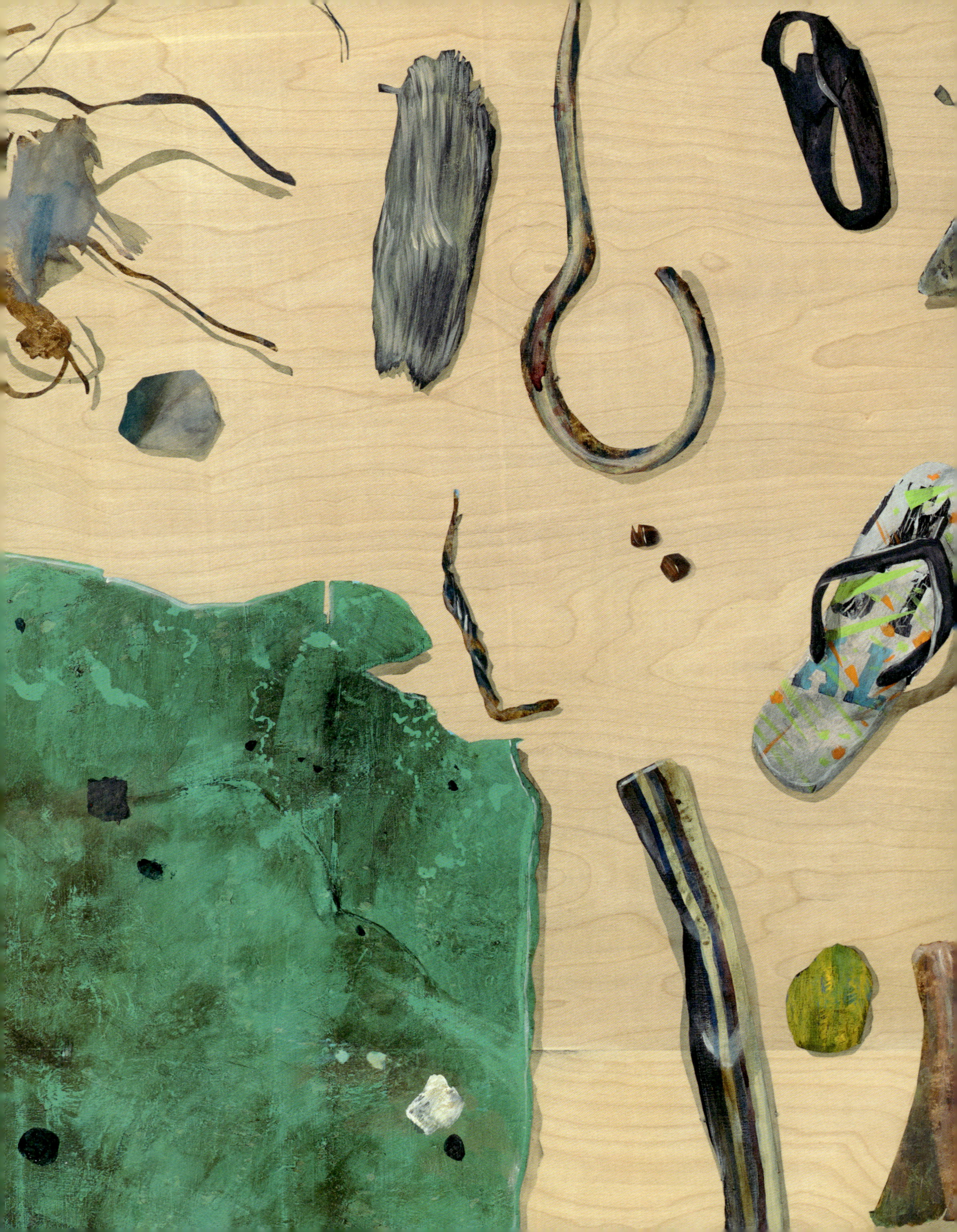

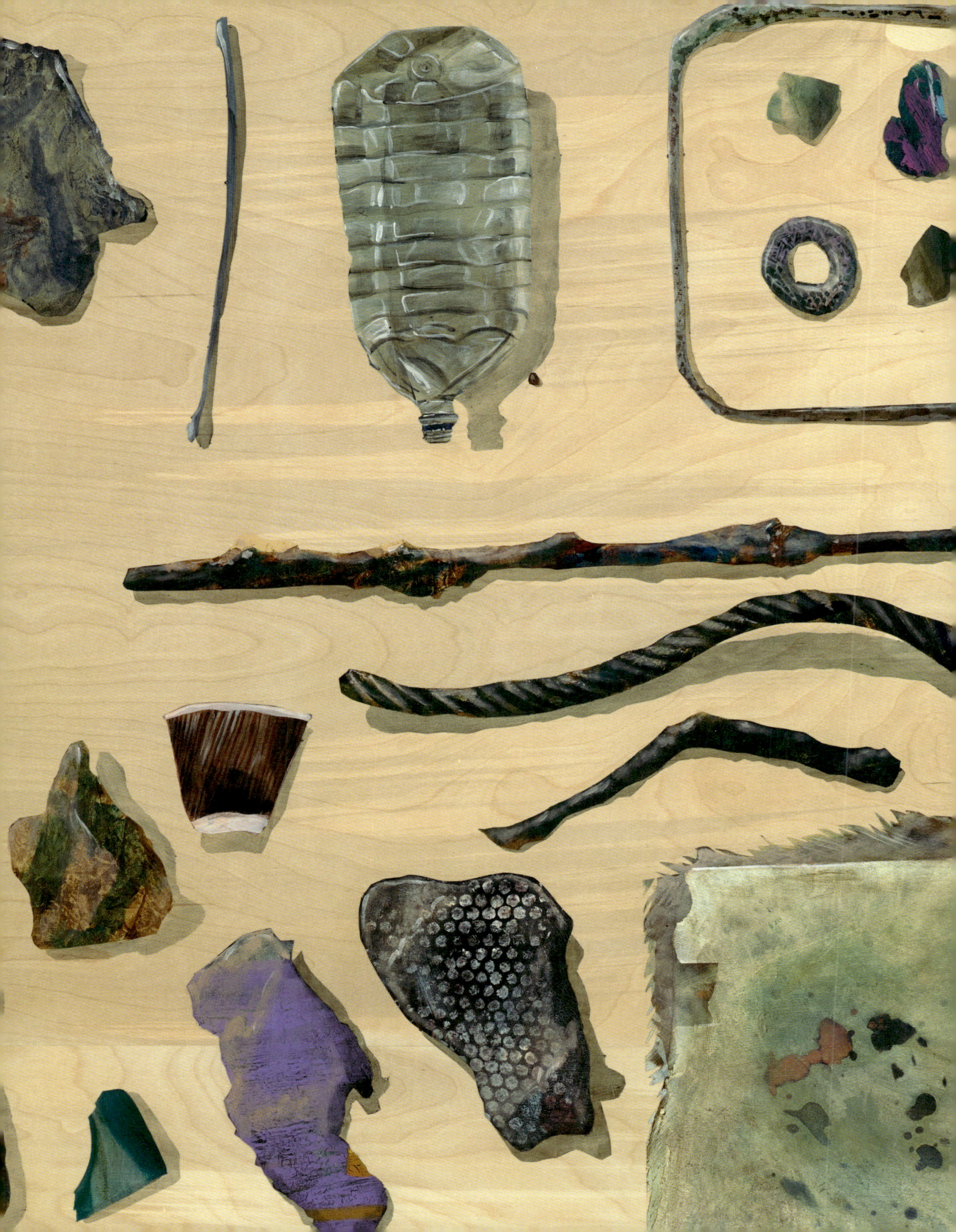

There have been moments when I have seen people trying to peel the tape away from my paintings. Even when I explain it's painted, they still aren't satisfied, and go back for a second attempt. *Trompe-l'oeil* allows for these moments of slow revelation; a point of 'aha', where reality is suspended just long enough for the viewer to be fooled. Yet I see this more as an action of revelation than deception; a moment to question the veracity of perception. In a way, these paintings are as much about seeing as about what they depict.

I paint everyday detritus. Those gloriously mundane moments of wonder overlooked. The flotsam of human activity, including recycled objects, postcards pinned to the cupboard door, old shoes, remnants of human migration from refugee camps, debris from street protests, spent matches, and, most recently, the leftovers from my studio practice.

Just as TS Eliot found fear in a handful of dust, I imagine possibilities in my studio detritus. I look at the notes sprawling across the paint-splattered floor, and the sketches taped to the walls. A candle flickers to shadow. Along the wall are the marks, papers, stains, splashes, splodges and scuffs – the residue of making. The papers flit, and new worlds are released.

The quodlibet genre of painting first emerged in seventeenth-century northern Europe. Initially a musical term, quodlibet means 'what you will', a specific form of illusionism associated with objects painted in flat relief, such as newspaper cuttings, letter racks or card tables. At first, objects appear randomly selected, without composition or connection. Look more closely, and certain meanings emerge. You might find a dialogue between seemingly unrelated artefacts, a philosophical musing, or an act of political subversion. Yet the veracity of the objects is always in doubt.

I especially admire quodlibets that give dignity to everyday objects, where I am invited to look at the overlooked. I think of paintings by Cornelis Norbertus Gijsbrechts, Edwaert Collier or Samuel Dirksz van Hoogstraten, with their seemingly casual assemblages of domestic objects. I think of later artists such as Georges Braque and Pablo Picasso, who found greater possibilities for the genre. To me, their early attention to still-life cubism is straight out of the quodlibet playbook. Items such as guitars, cups and bowls of fruit were painted with a fragmented sense of realism alongside collaged elements and found objects, including newspaper cuttings and sun-bleached papers. When I look at these paintings, questions arise about illusion and replication, the real and the fake, and how we perceive the world around us.

The things we leave behind

At times, my paintings look like something is about to begin; a blank sheet of paper with the promise of something new. In other paintings, it appears like an aftermath; strips of masking tape and oily residue where the paper has been. In a way, they are paintings about painting. Objects that oscillate between artifice and artefact.[1] Beginnings of endings, potential and reflective, the cycles of making.

1 Geraint Evans, introduction to *Alastair Gordon: Danish Departed*, at Husk/Departed, London, 30 September – 7 November 2013, accessed 26 January 2023, https://www.geraintevans.net/danish-departed.

34

Nail 2012 Oil on found wood 22.5 × 9 cm

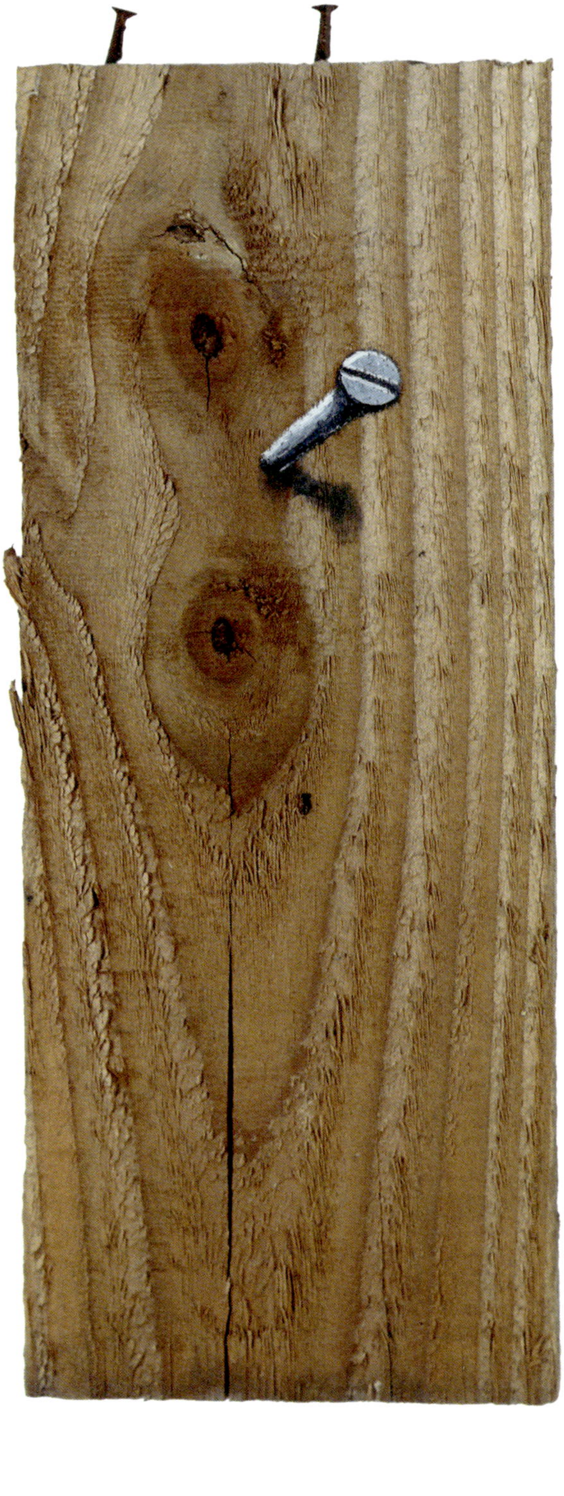

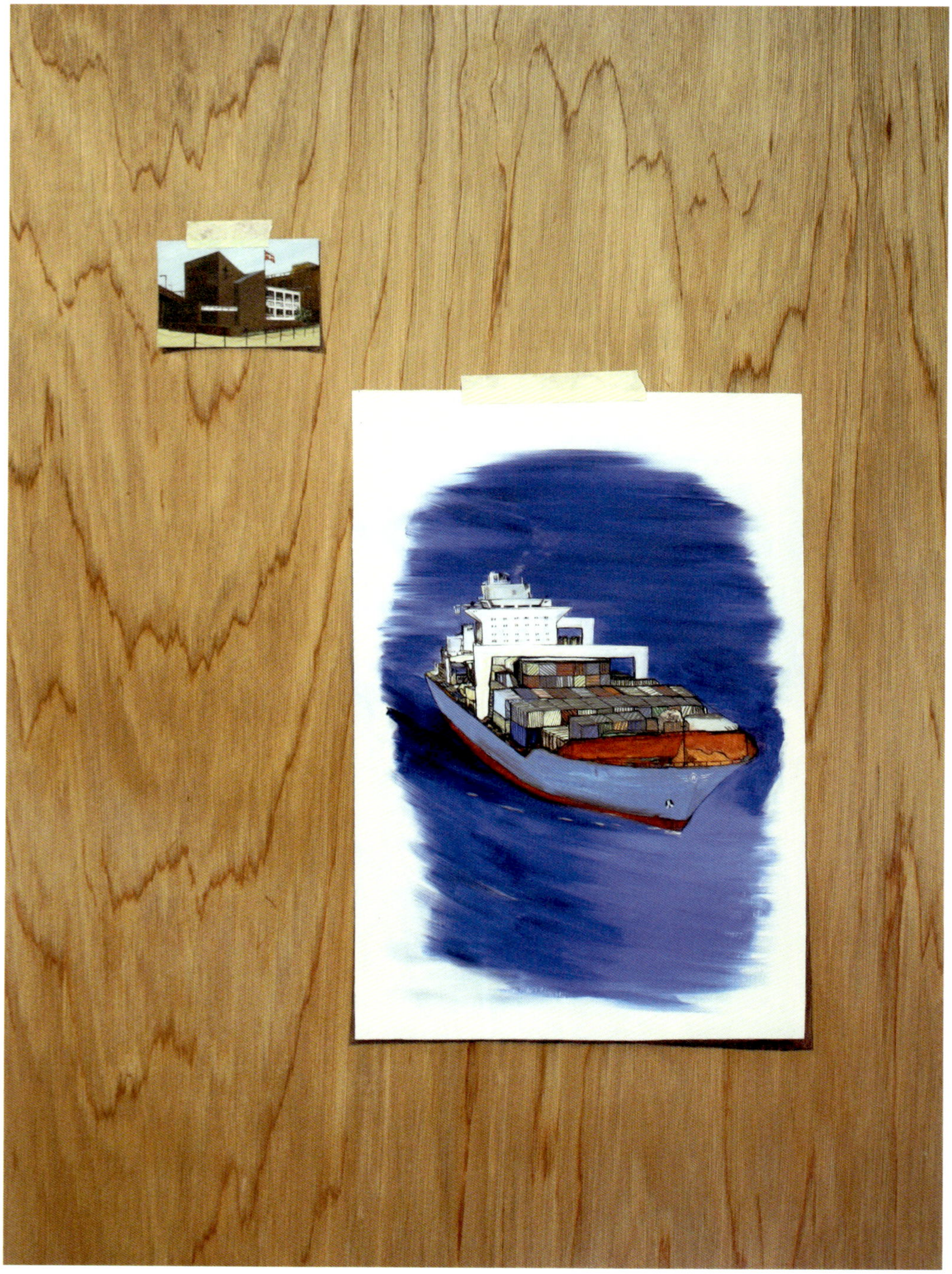

Postcard and Poster 2013 Oil on wood 120 × 90 cm

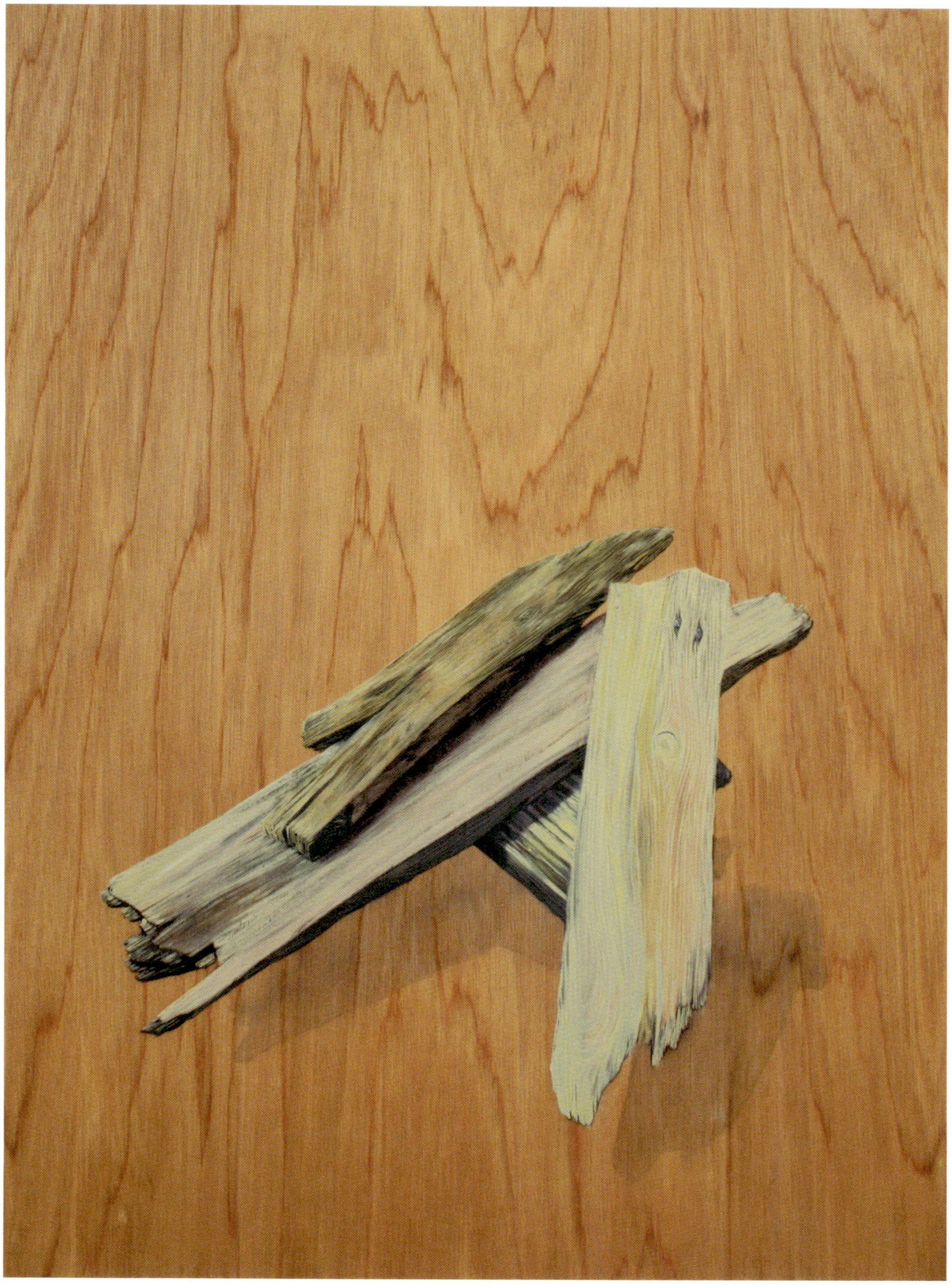

Fragments 2013 Oil on wood 120 × 90 cm

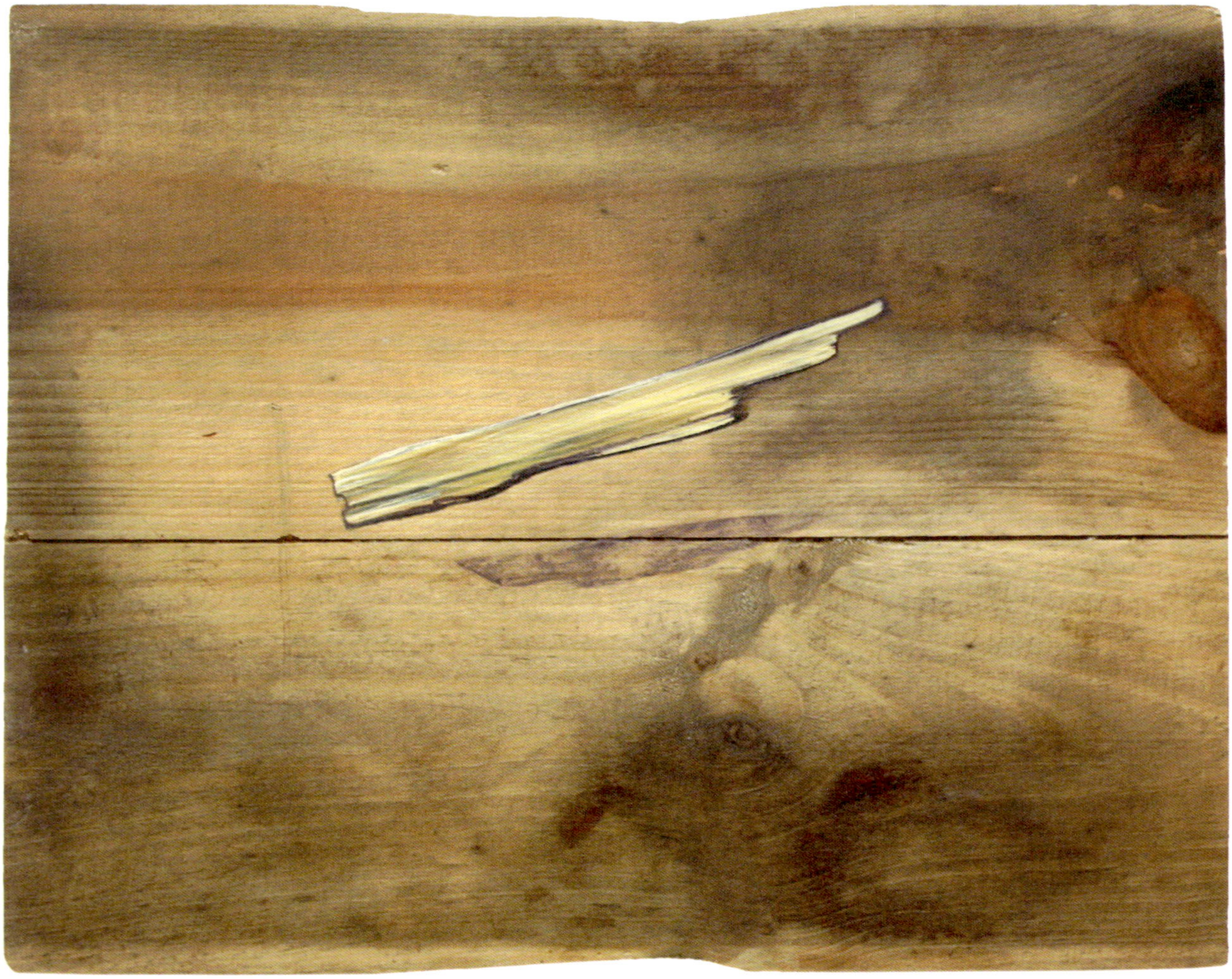

Splinter, Ascending 2013 Oil on found wood 22 × 30 cm

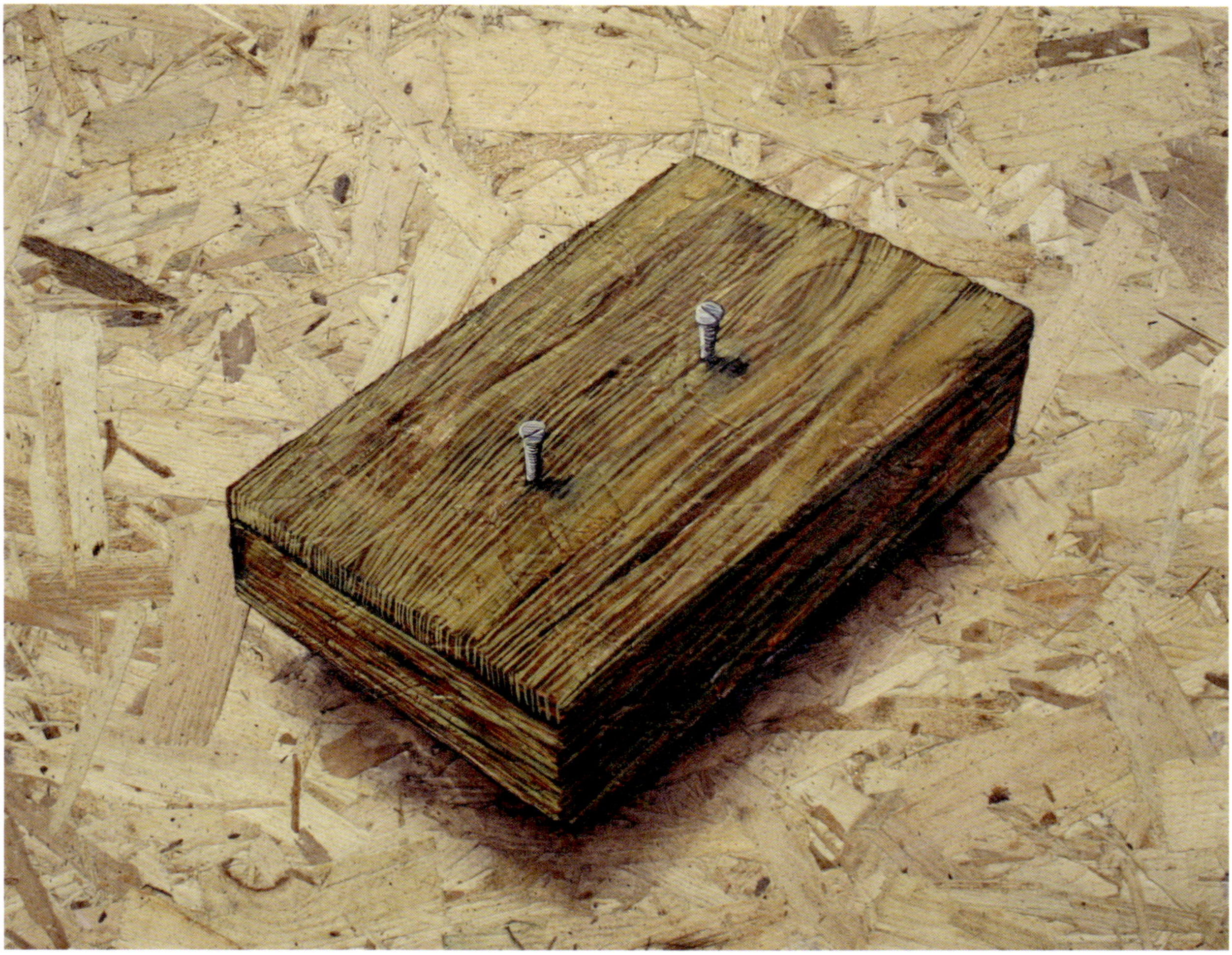

Block 2013 Oil on found wood 39 × 50 cm

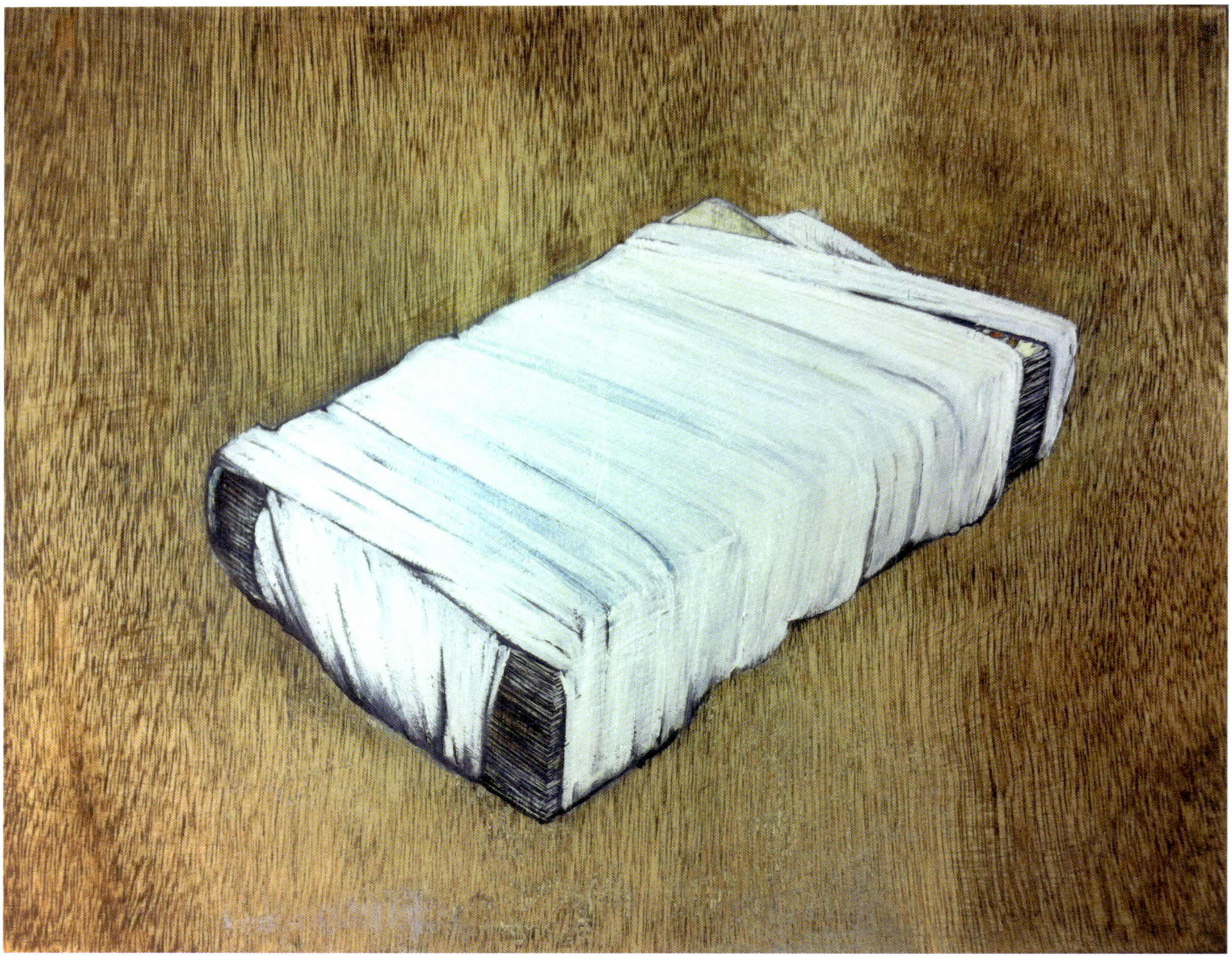

Book, Bound 2013 Oil on found wood 21 × 30 cm

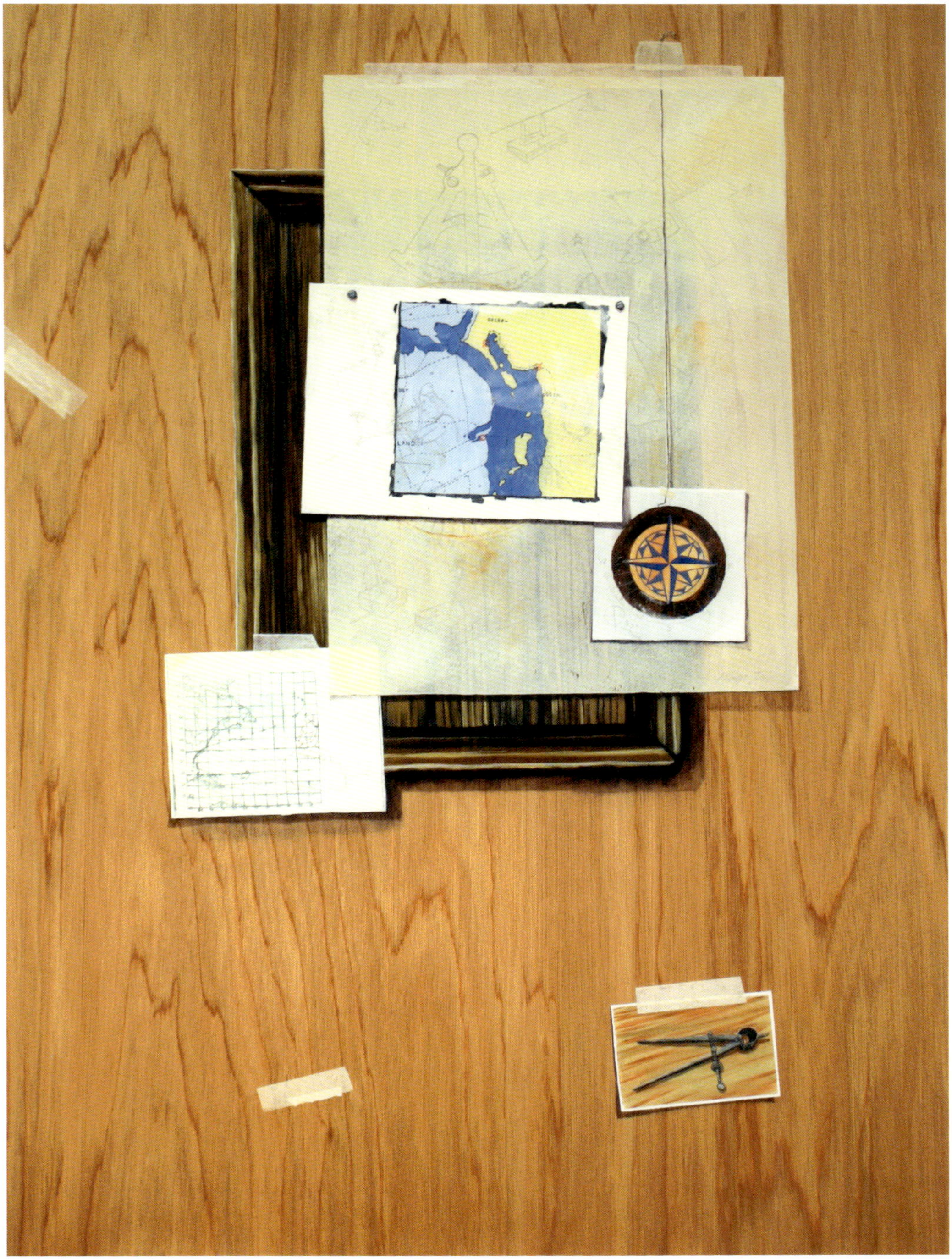

Charts and Drawings 2013 Oil on wood 120 × 90 cm

Match, Levitating 2014 Oil on found wood 31 × 22 cm

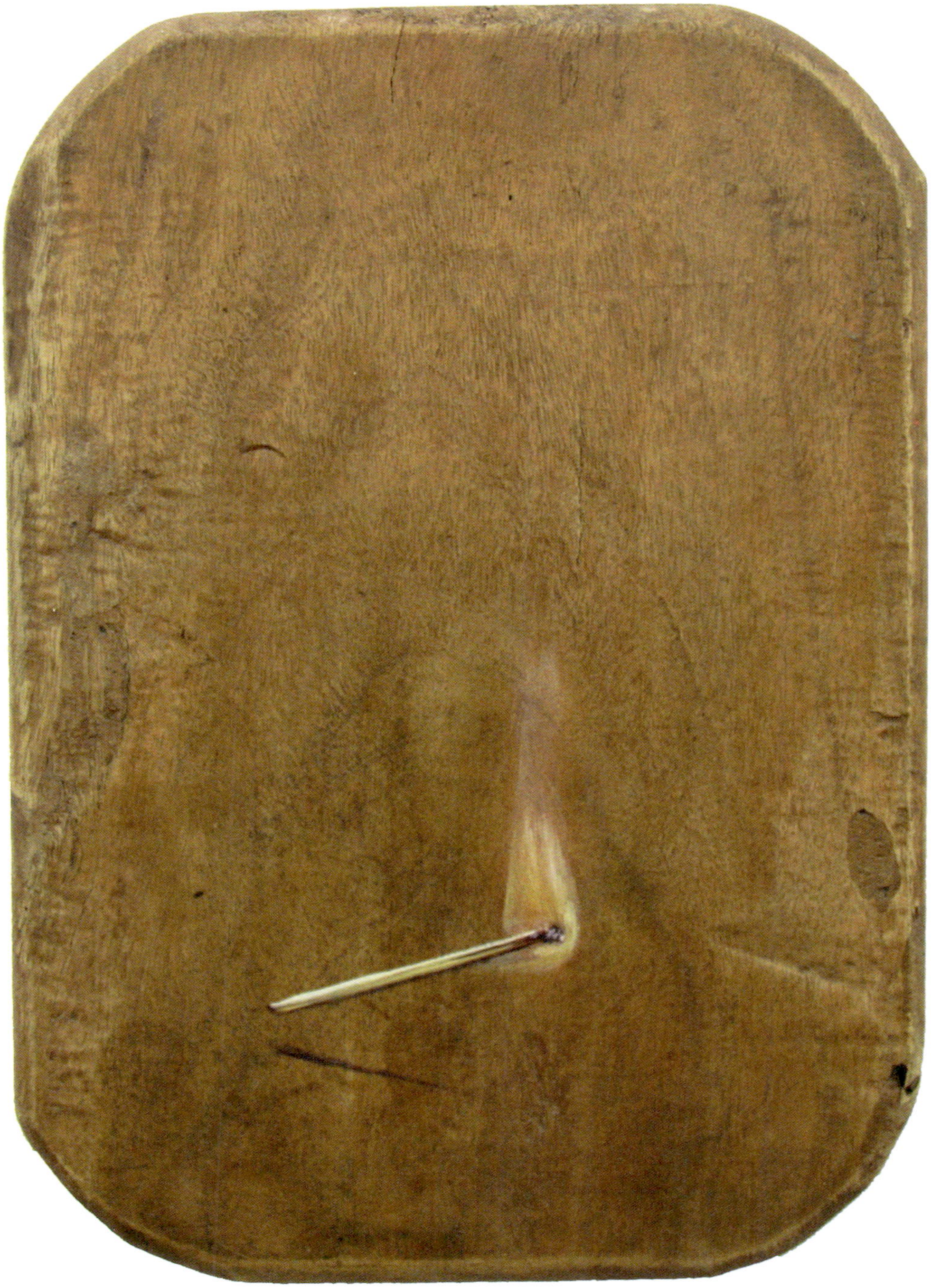

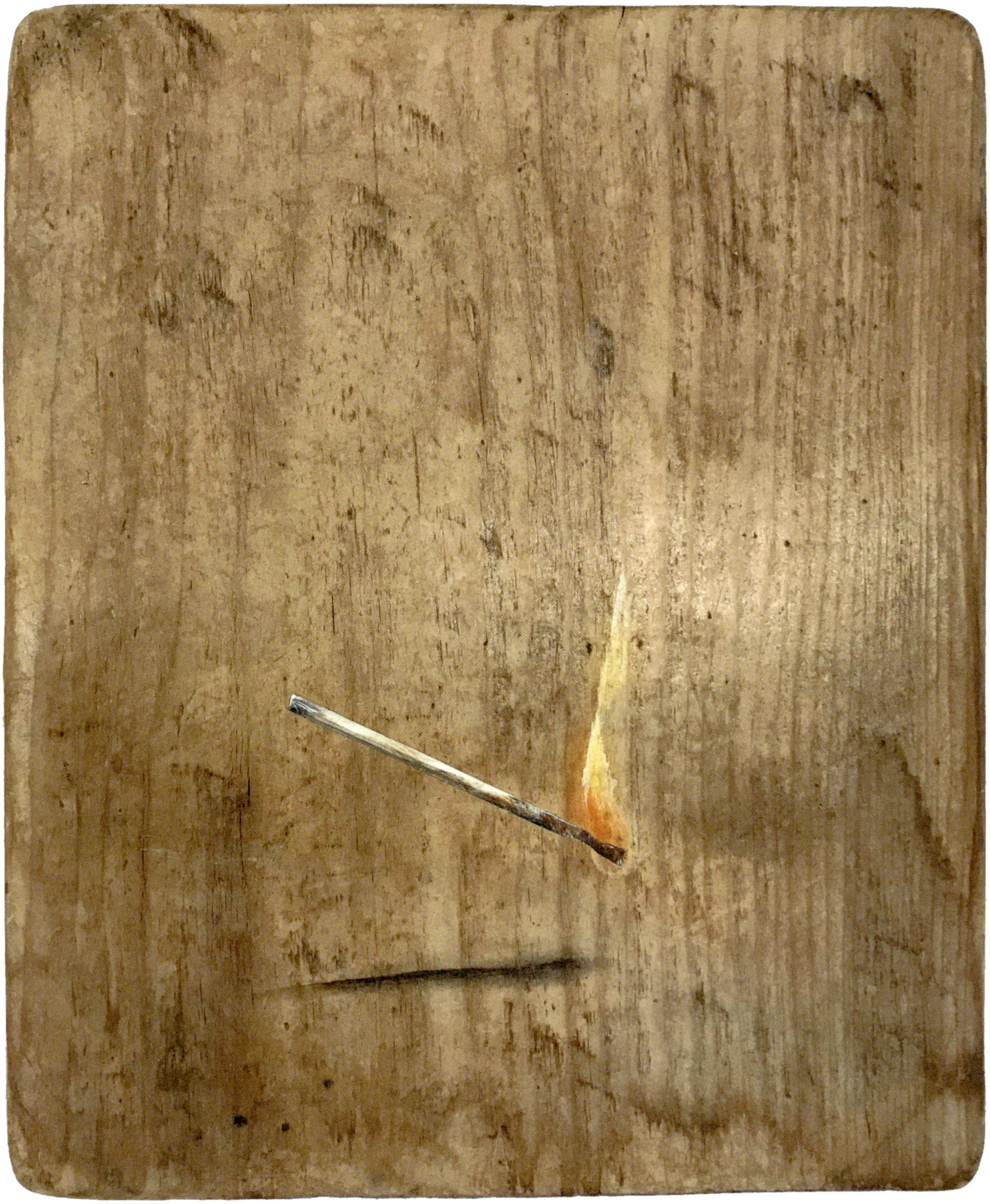

Presence 2020 Acrylic and oil on found wood 31 × 22 cm

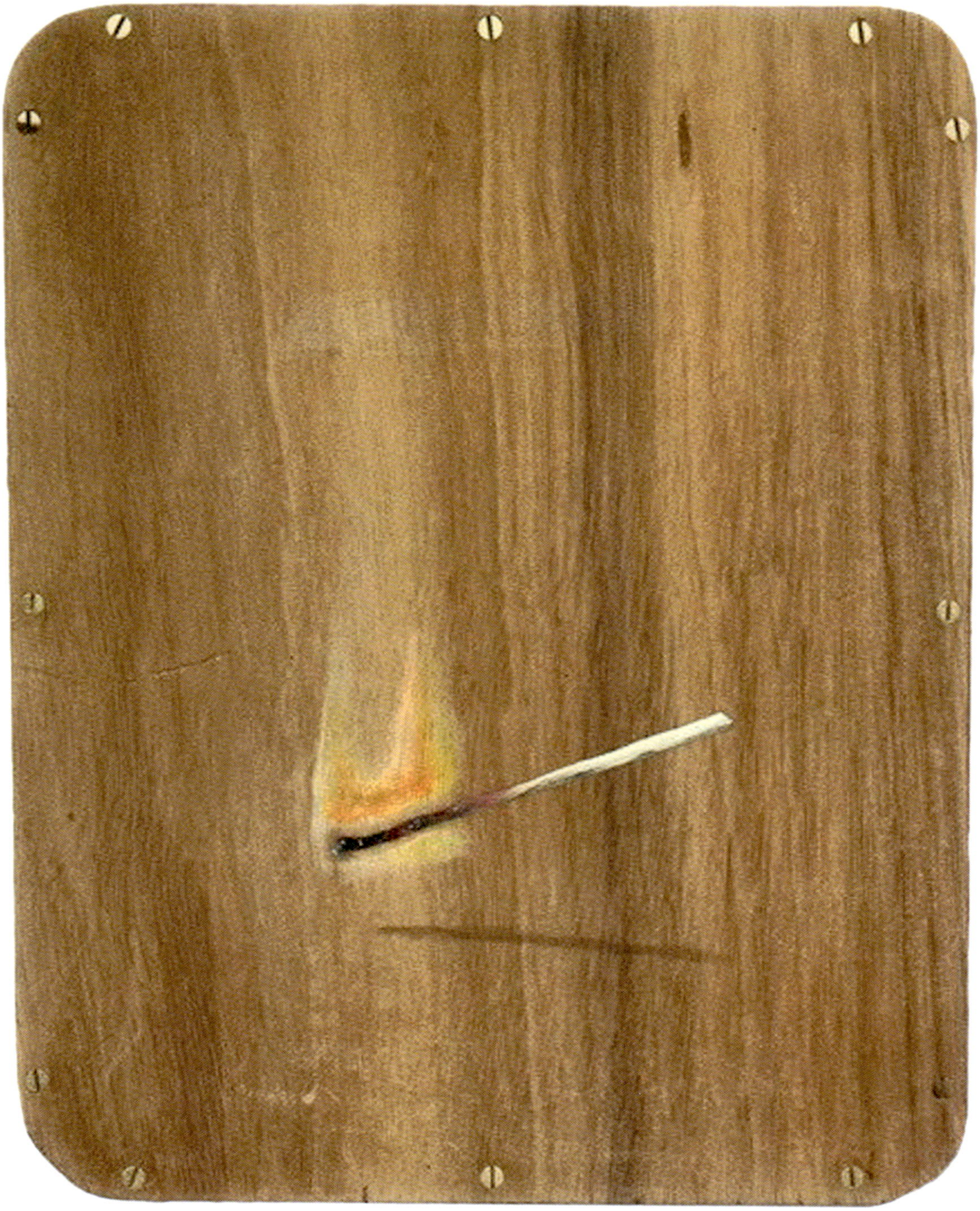

Match, Levitating 2020 Oil on found wood approx 31 × 22 cm

Splinter, Descending 2013 Oil on found wood approx 35 × 28 cm

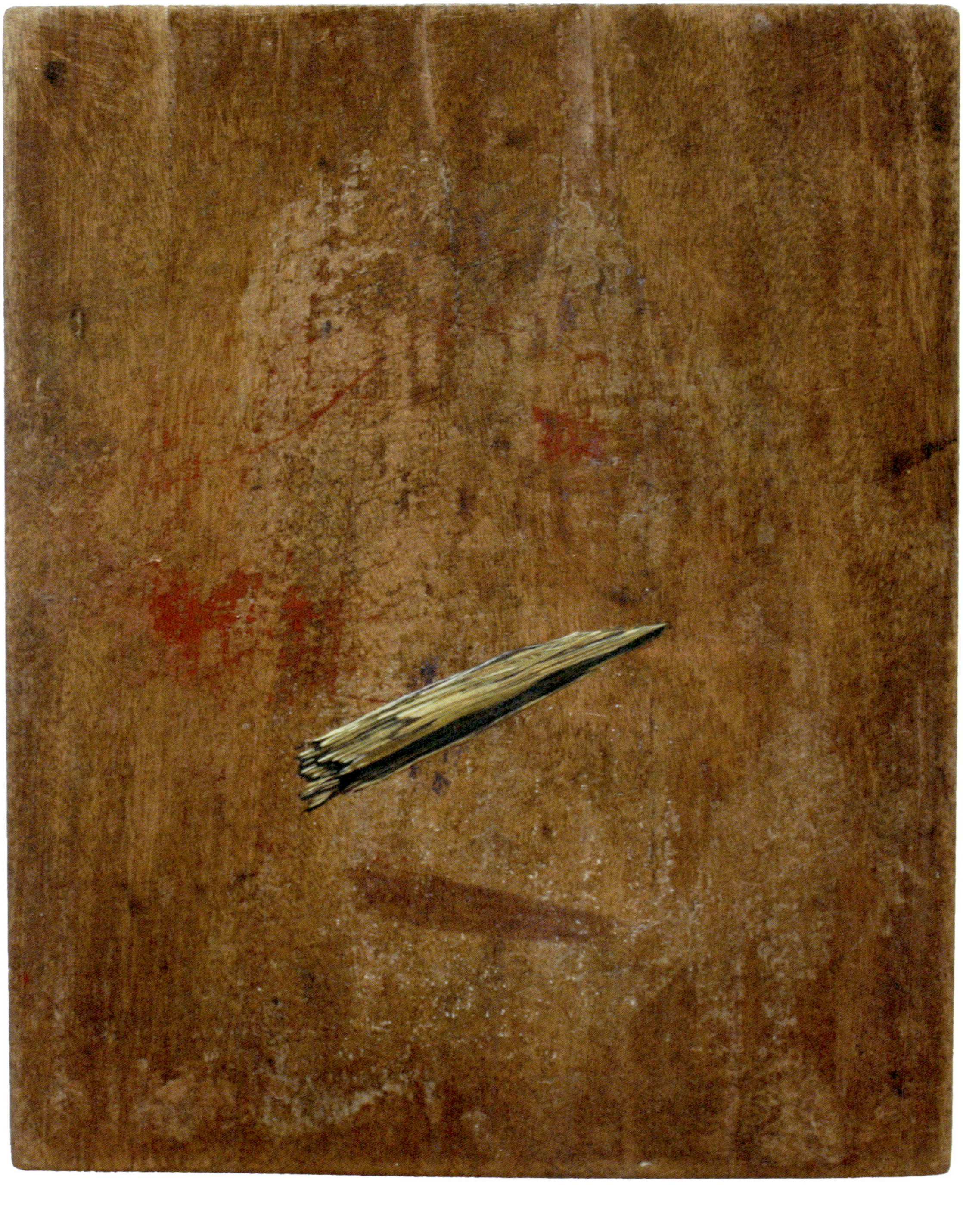

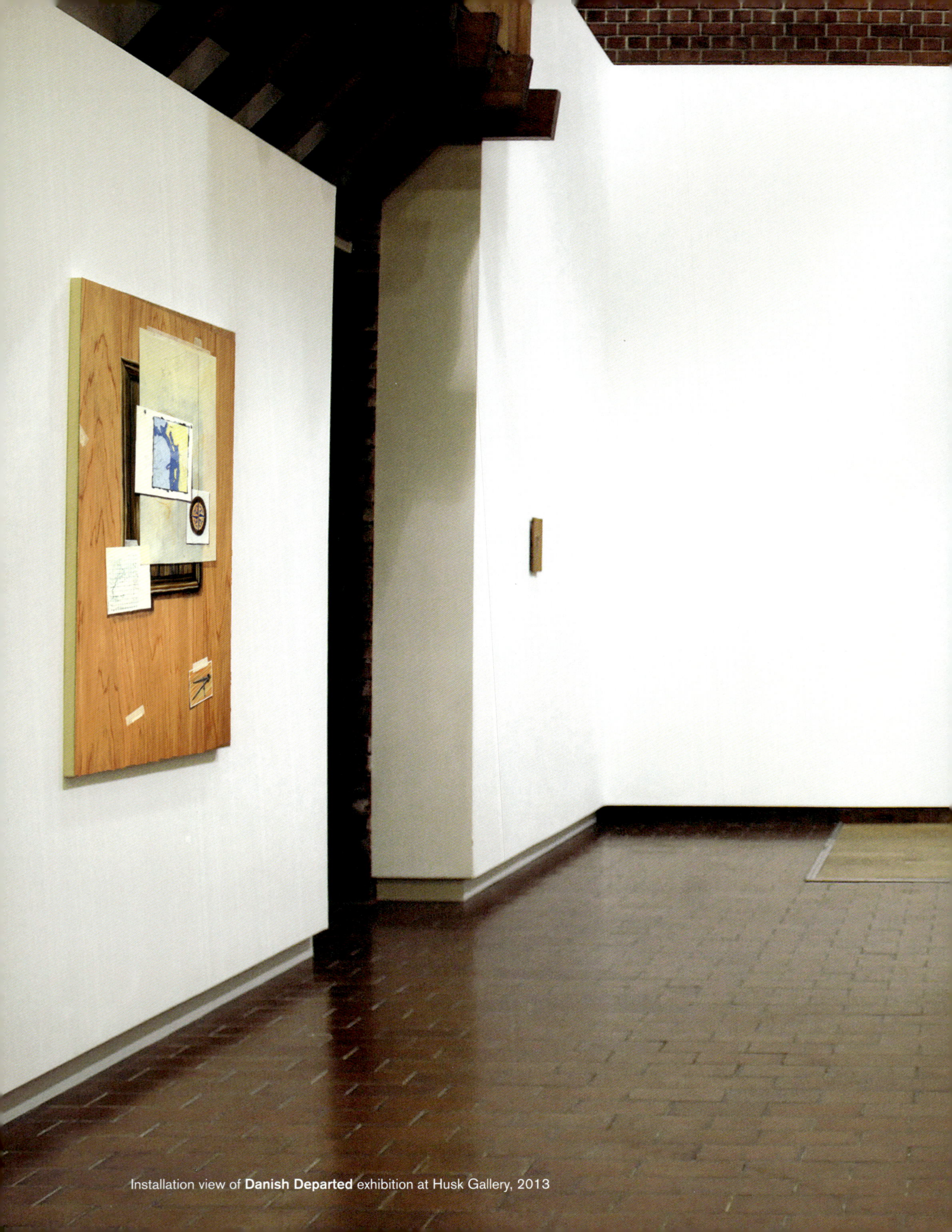

Installation view of **Danish Departed** exhibition at Husk Gallery, 2013

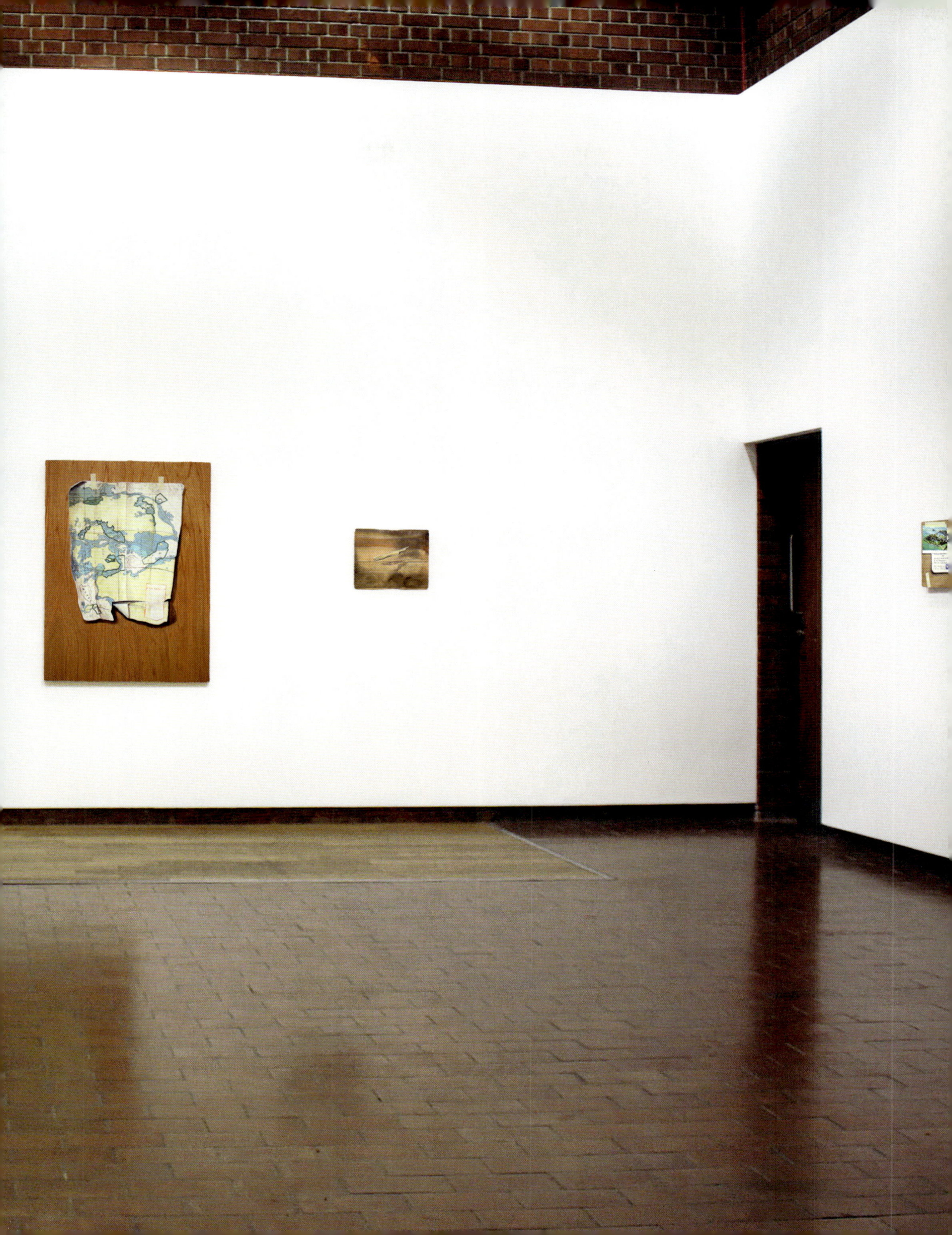

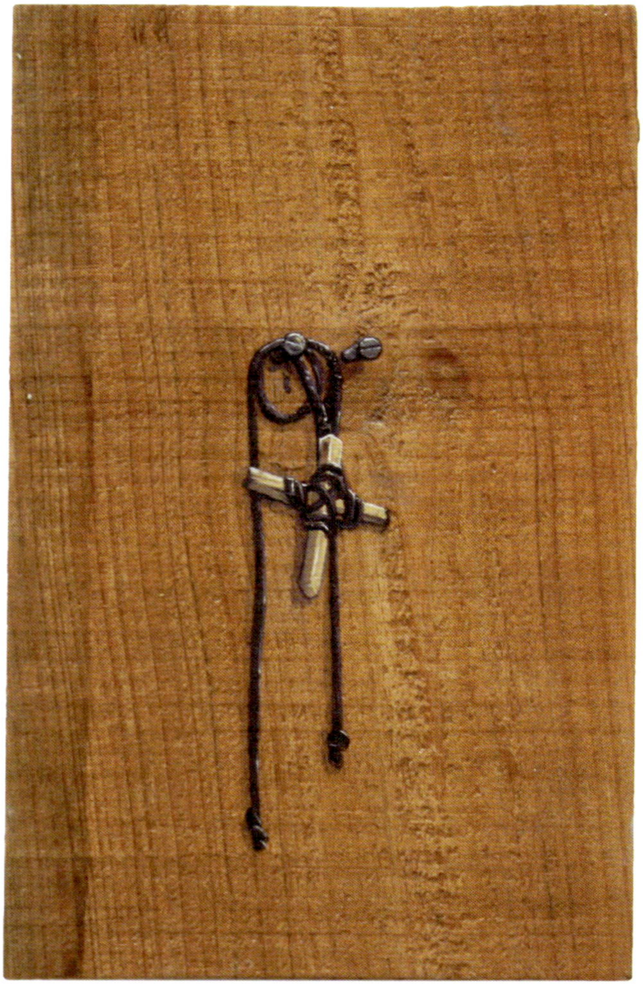

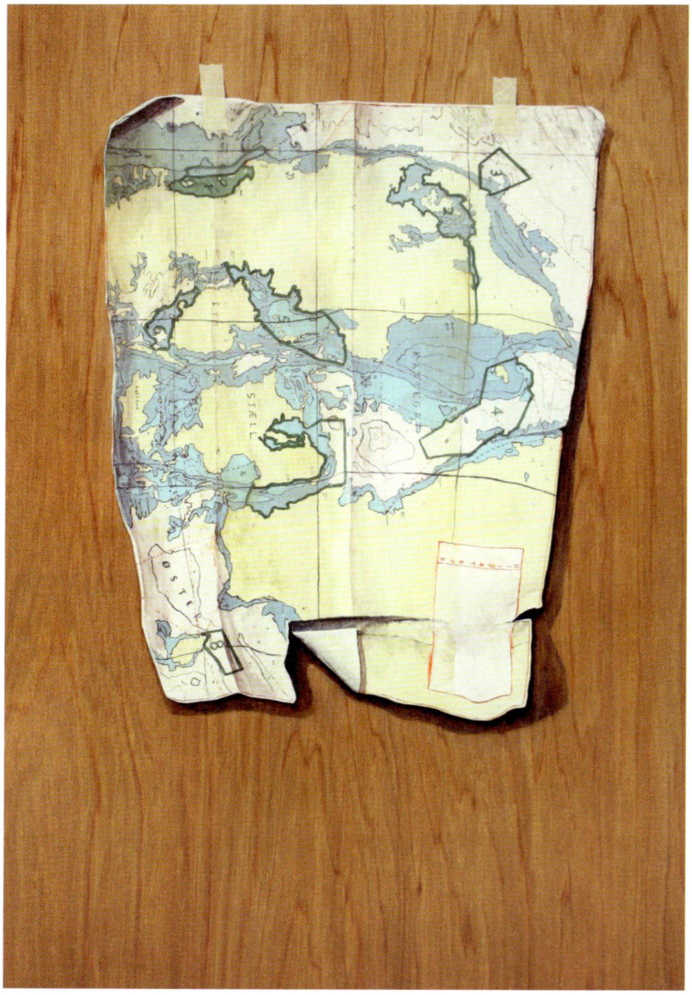

Charm 2013 Oil on found wood approx 15 × 8 cm

Nautical Map 2013 Oil on wood 120 × 90 cm

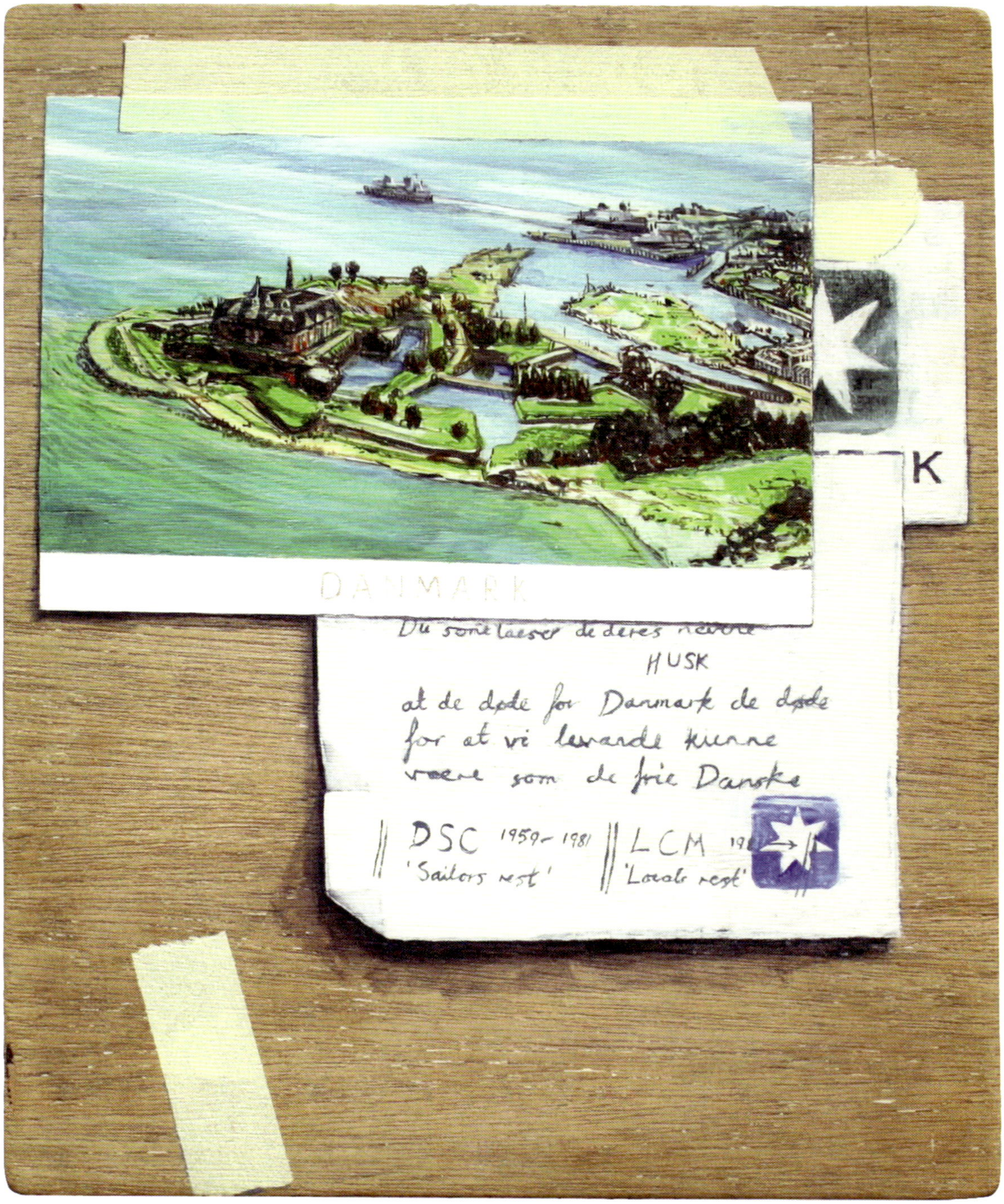

Postcard and Letter 2013 Oil on found wood 30 × 26 cm

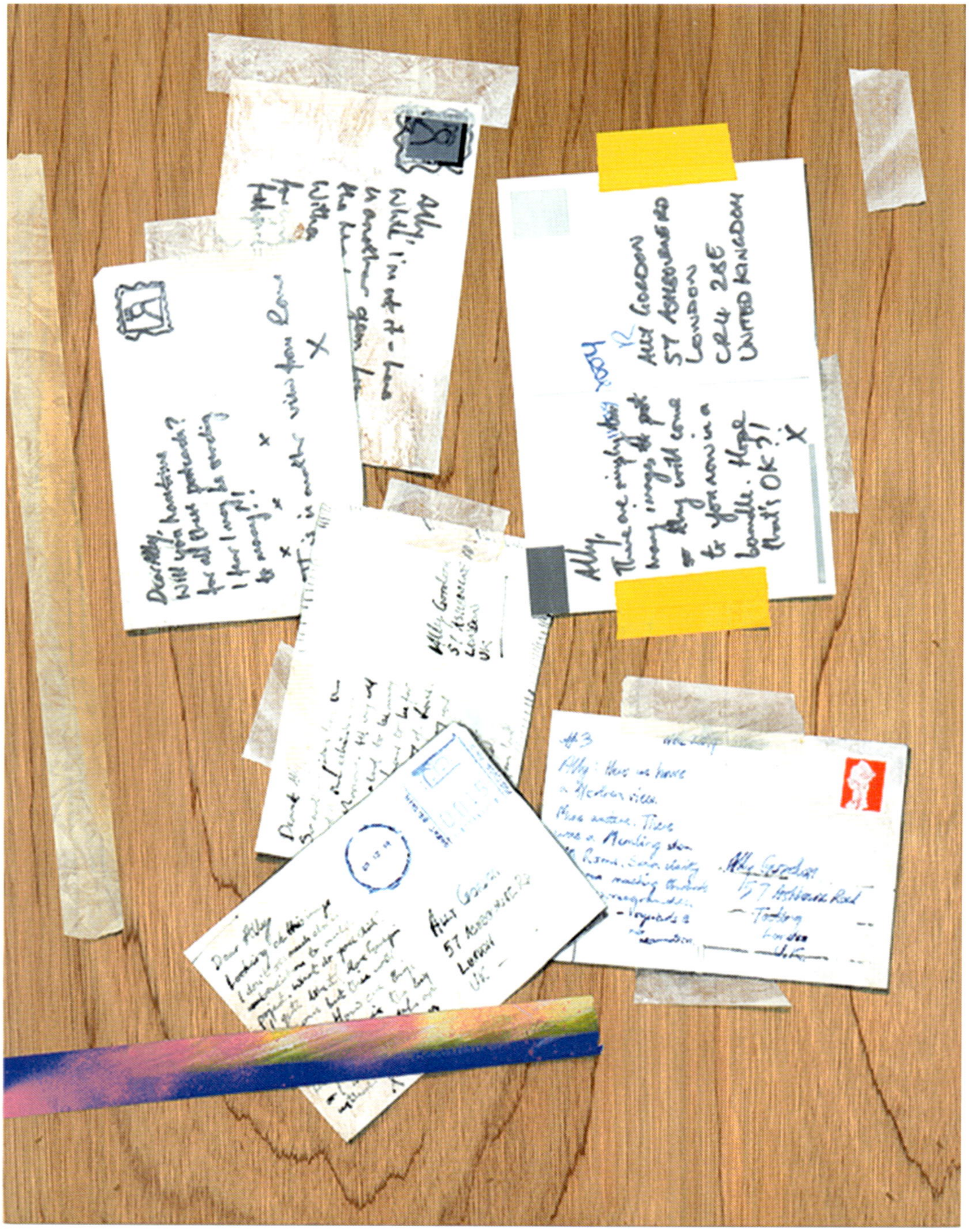

Letters From a Friend 2020 Acrylic on wood 50 × 40 cm

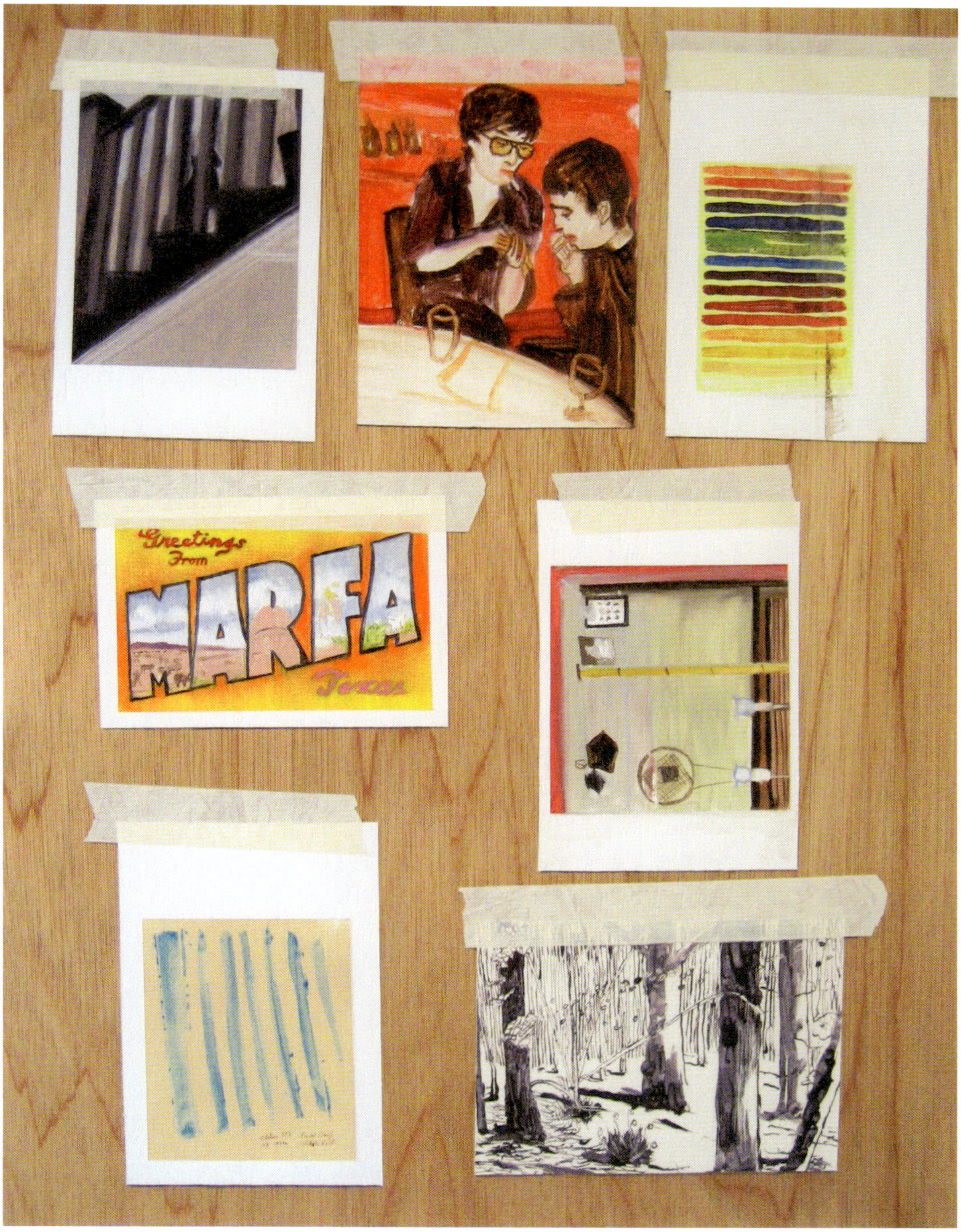

All the Postcards Sent to a Friend (After Carnegie, Peyton, Judd and Blackadder) 2015
Oil and acrylic on wood 50 × 40 cm

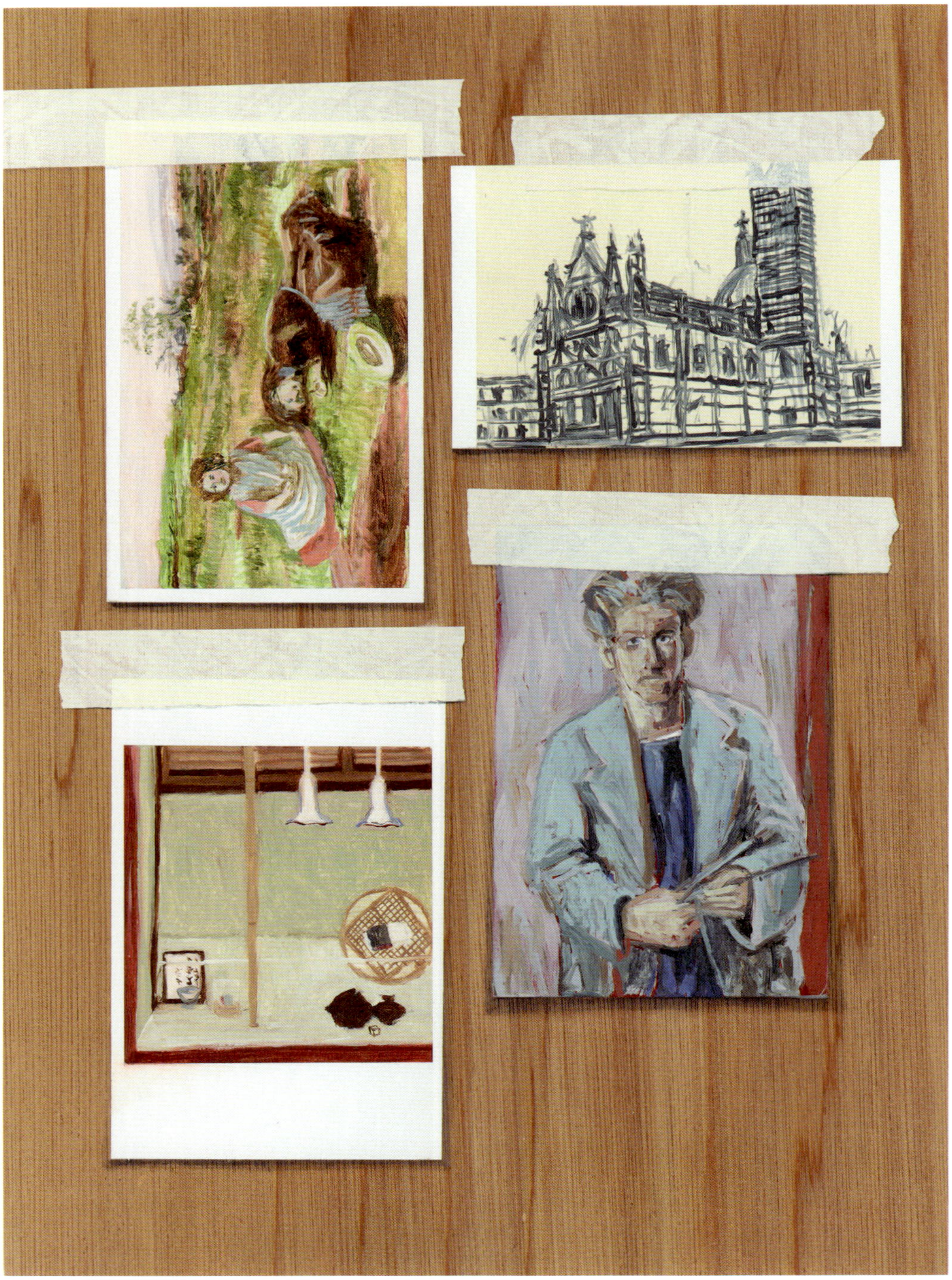

All the Postcards Sent to a Friend (After MacTaggart, Blackadder and Gillies) 2015
Oil and acrylic on wood 40 × 30 cm

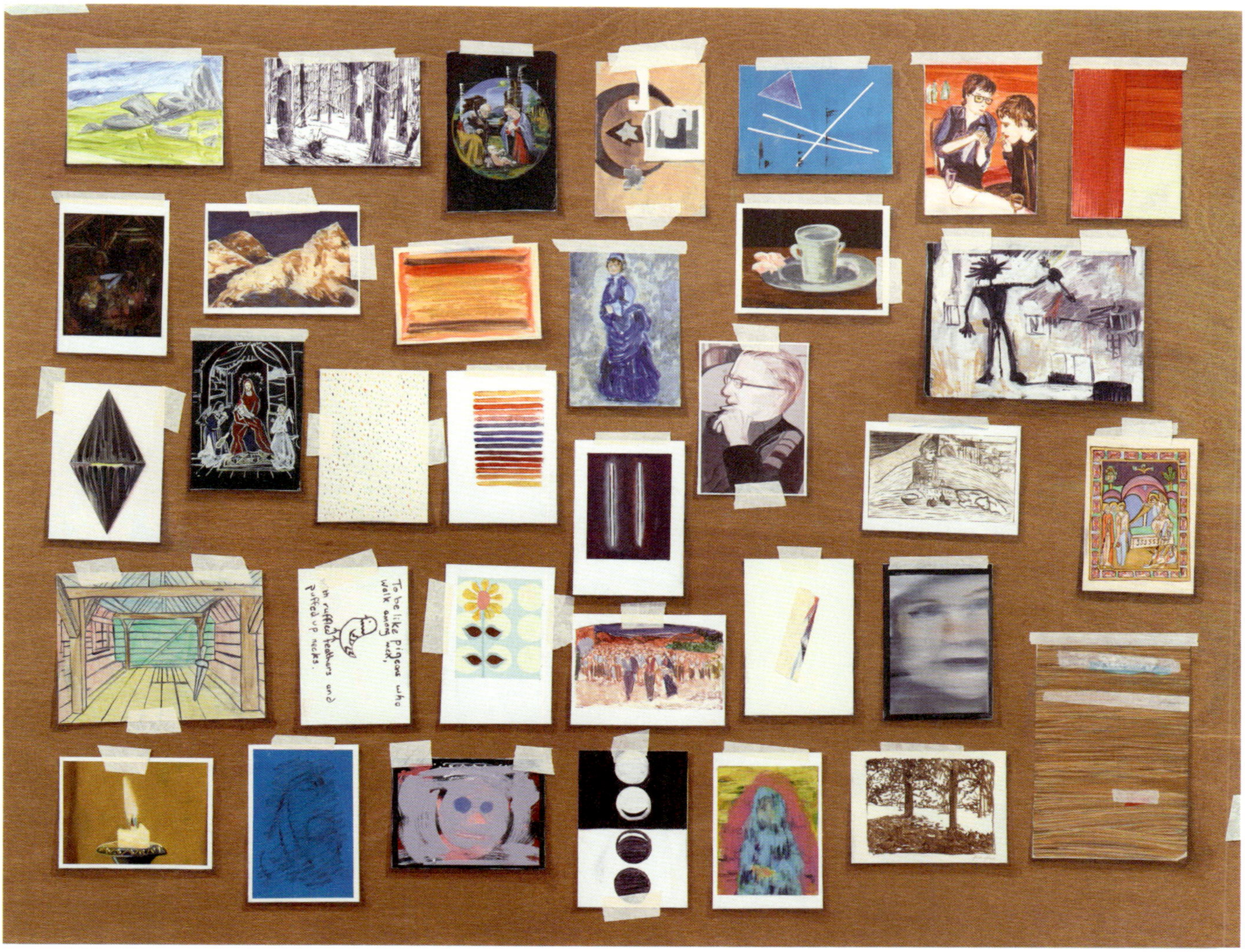

All the Postcards Sent to My Studio (01.12.14 to 25.12.14) 2015
Oil and acrylic on wood 90 × 120 cm

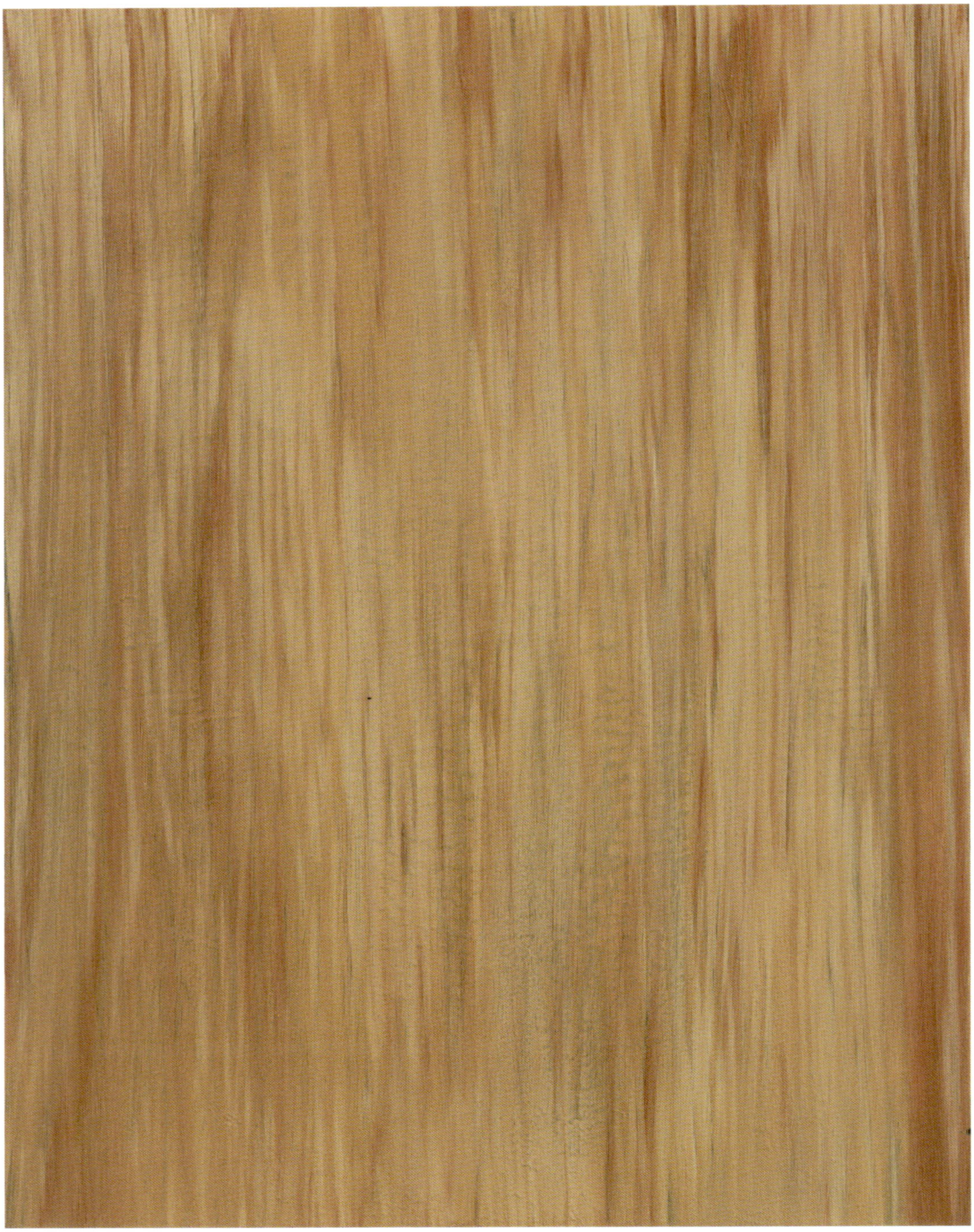

Ground 2015 Oil on board 50 × 40 cm

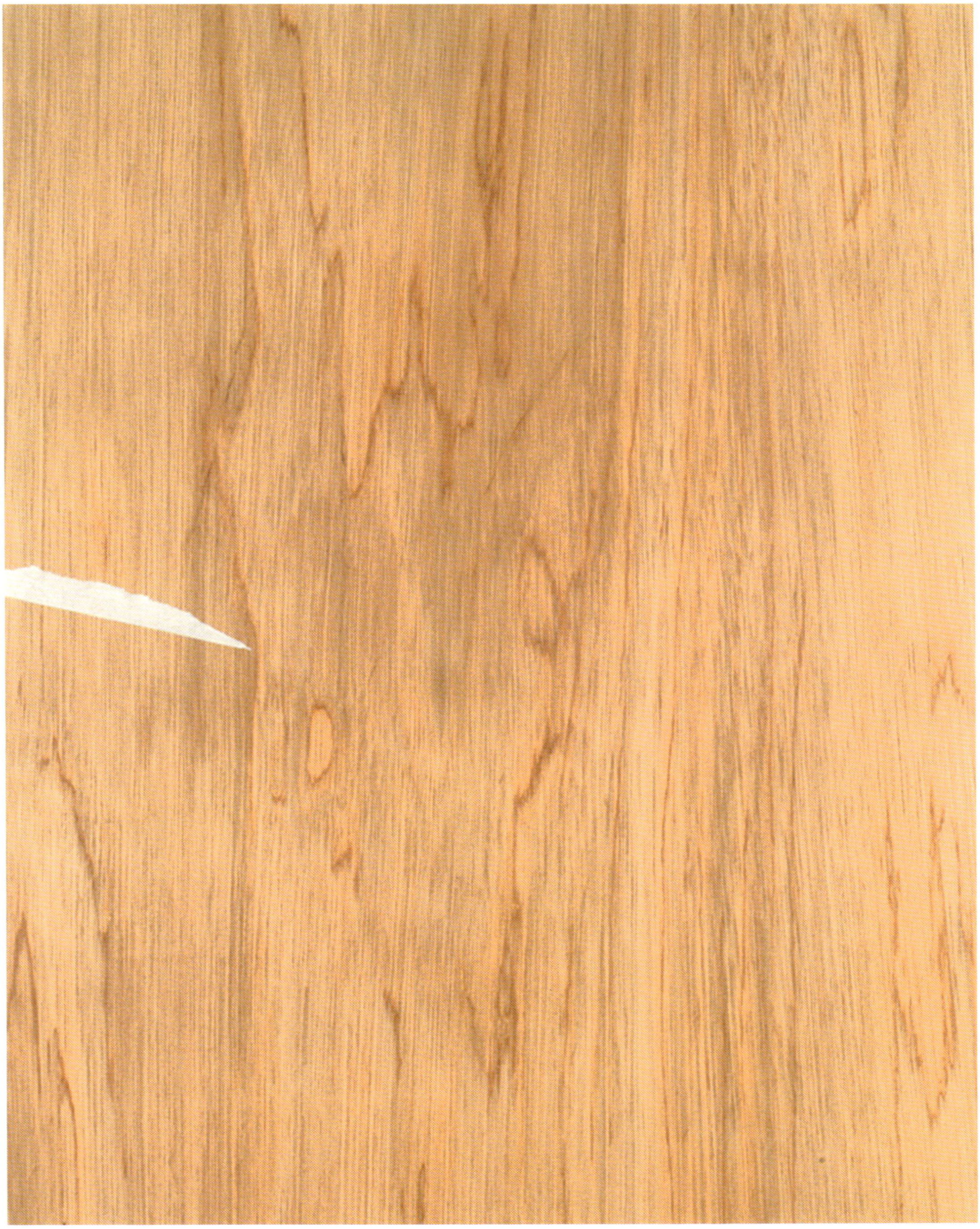

Tear 2014 Oil on wood 50 × 40 cm

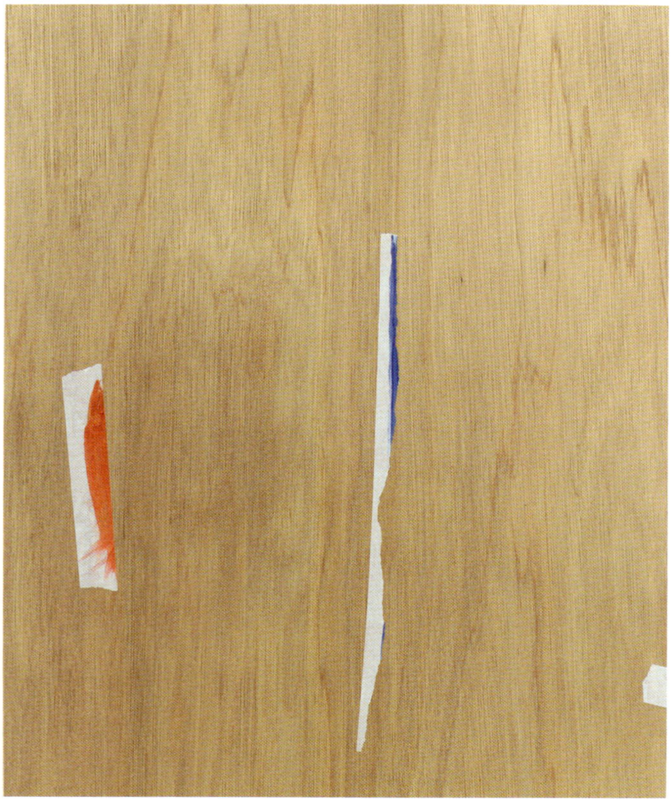

Vibac, Single Strips 2015 Oil on wood 50 × 40 cm

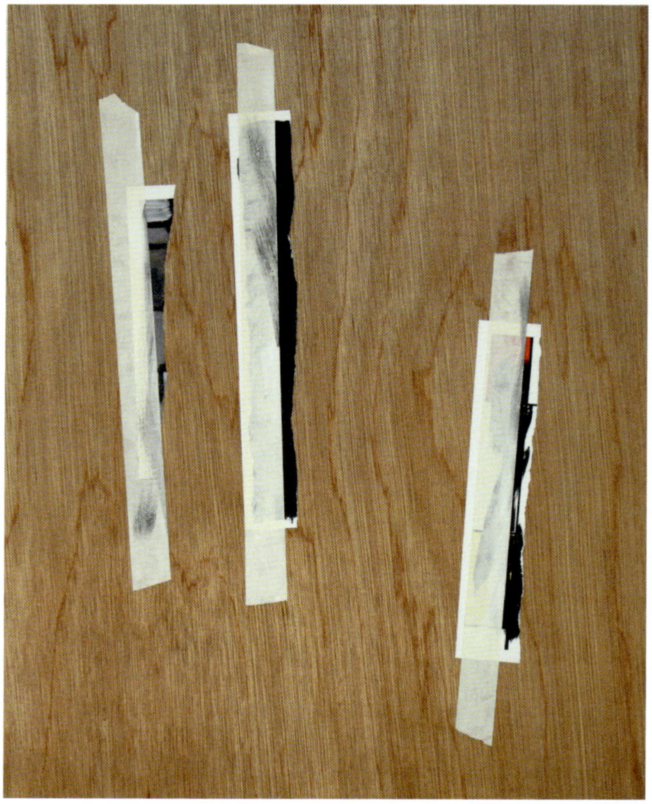

Vibac, PM71 2015 Oil on wood 50 × 40 cm

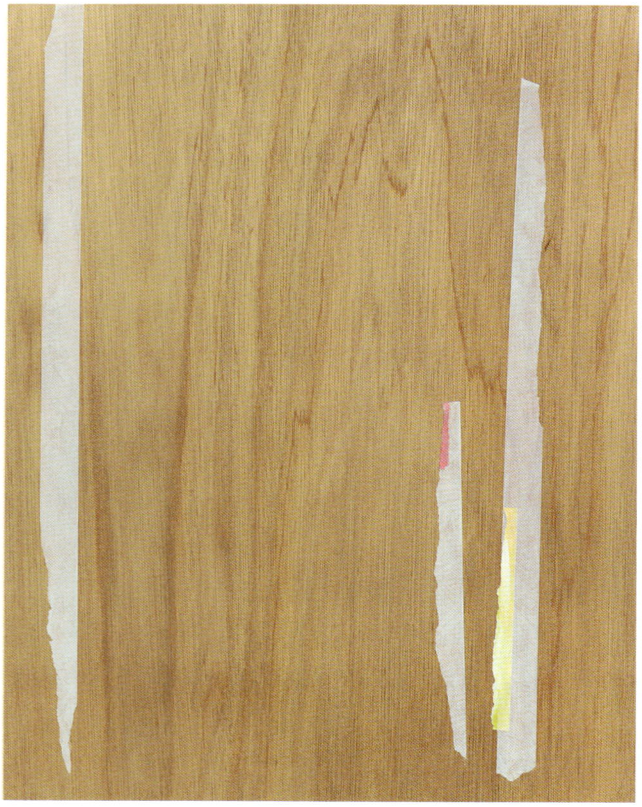

Vibac, Red Yellow 2015 Oil on wood 50 × 40 cm

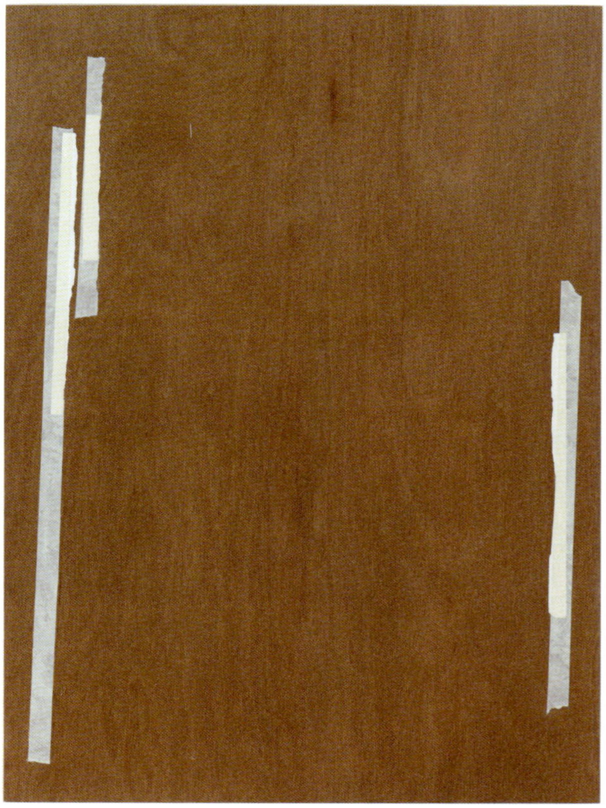

Vibac, Three Strips 2015 Oil on wood 120 × 90 cm

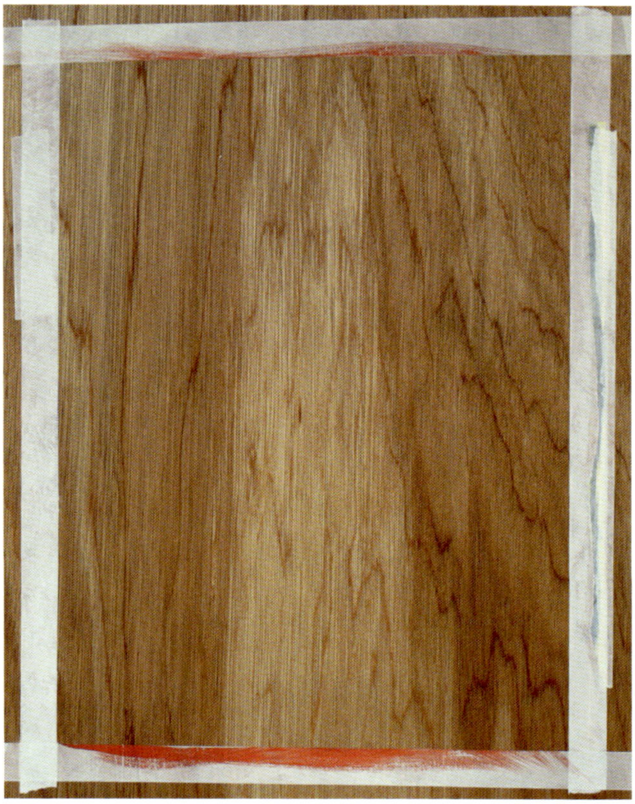

Vibac, Perimeter Formation 2015 Oil on wood 50 × 40 cm

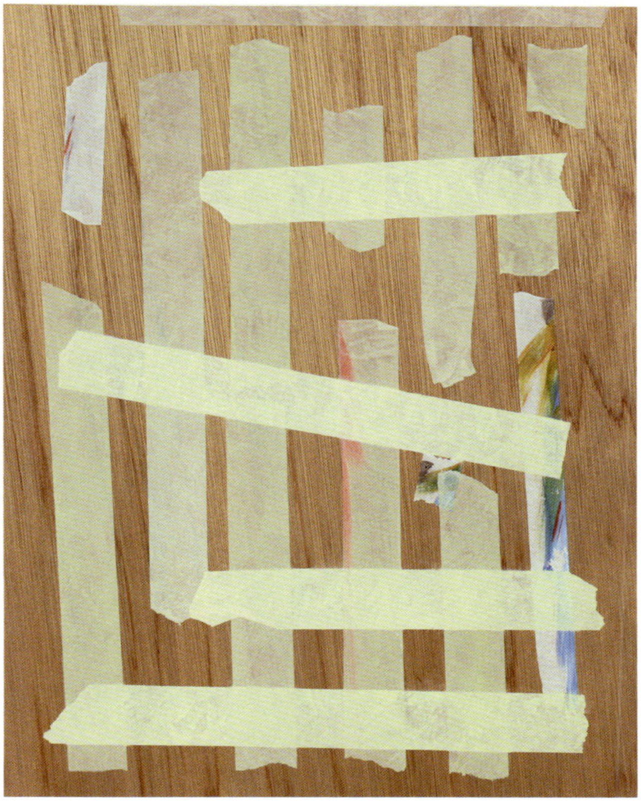

All the Tape Left Over From My Last Painting, White 2015
Oil on wood 40 × 30 cm

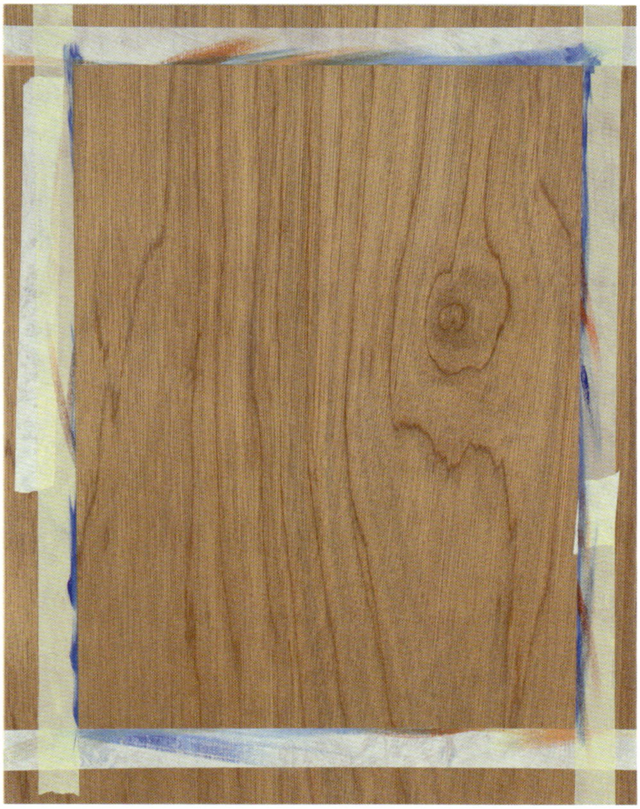

Vibac, Perimeter With Torn Paper 2015
Oil on wood 50 × 40 cm

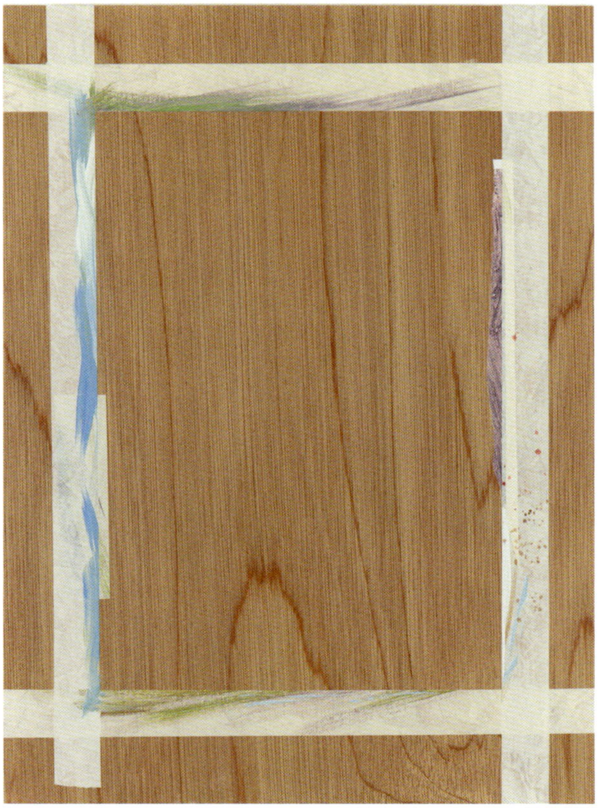

Vibac, Perimeter With Blue and Red 2015
Oil on wood 30 × 23 cm

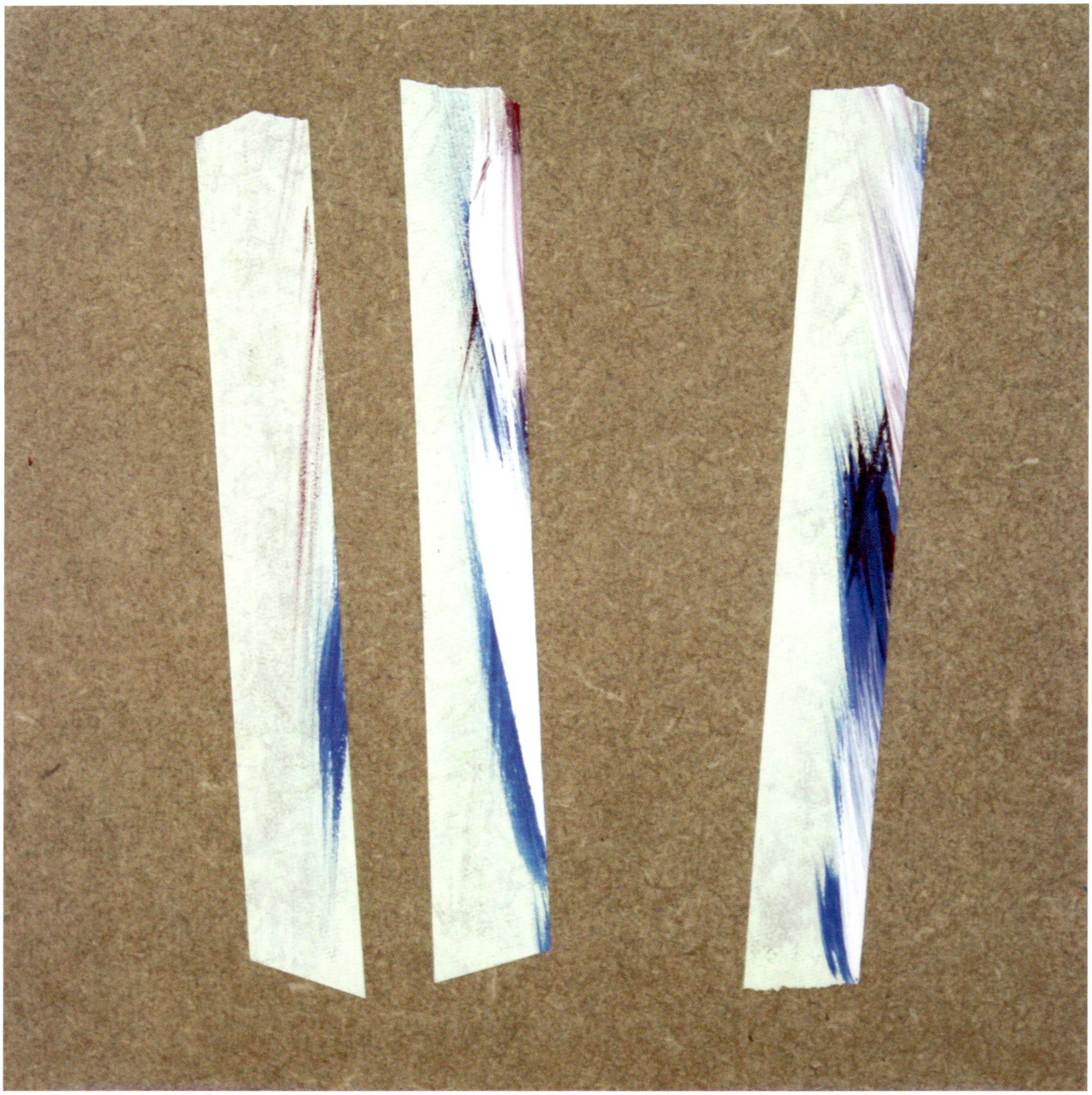

Three Strips of Masking Tape 2015 Oil on MDF board 22 × 22 cm

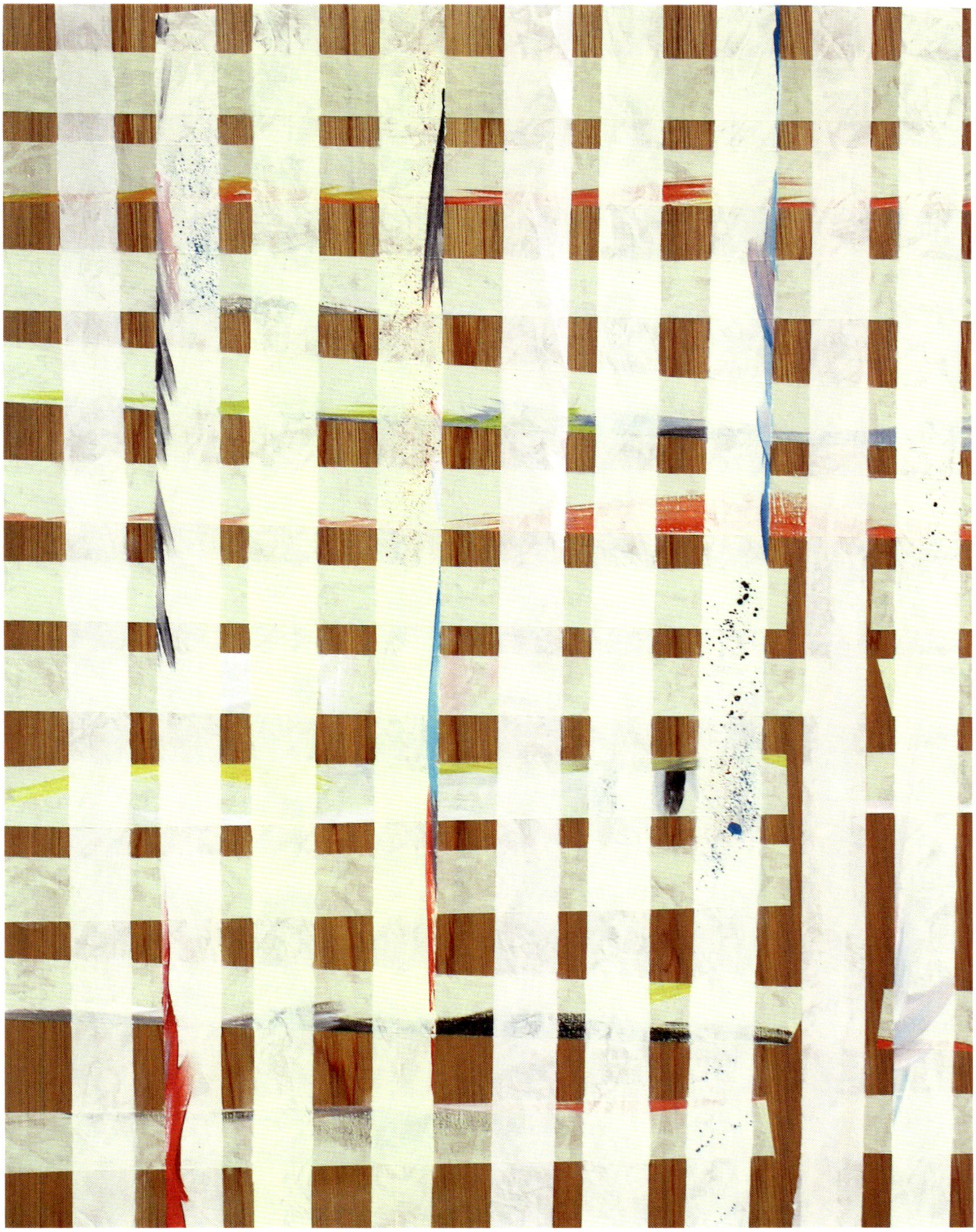

Vibac, Grid Formation 2015 Oil on wood 50 × 40 cm

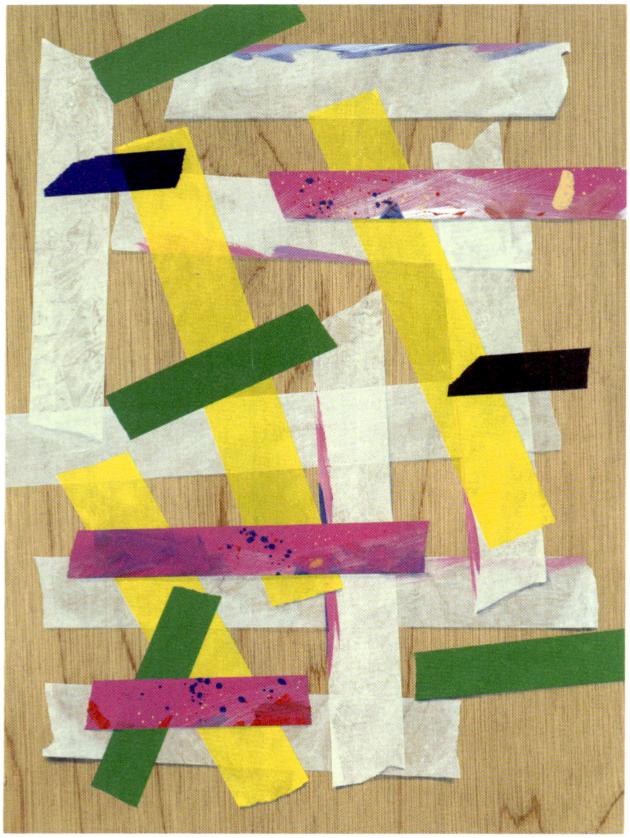

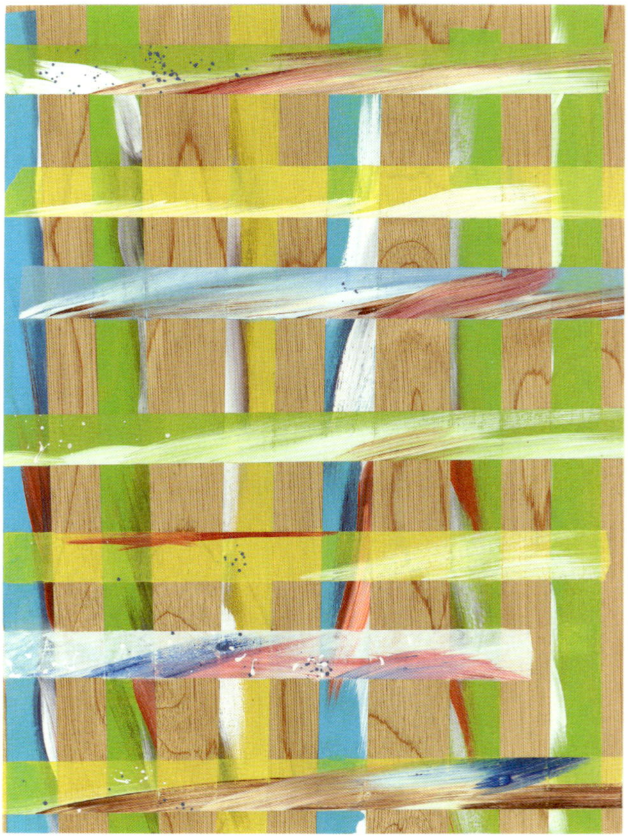

All the Tape Left Over From the BA Students' Paintings
2019 Acrylic on wood 40 × 30 cm

All the Tape Left Over From My Last Painting, Yellow, Blue and Green Stripes 2015
Oil on wood 40 × 30 cm

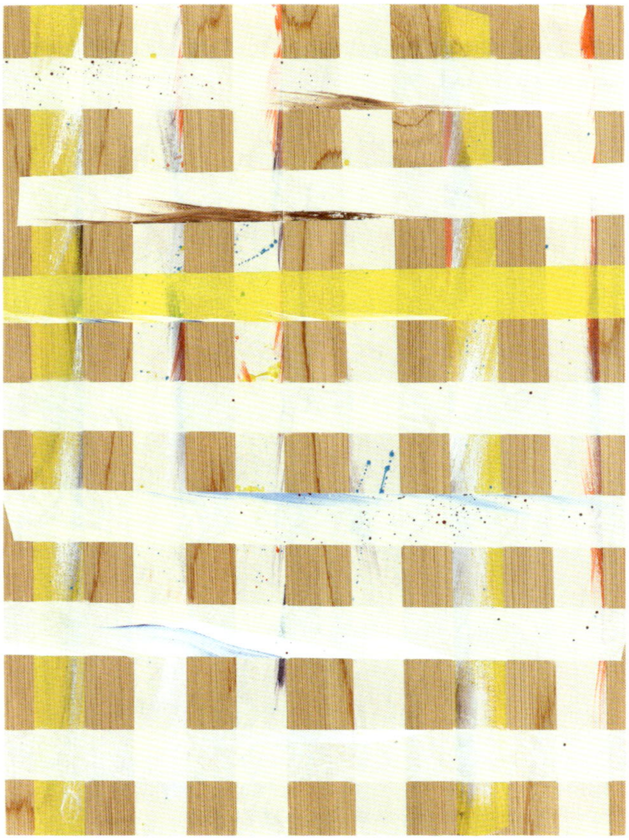

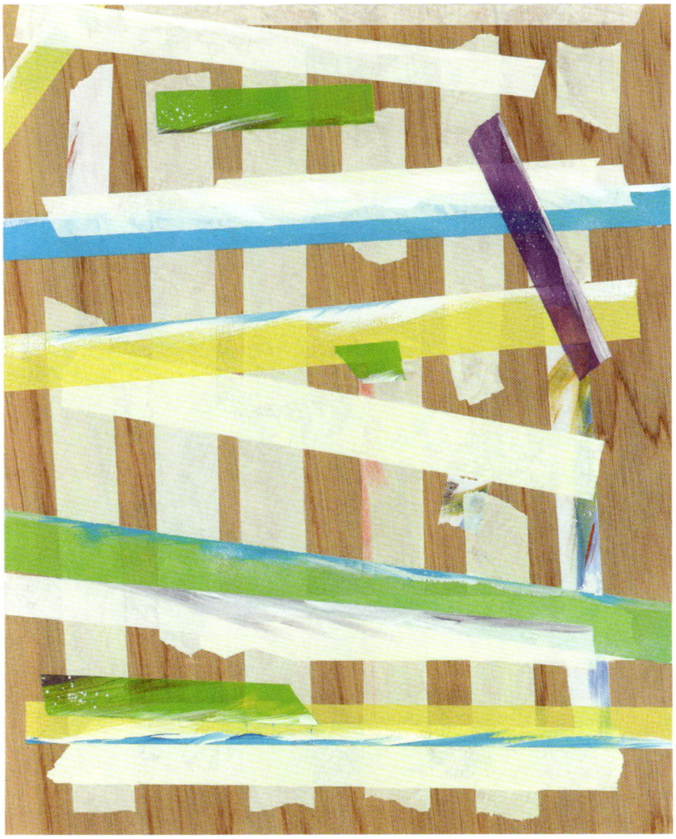

All the Tape Left Over From My Last Painting (Broken Stripes)
2015 Oil on wood 50 × 40 cm

All the Tape Left Over From My Last Painting (Diagonal Assembly)
2015 Oil on wood 50 × 40 cm

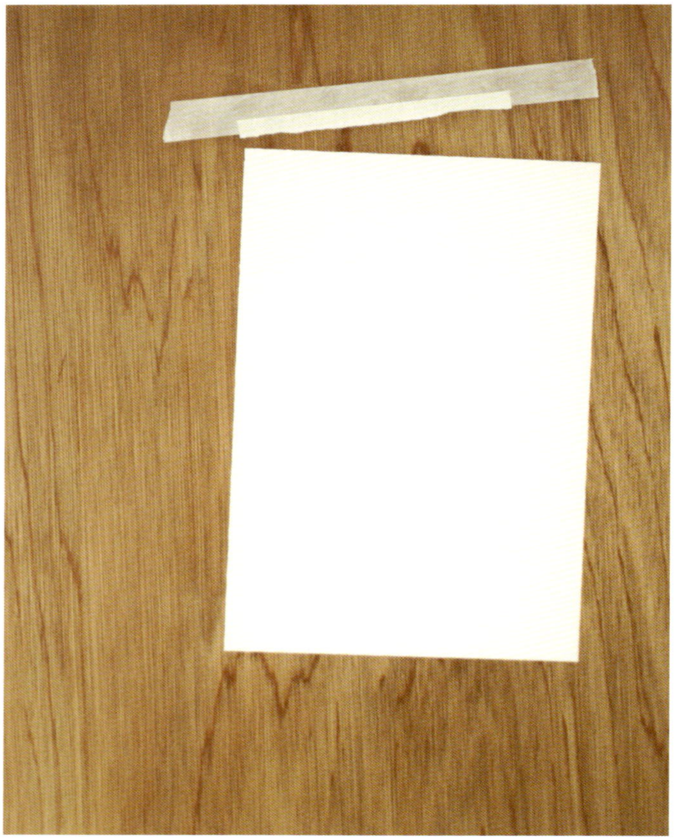

Sacrament, Paper Suspension 2014 Oil on wood 40 × 30 cm

Paper 2013 Oil on found wood approx 37 × 25 cm

Sacrament: Hidden, Revealed and Concealed 2014 Oil on wood 120 × 90 cm

Papers From My Studio (Staedtler Tracing Paper 120gsm) 2016 Oil on wood 50 × 40 cm

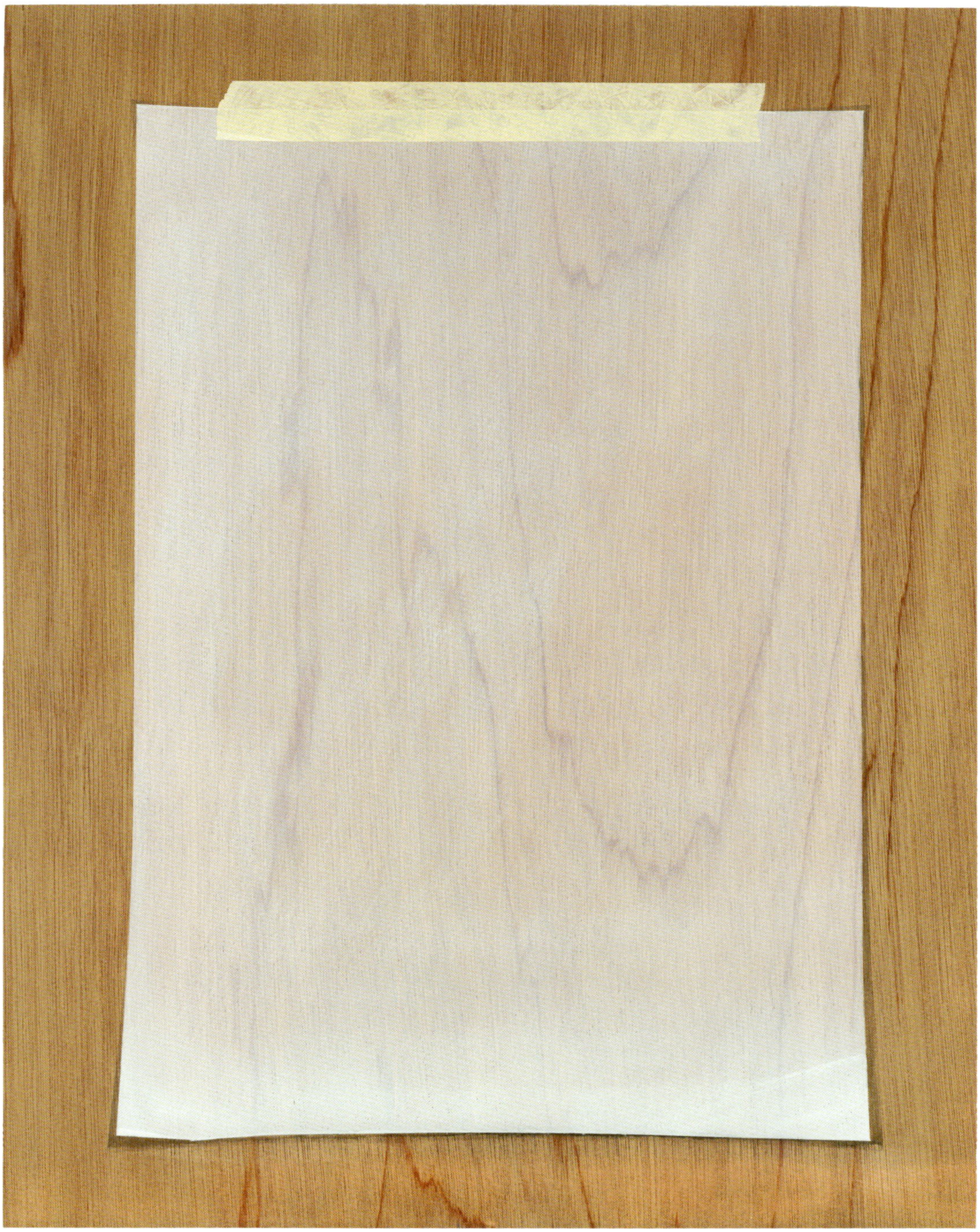

Papers From My Studio (Langston 140gsm) 2016 Oil on wood 50 × 40 cm

Papers From My Studio (Saunders Waterford 300gsm) 2016 Oil on wood 50 × 40 cm

Papers From My Studio (Rymans Copy Paper 80gsm) 2016 Oil on wood 50 × 40 cm

Papers From My Studio (Arches Aquarelle 640gsm) 2016 Oil on wood 50 × 40 cm

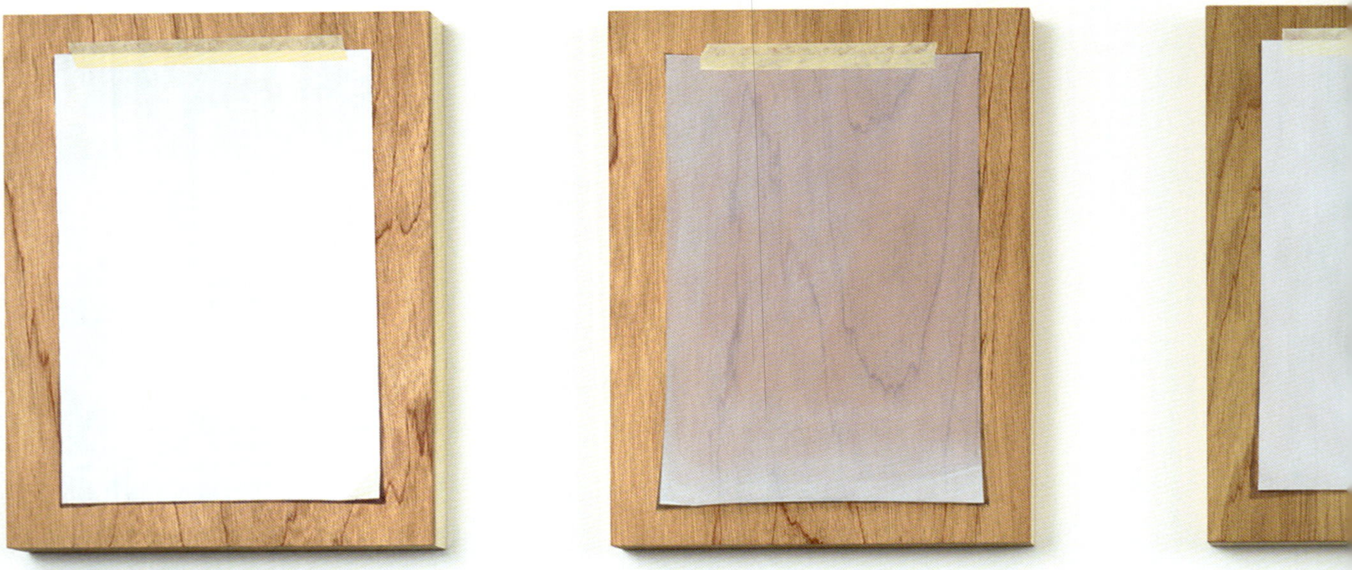

A Collection of Papers From My Studio 2016 Oil on wood Five paintings, each 50 × 40 cm

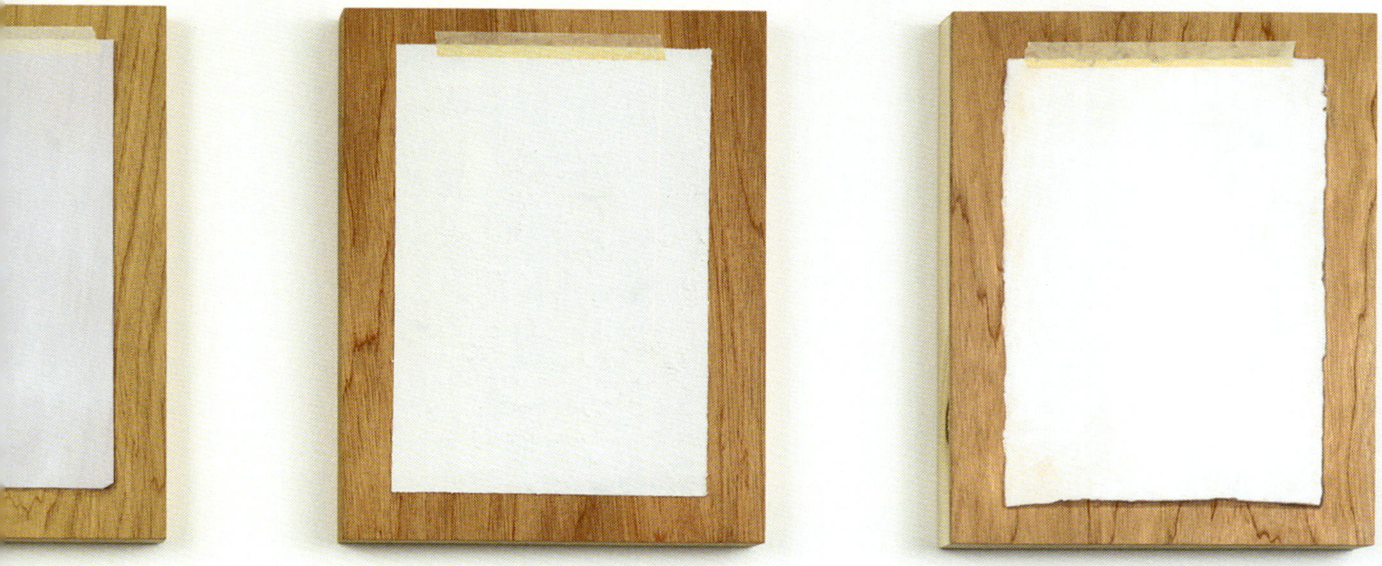

A few years ago, I took to mudlarking on the banks of the River Thames. You would be amazed at what those mudflats hold in secret perpetuity. Second World War shrapnel, Victorian clay pipes, bones, rusted metals, flip-flops, ancient coins and all manner of weird plastic objects, reformed by the elements, all waiting to be discovered amid the other less-curious sediments of the city. Compared to other mighty thoroughfares such as the Ganges or the Mississippi, the Thames is a relatively short waterway. It must be the shortest river in the world to acquire such a history.

I took those washed-up objects to my studio and painted them to appear like museum artefacts or archaeological remains. One of these paintings found its way to China for a touring exhibition with works by other artists concerned with the degradation of the oceans. The exhibition, *Matter Matters*, first exhibited at the Czech-China Contemporary Art Museum in Beijing and then toured to Norway, the mudlarked objects travelling with the painting itself.

That same year, I worked for the City & Guilds of London Art School as artist in residence. I was especially drawn to the objects left in the studios after the students had completed their final shows. Discarded paint rags and papers littered the wooden floors, residual marks and paint-thumbed postcards adorning the walls like an incidental cabinet of curiosity or archive of forgotten objects. Each item suggesting a personal history or speculative diary of the student's time at the school. I began to paint these objects, seeing them as a kind of flotsam and jetsam of the art school. My final show recreated the studio detritus as an expanded quodlibet mural, painted directly onto the vinyl floor, and recreating the wooden floorboards of the original Georgian building. This was my largest painting to date, pushing me to the limits of my technical and physical capacity. A few years earlier, I had made another large-scale work, while artist in residence for the charity London City Mission, involving large-scale planning, assistants and long hours in the studio.

Souvenirs from the Waste Land

Best known for its work with the homeless community, LCM is a remarkable charity, and it was a privilege to work with so many generous-hearted people. My residency studio, based at Departure arts centre (later to become Husk), was housed alongside rehearsal rooms for musicians, English classes for the local Bangladeshi community, a discreet counselling service for women caught in sex trafficking, a gallery space for recent art graduates, and a café. Alongside painting and community projects, my role also involved curating art shows for the gallery and making tea for the homeless. In my second year, I was commissioned by the charity to make a painting to celebrate its 180th anniversary. My response was a painting to celebrate everyone working for the charity at that time; seventy individual paintings of their shoes to make a collective portrait titled *The Feet of Those*.

In the years that followed, I was granted the opportunity to exhibit further afield, and an exhibition at the Ahmanson Gallery in Irvine, California, opened a door to new possibilities in scale and subject. With grander proportions than any gallery I had worked with before, I could play with the idea of quodlibet on a bigger scale. Most European quodlibets are limited to the modest proportions of a seventeenth-century mercantile home, but here, in California, my paintings could expand the humble postcard to the size of a billboard or roadside advertisement. The exhibition came in the same year Trump had been inaugurated president and the UK announced it would leave the European Union. An extraordinary year of political and economic turbulence. We titled the exhibition *Souvenirs from the Waste Land*, in tribute to TS Eliot's *The Waste Land*, a poem written at another time of geo-political unrest.

Back in London, I was collaborating with my friend, the artist Hugh Mendes. In the series *Remains*, we worked on a cluster of diptychs. I recreated the studio walls of late, great London artists, such as Francis Bacon, Lucian Freud, Craigie Aitchison and Michael Andrews. Hugh painted replicas of their obituaries as printed in *The Observer* newspaper. The resulting collaboration was presented by Charlie Smith Gallery in London and was something of a painterly homage to artists we admired. I remain grateful to Hugh for this nourishing partnership.

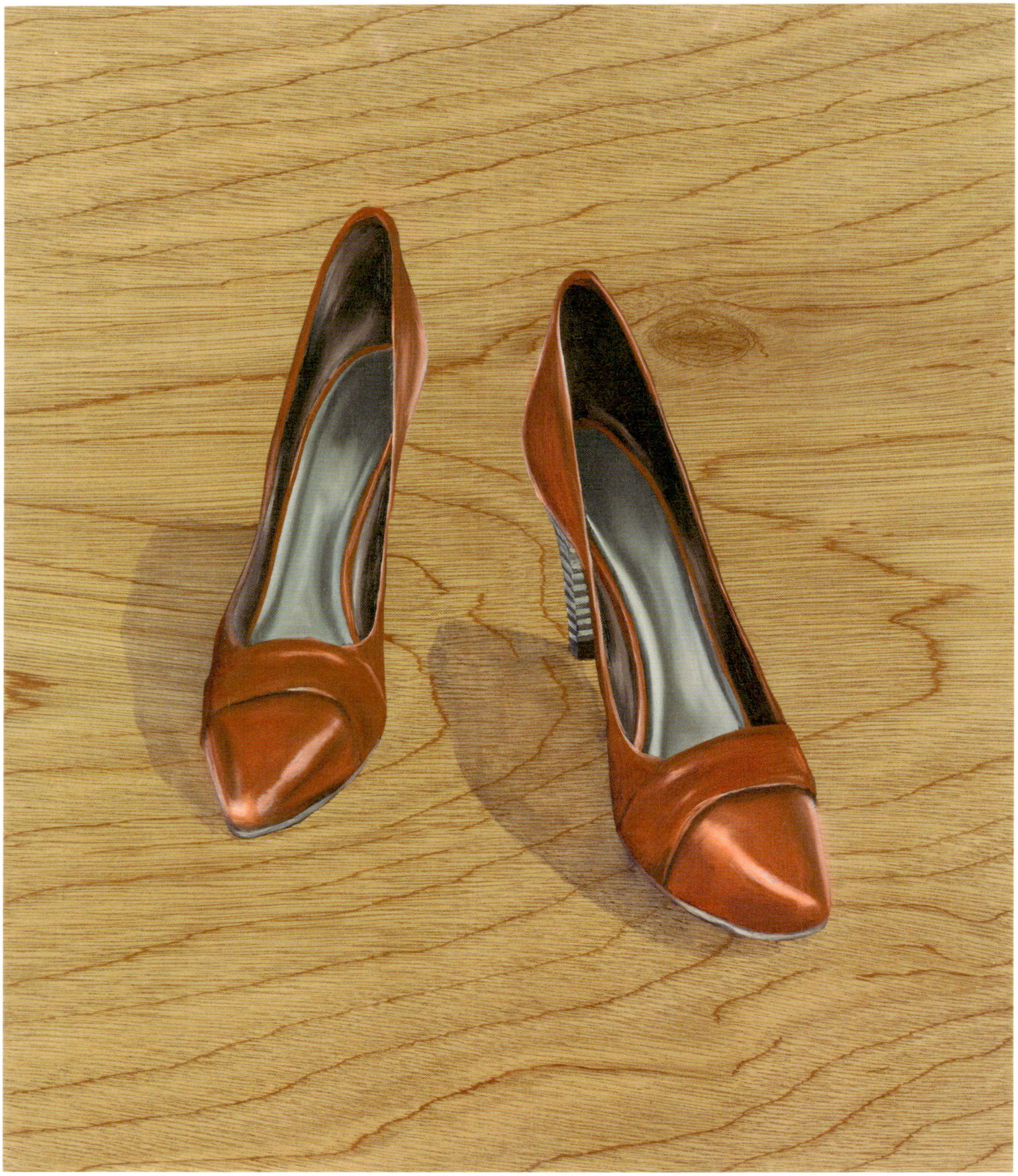

The Feet of Those details 2016 Oil on wood 71 paintings, each 40 × 50 cm

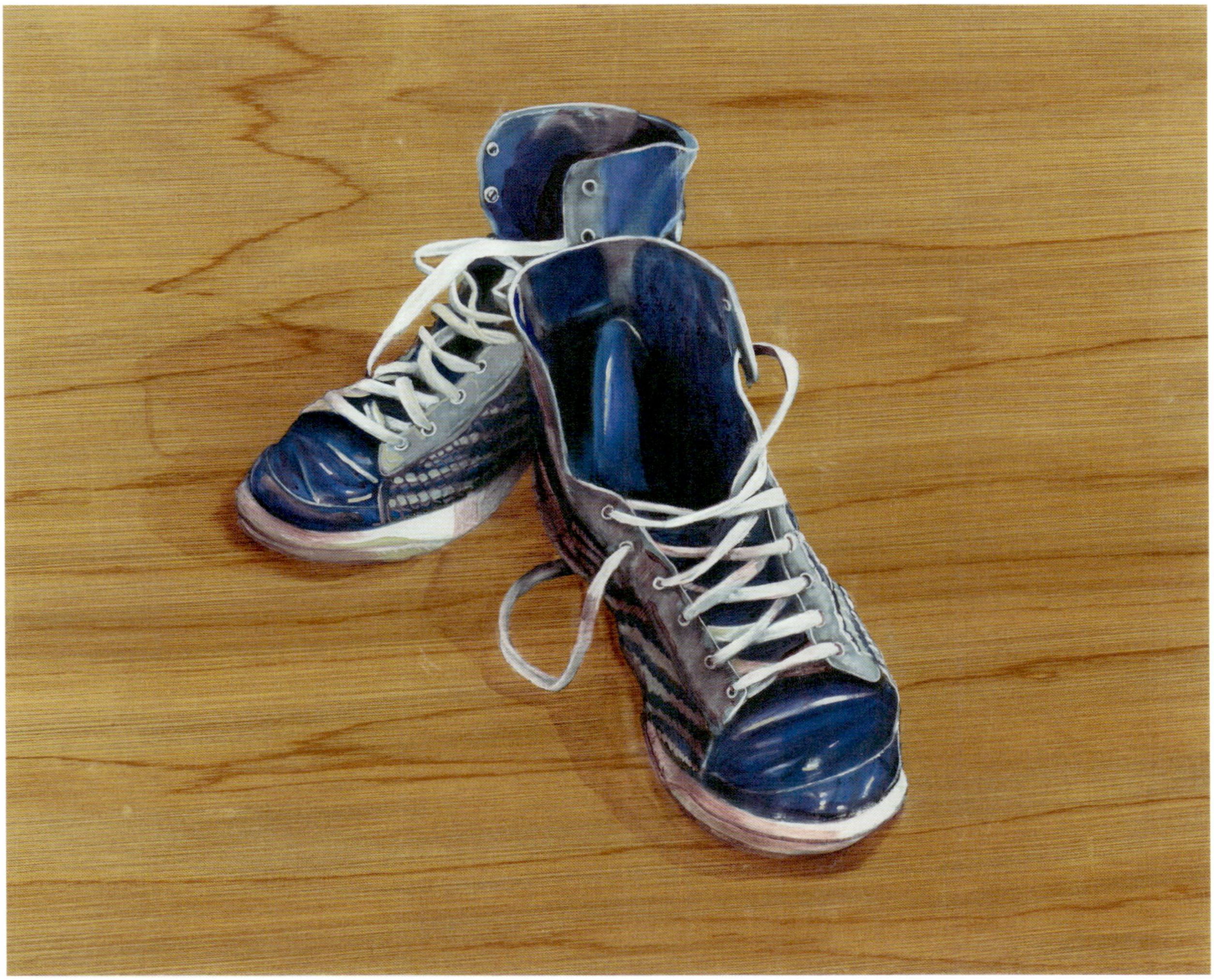

78

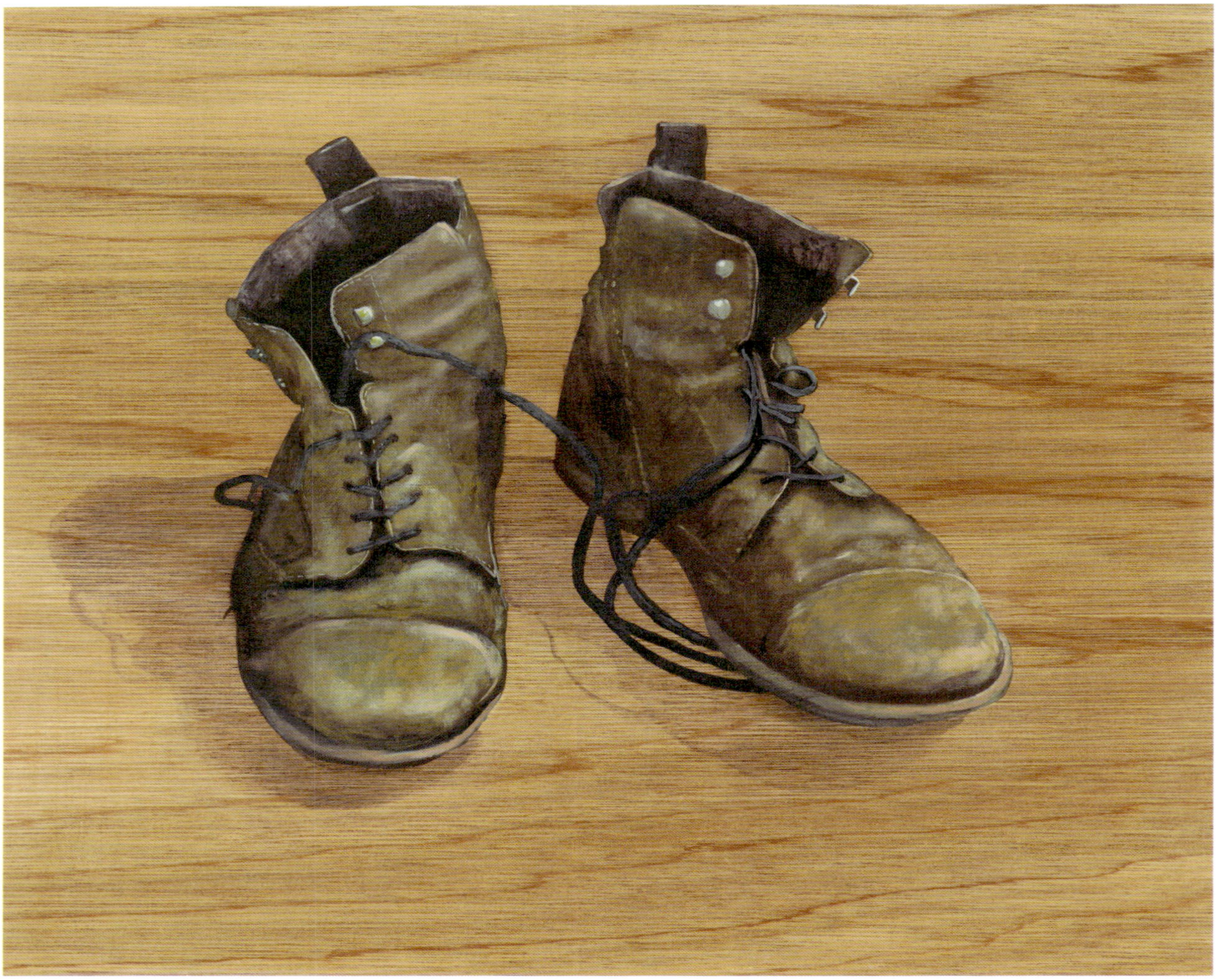

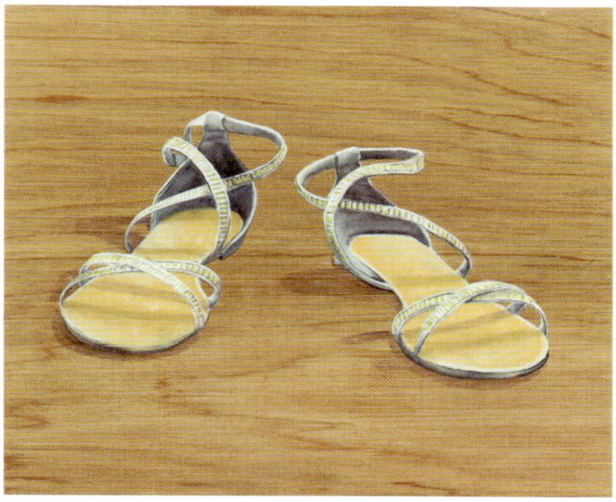
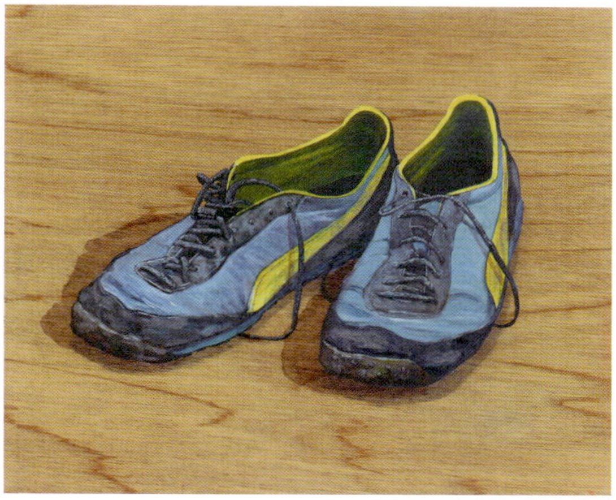
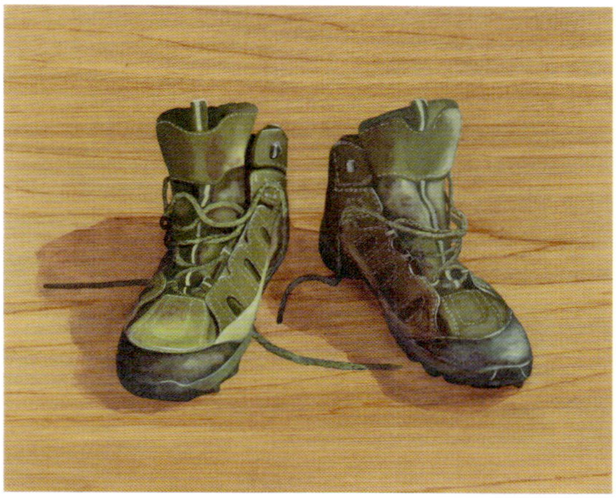
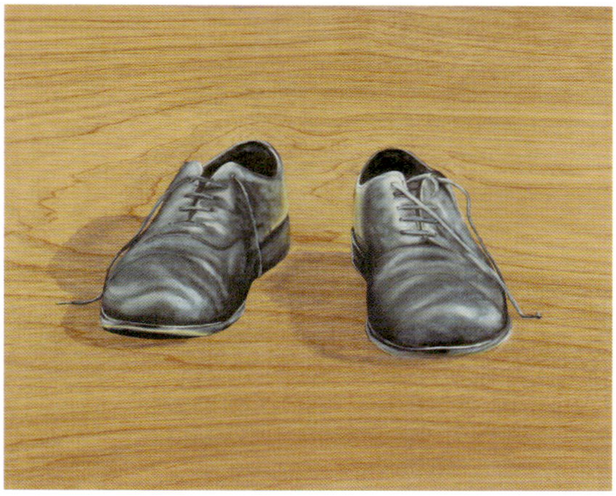
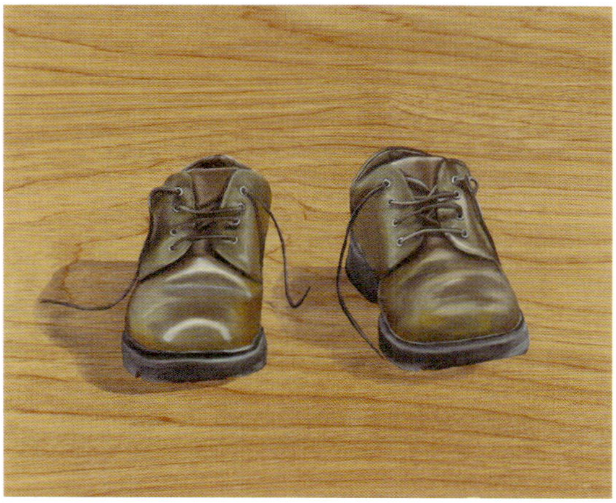
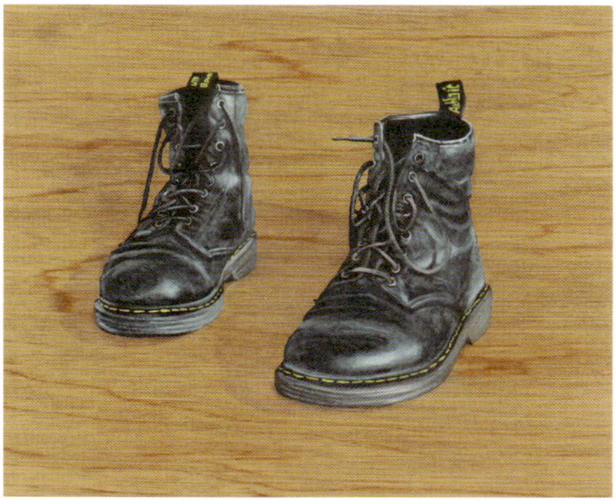
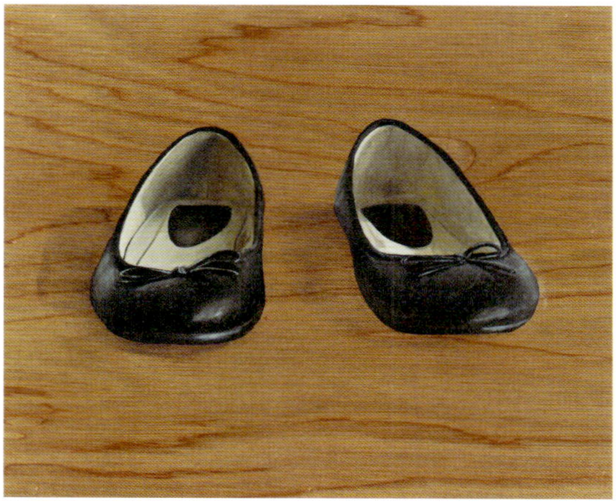
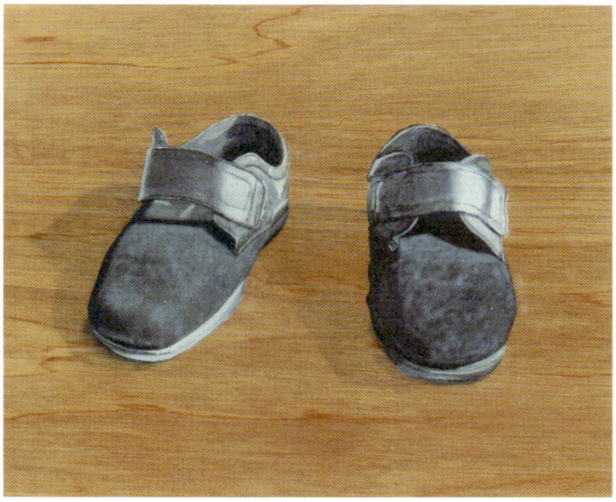

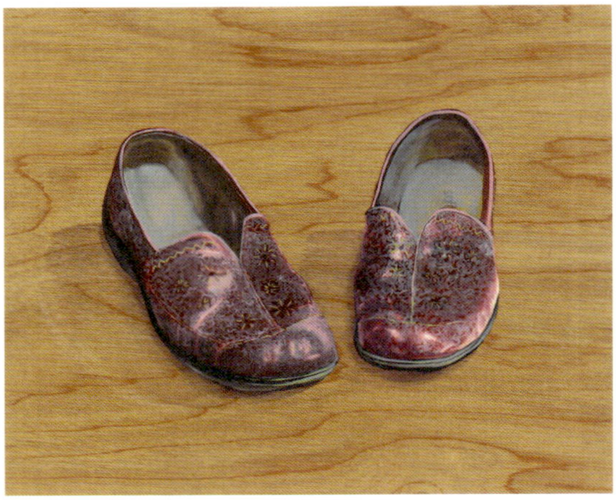
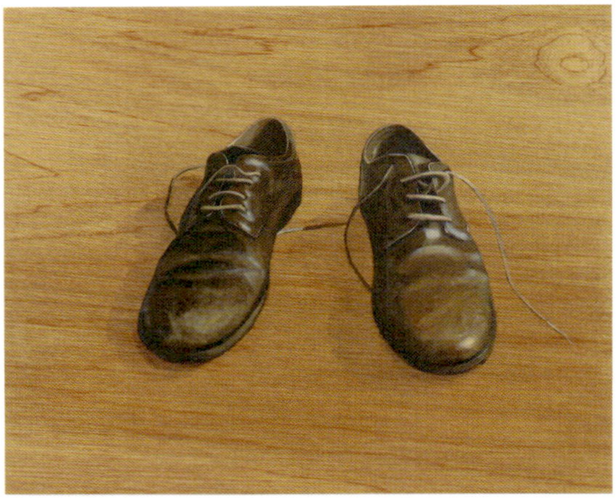
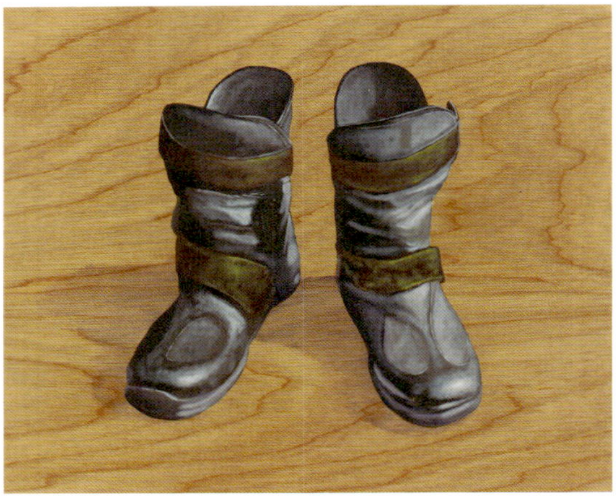
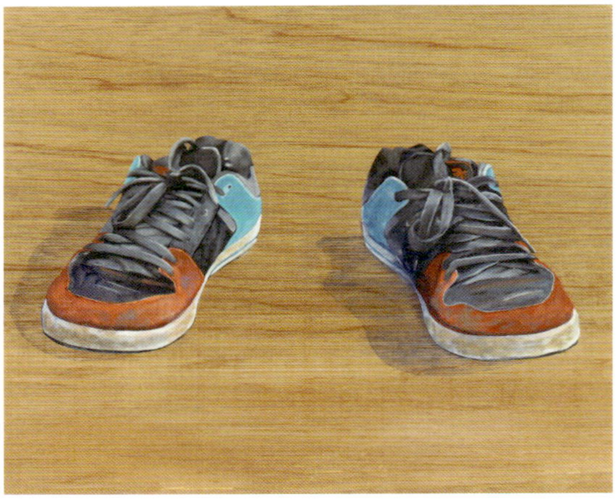
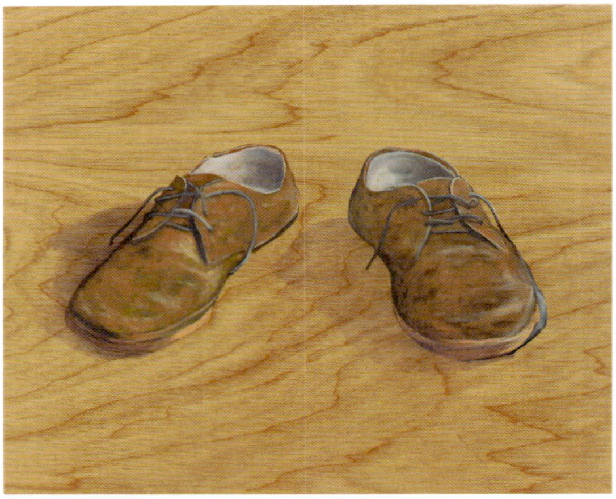
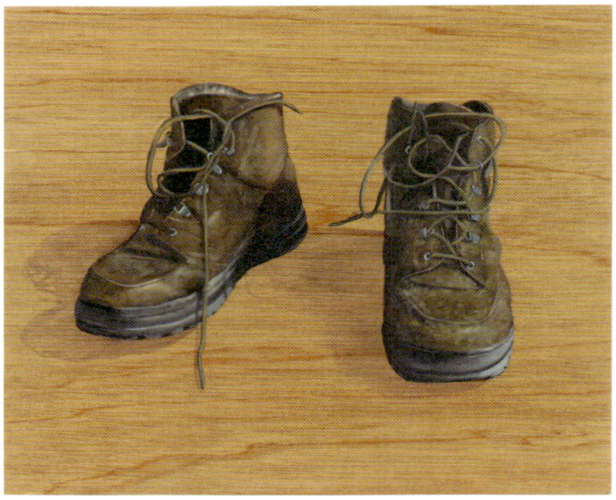
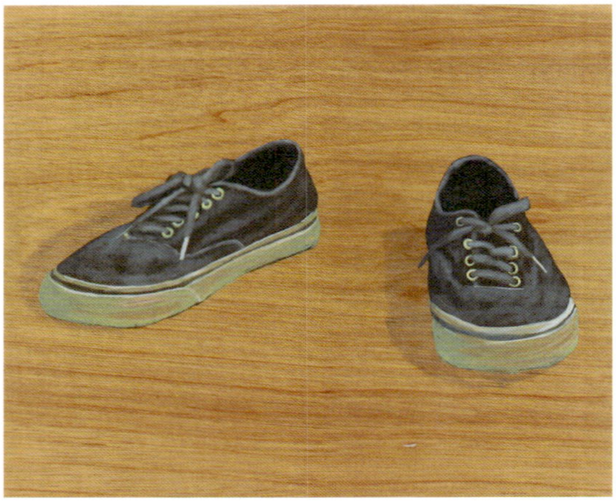
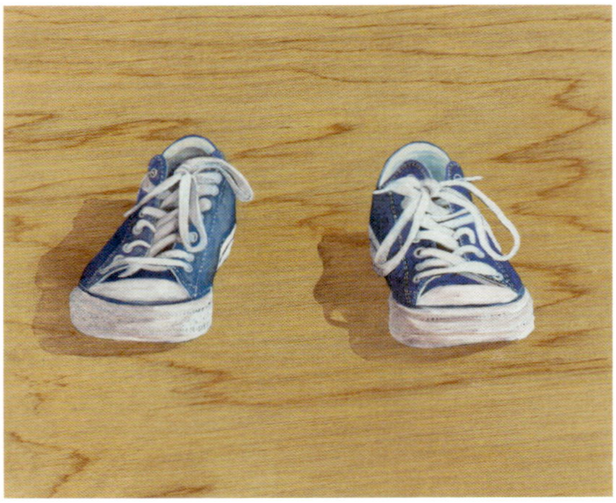

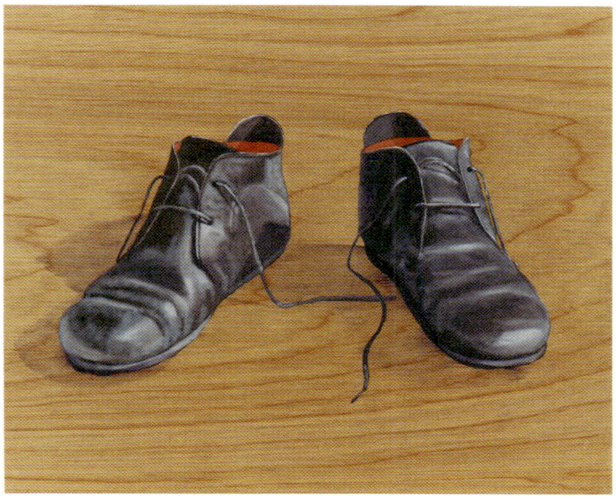
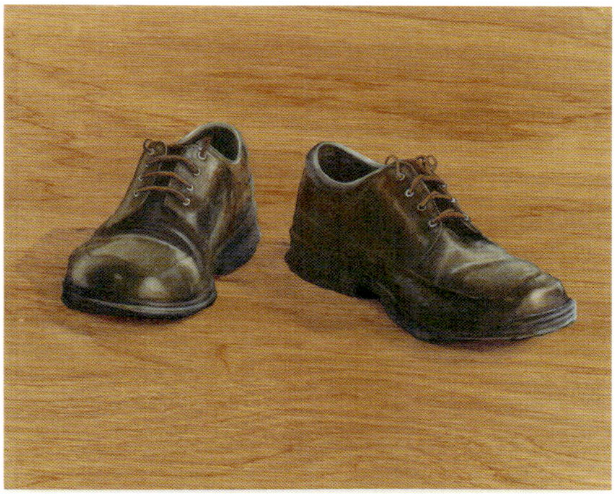
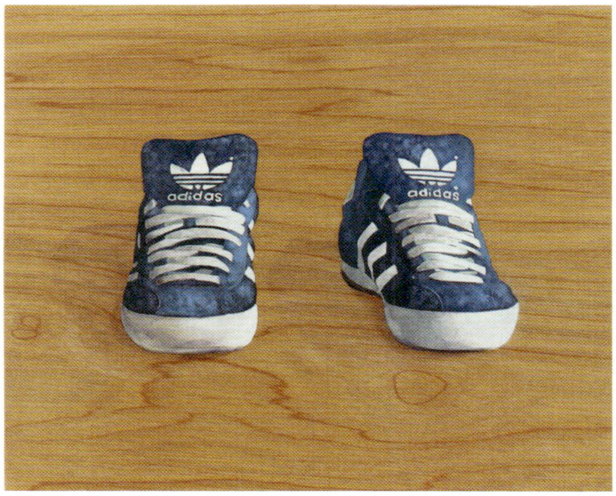
adidas
adidas
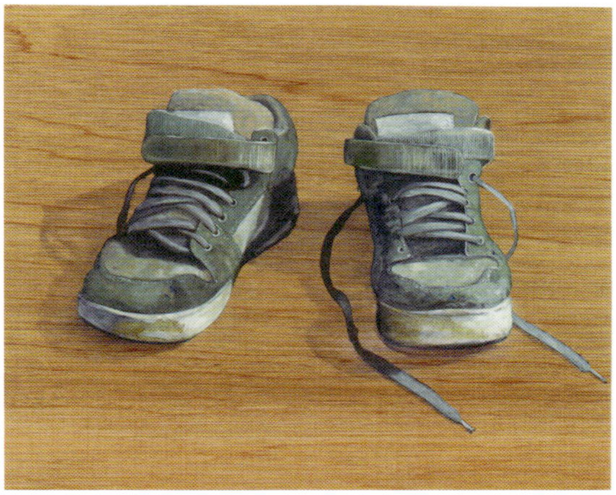

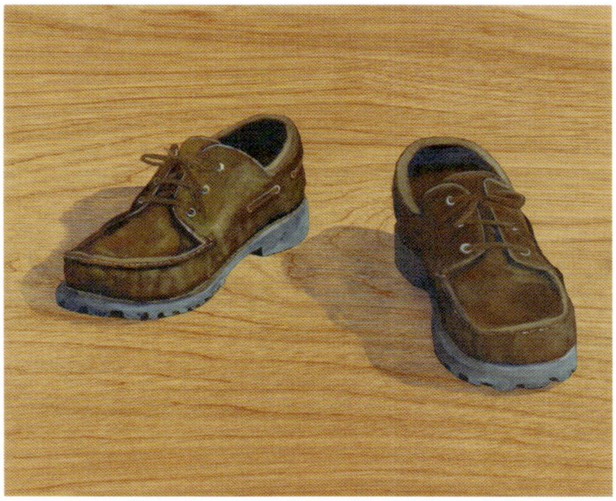
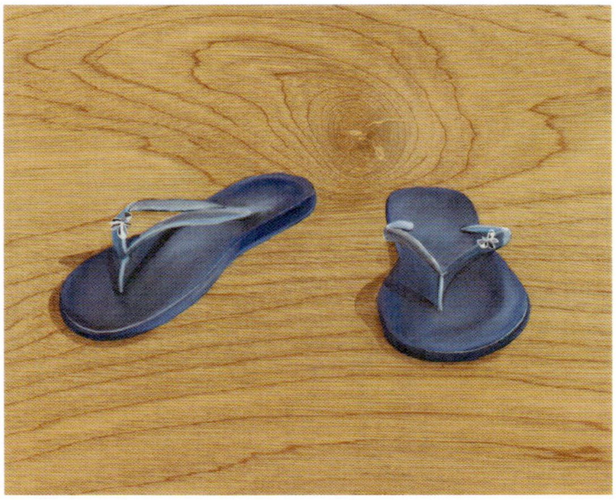
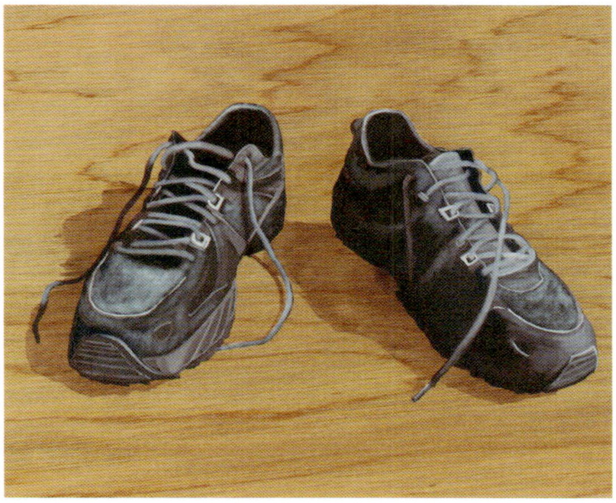
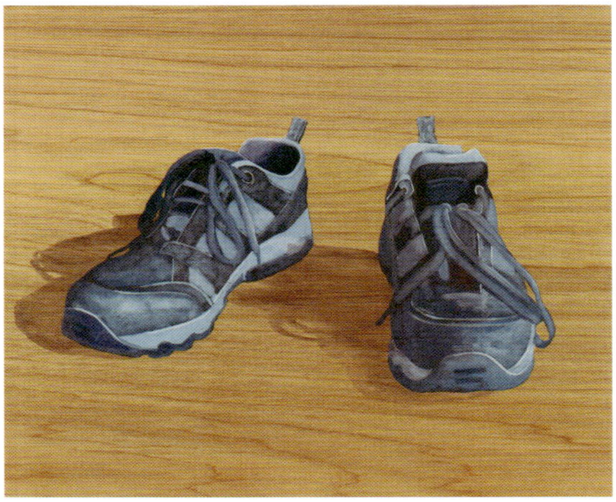

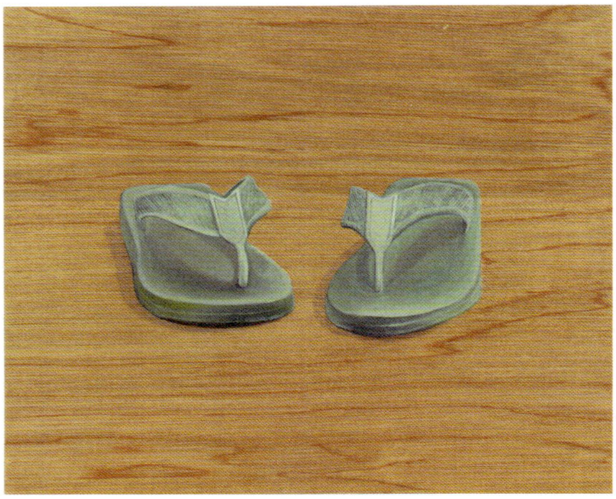
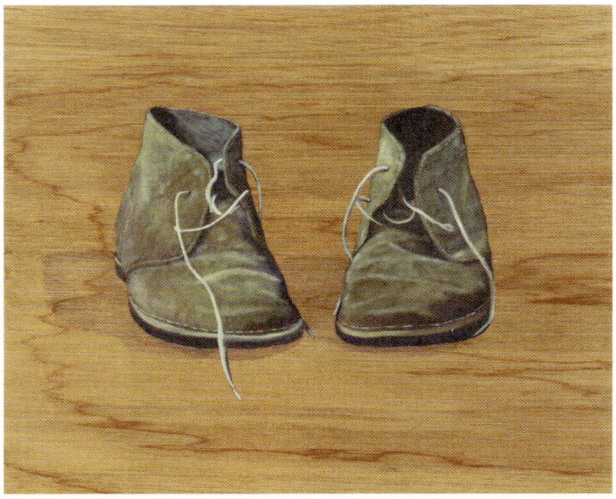
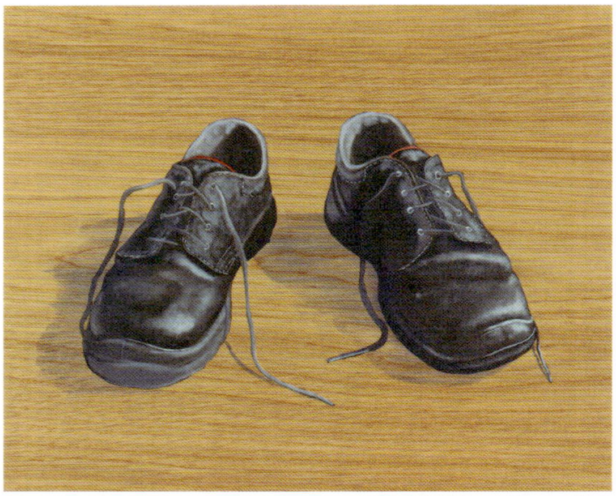
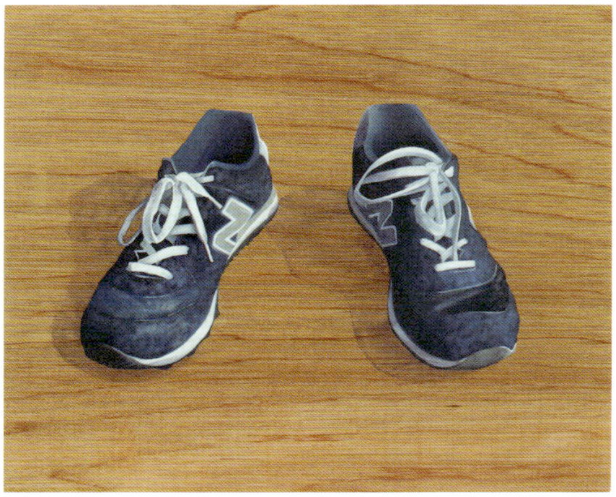

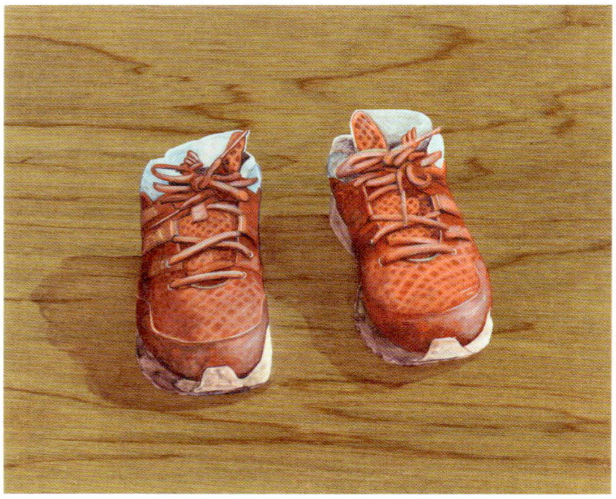
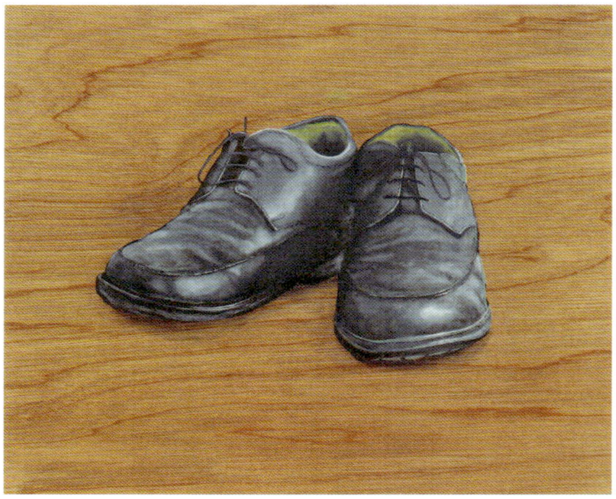
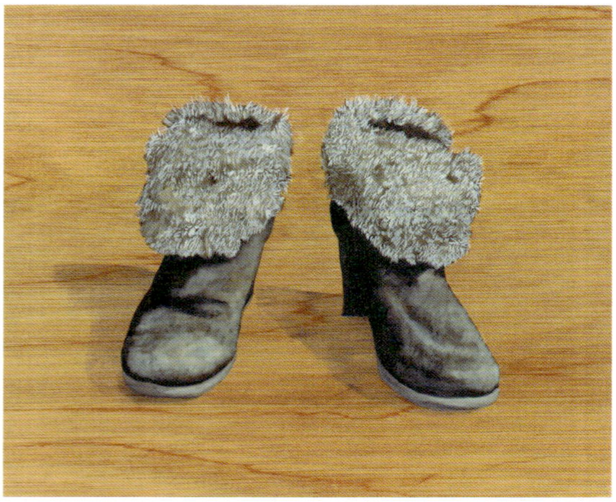
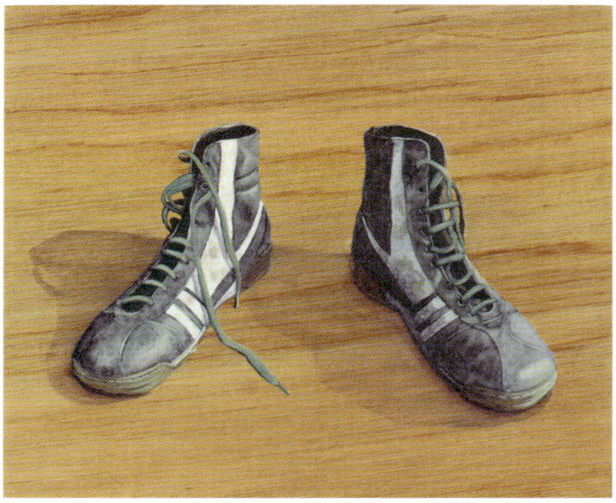

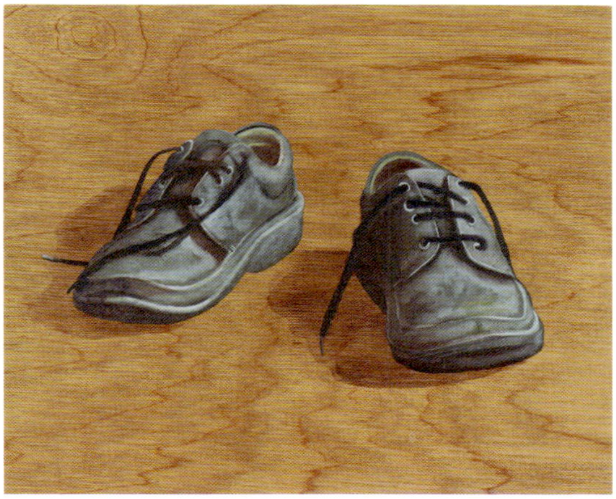
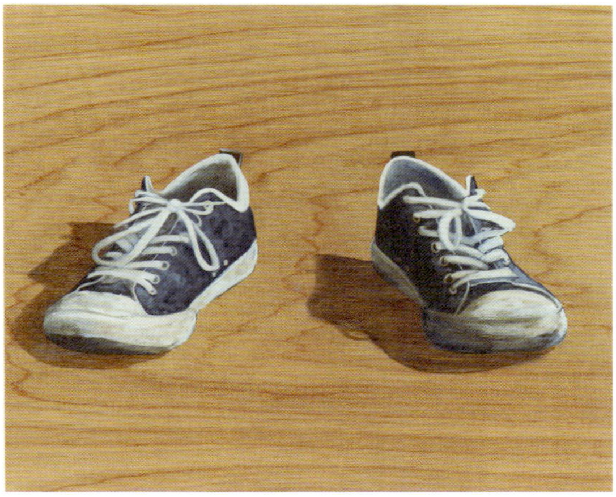
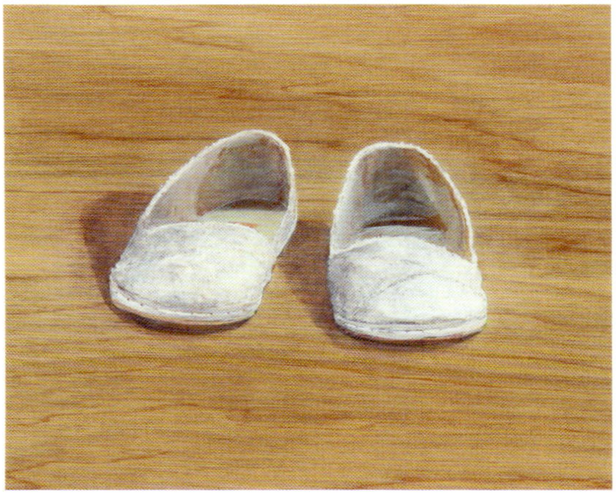
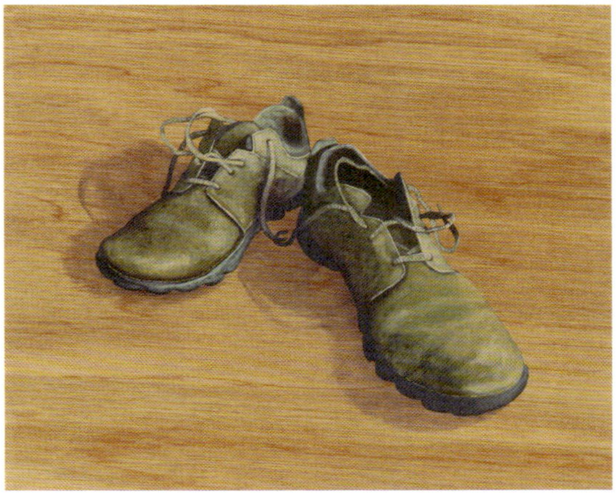
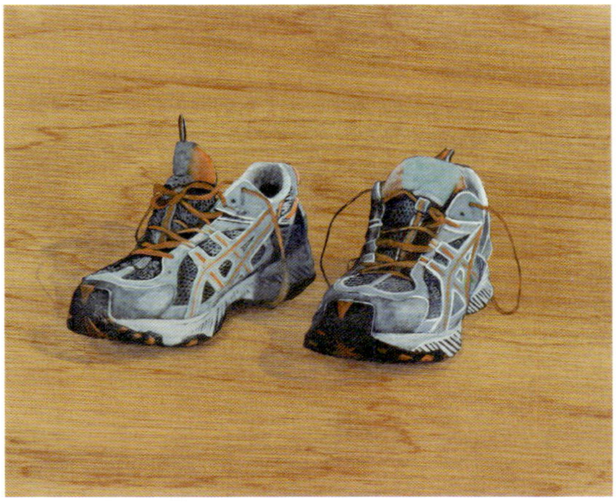
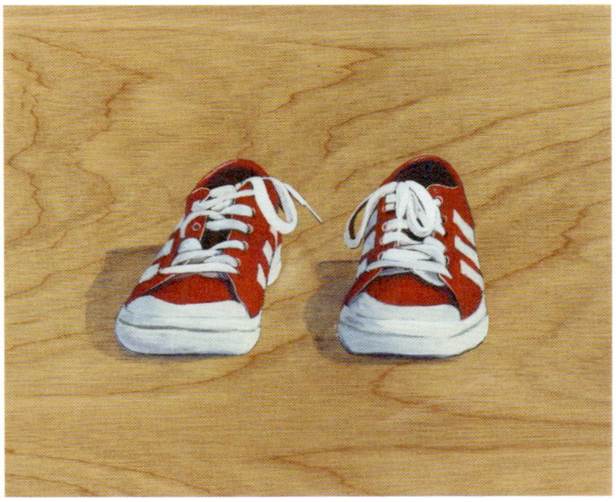
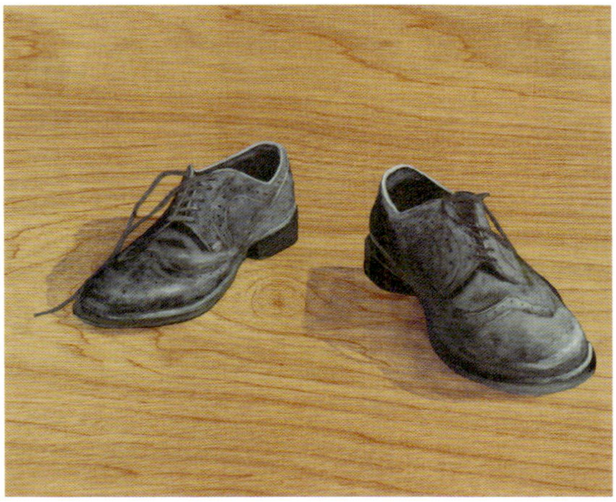
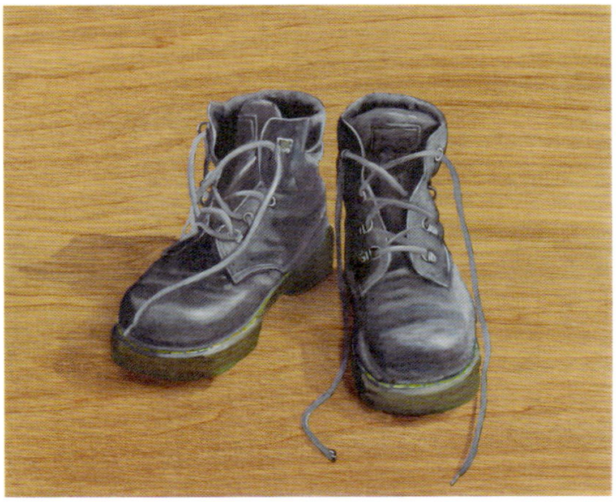

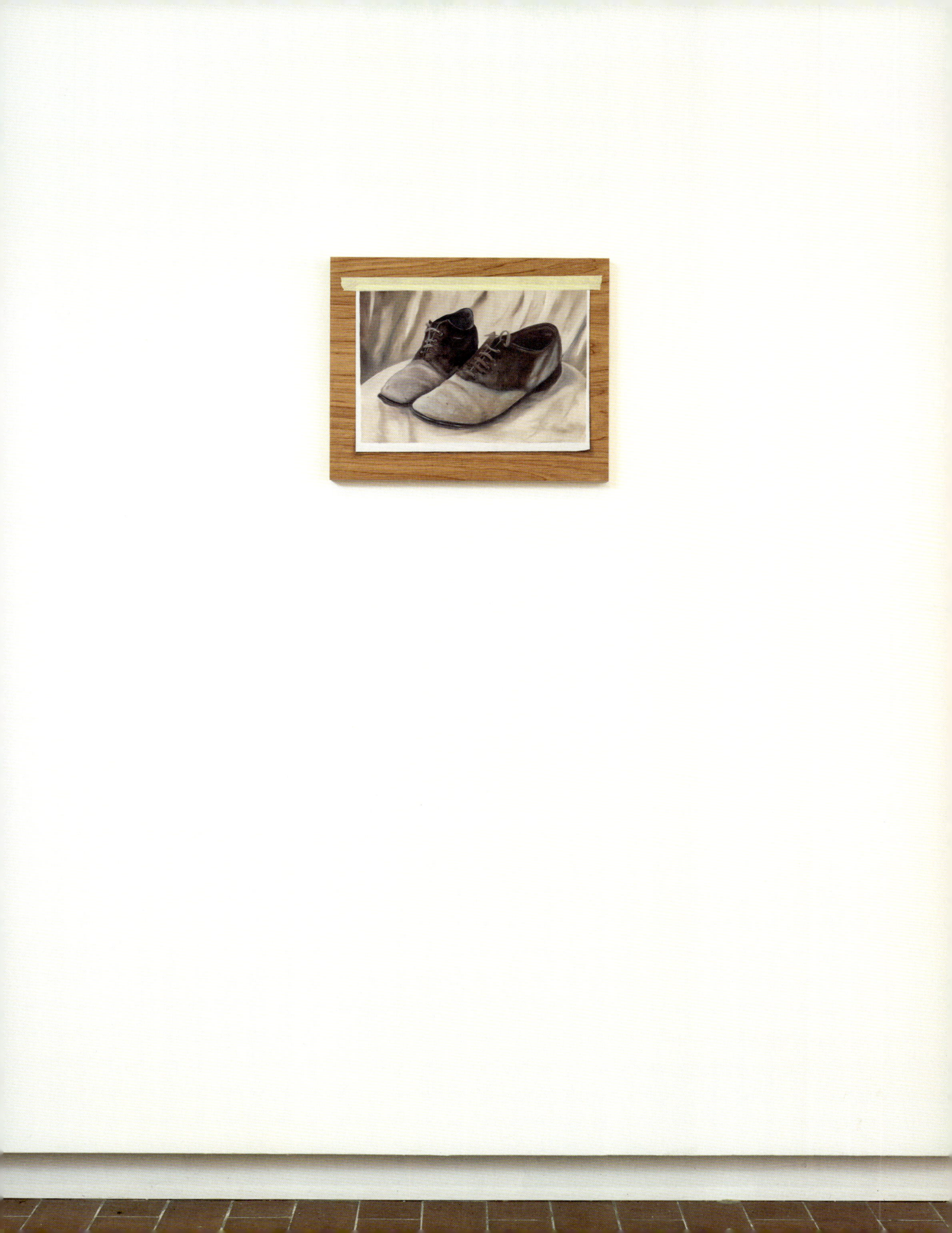

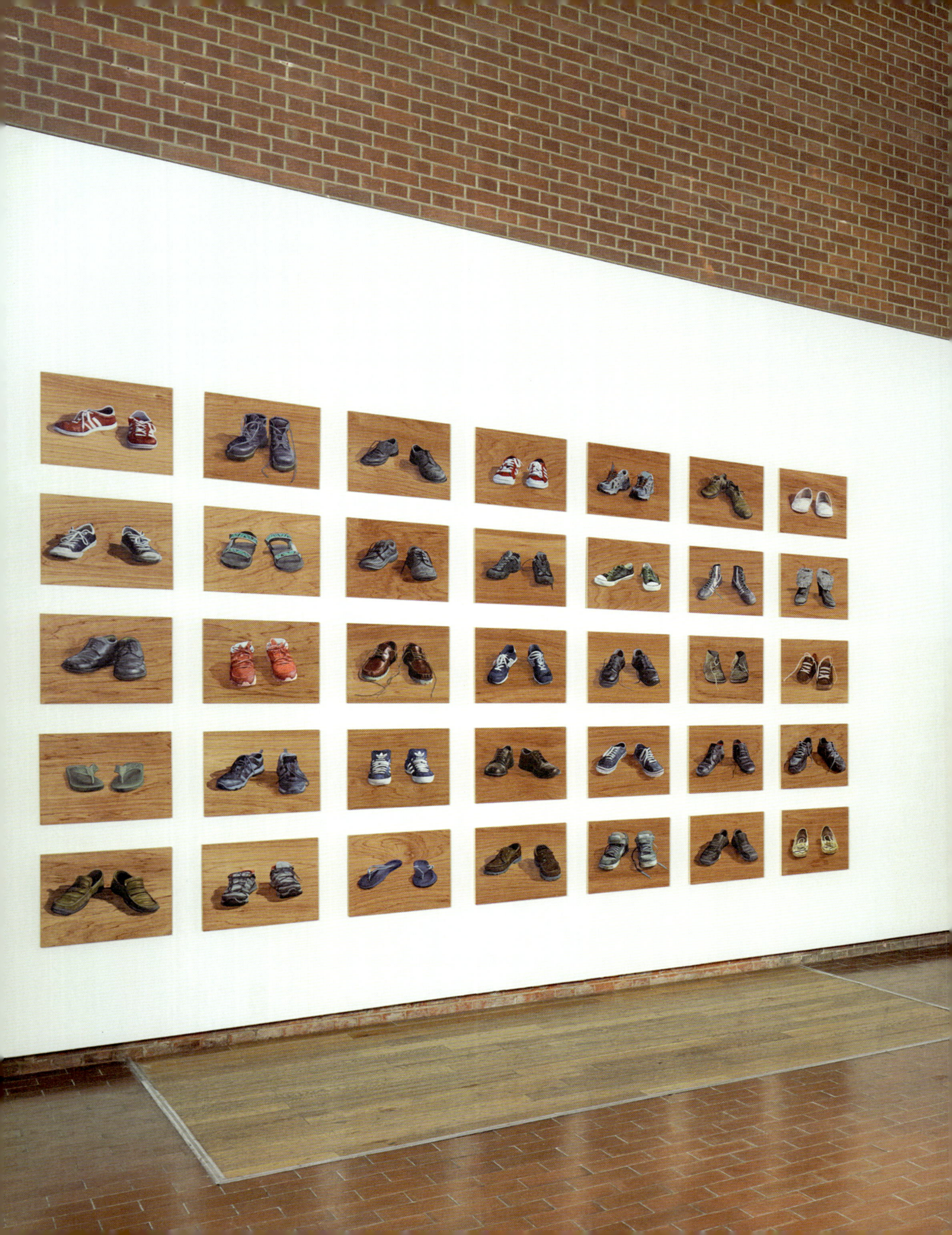

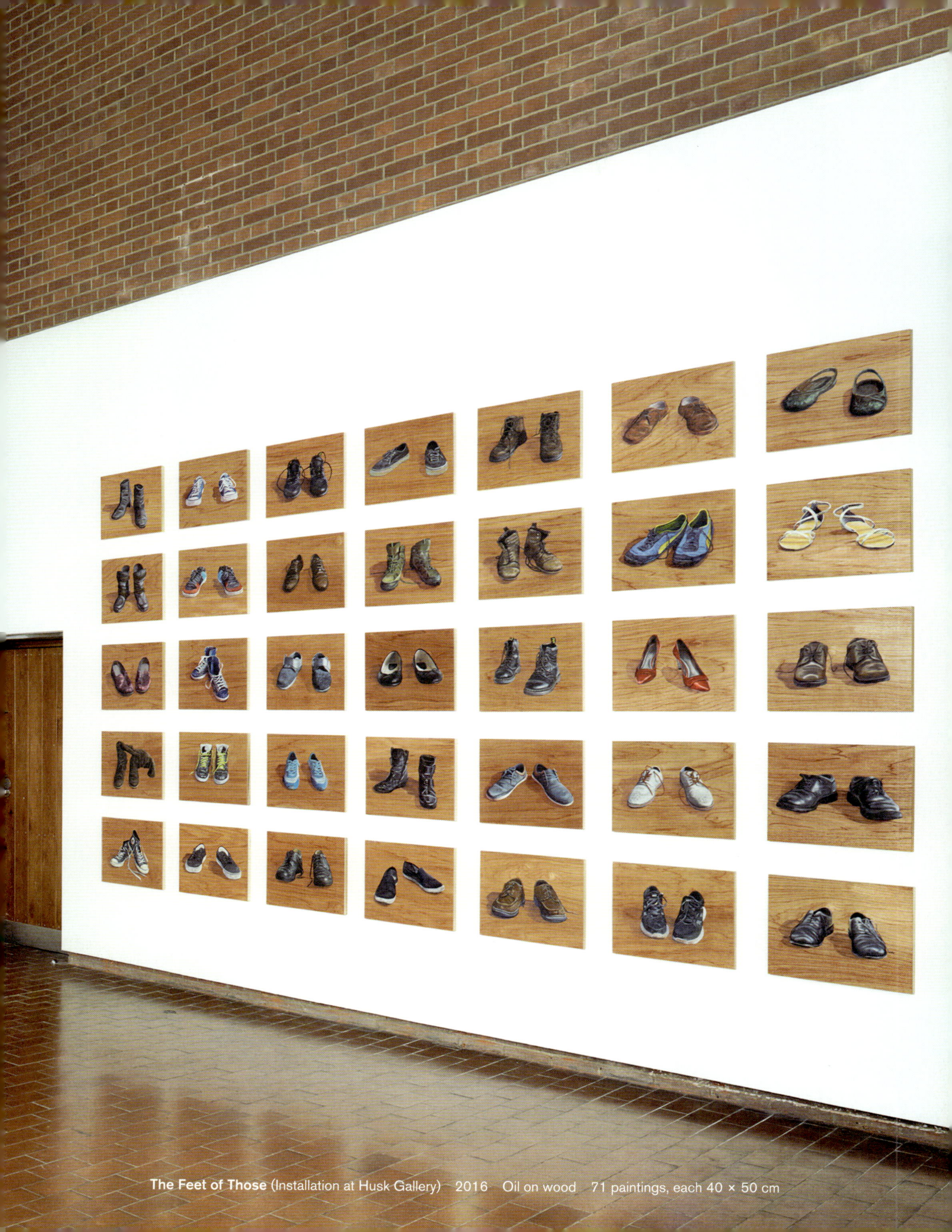

The Feet of Those (Installation at Husk Gallery) 2016 Oil on wood 71 paintings, each 40 × 50 cm

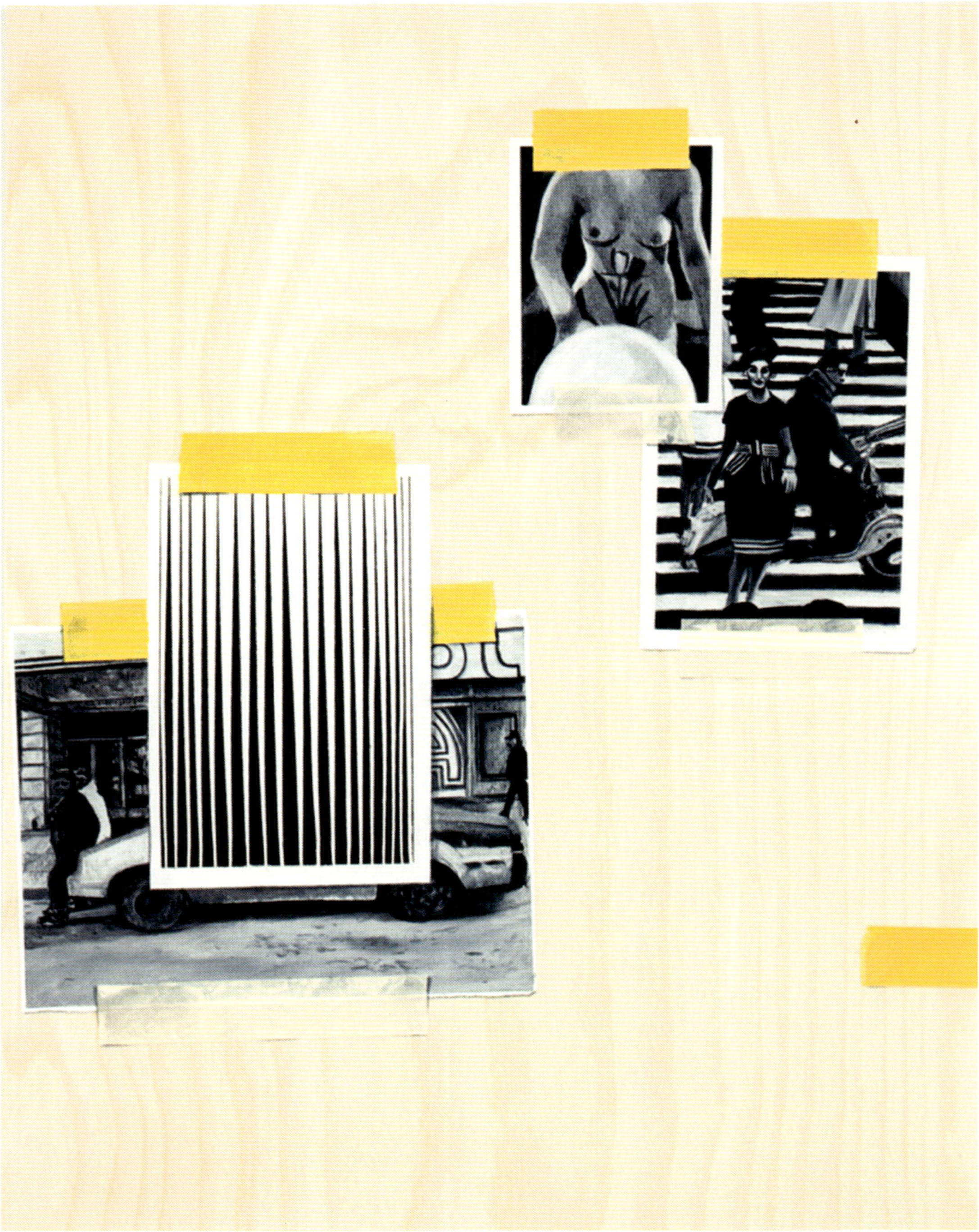

Postcards From a Collector (Two) 2018 Oil on wood 50 × 40 cm

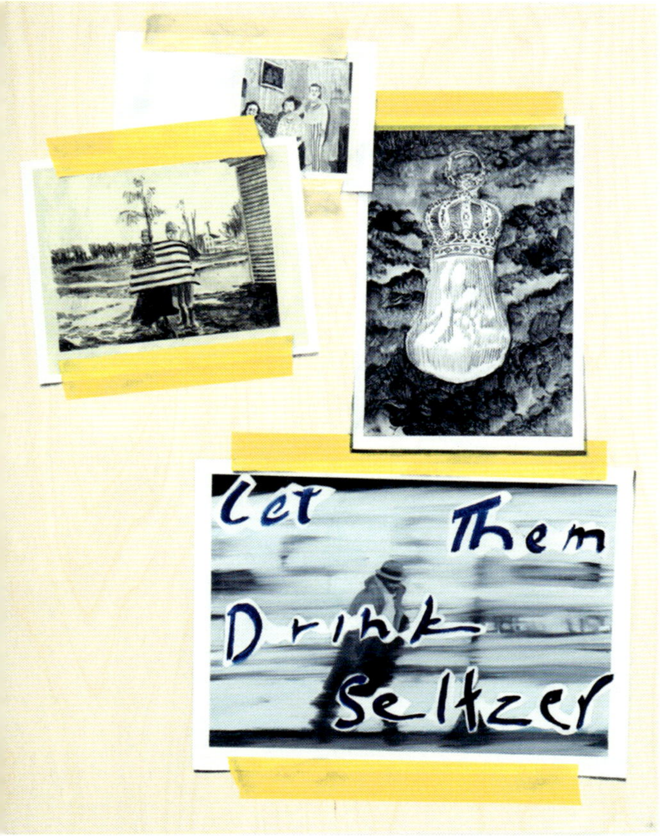

Postcards From a Collector (Three) 2018
Oil on wood 50 × 40 cm

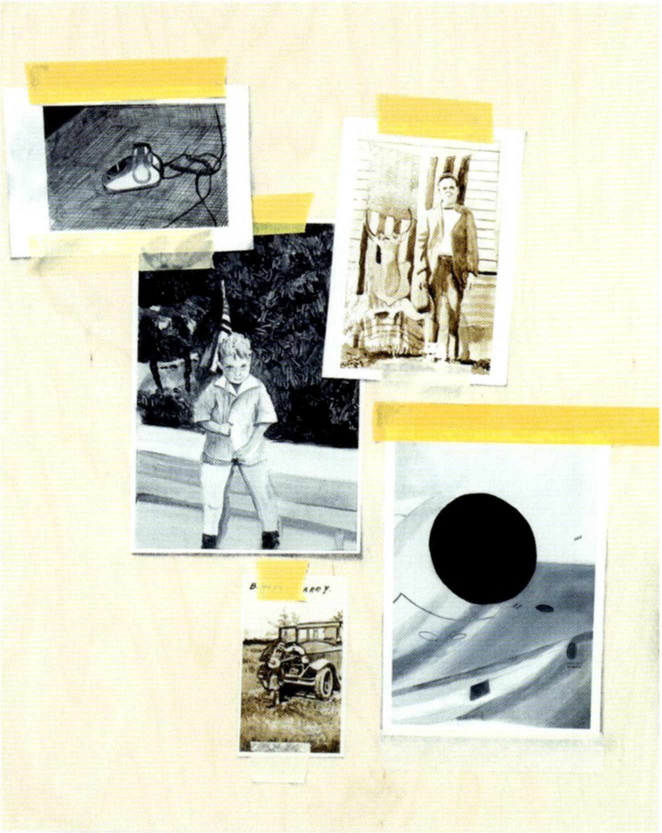

Postcards From a Collector (One) 2018
Oil on wood 50 × 40 cm

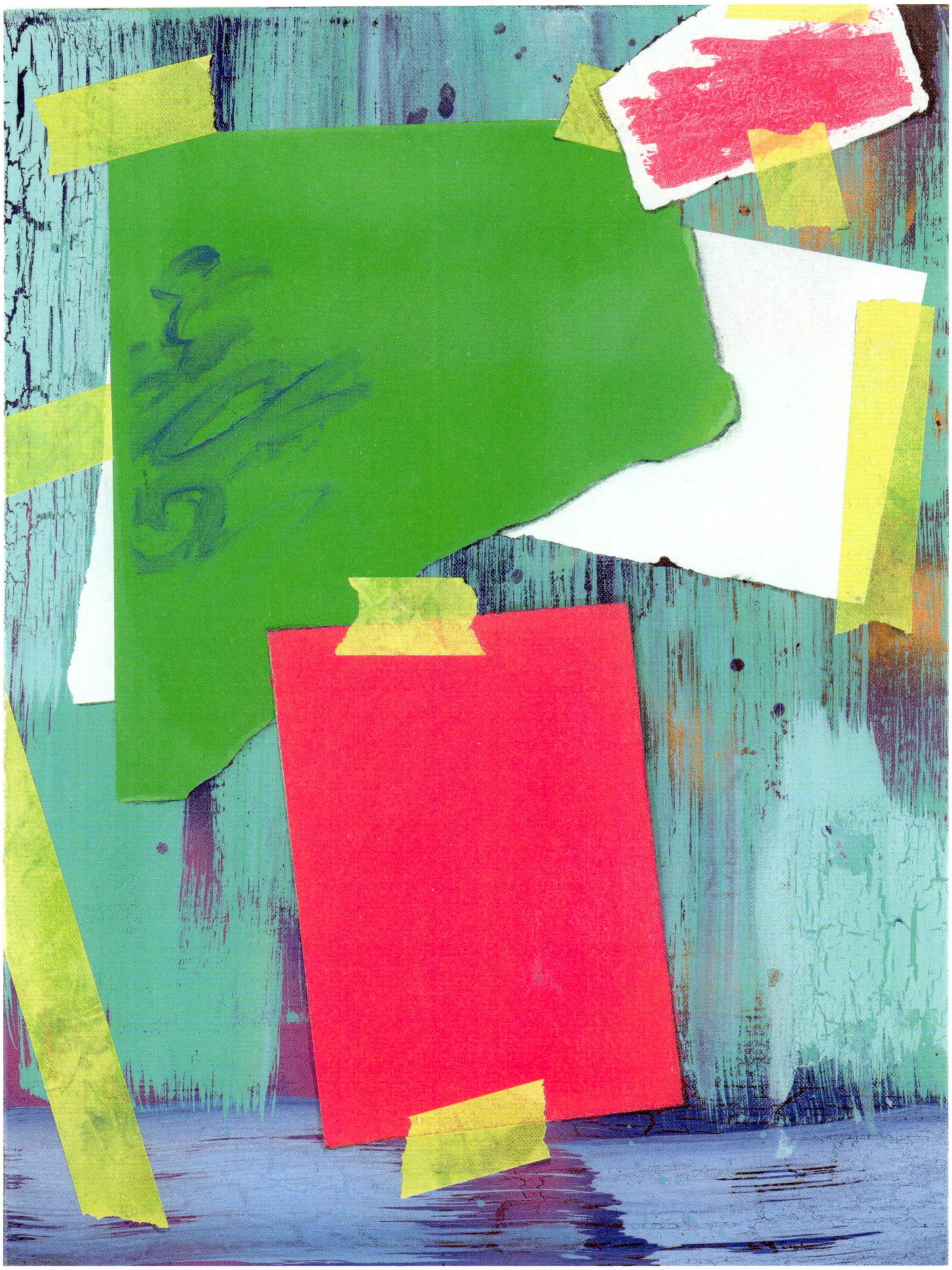

I Could Be the Walrus 2018 Oil and acrylic on linen 40 × 30 cm

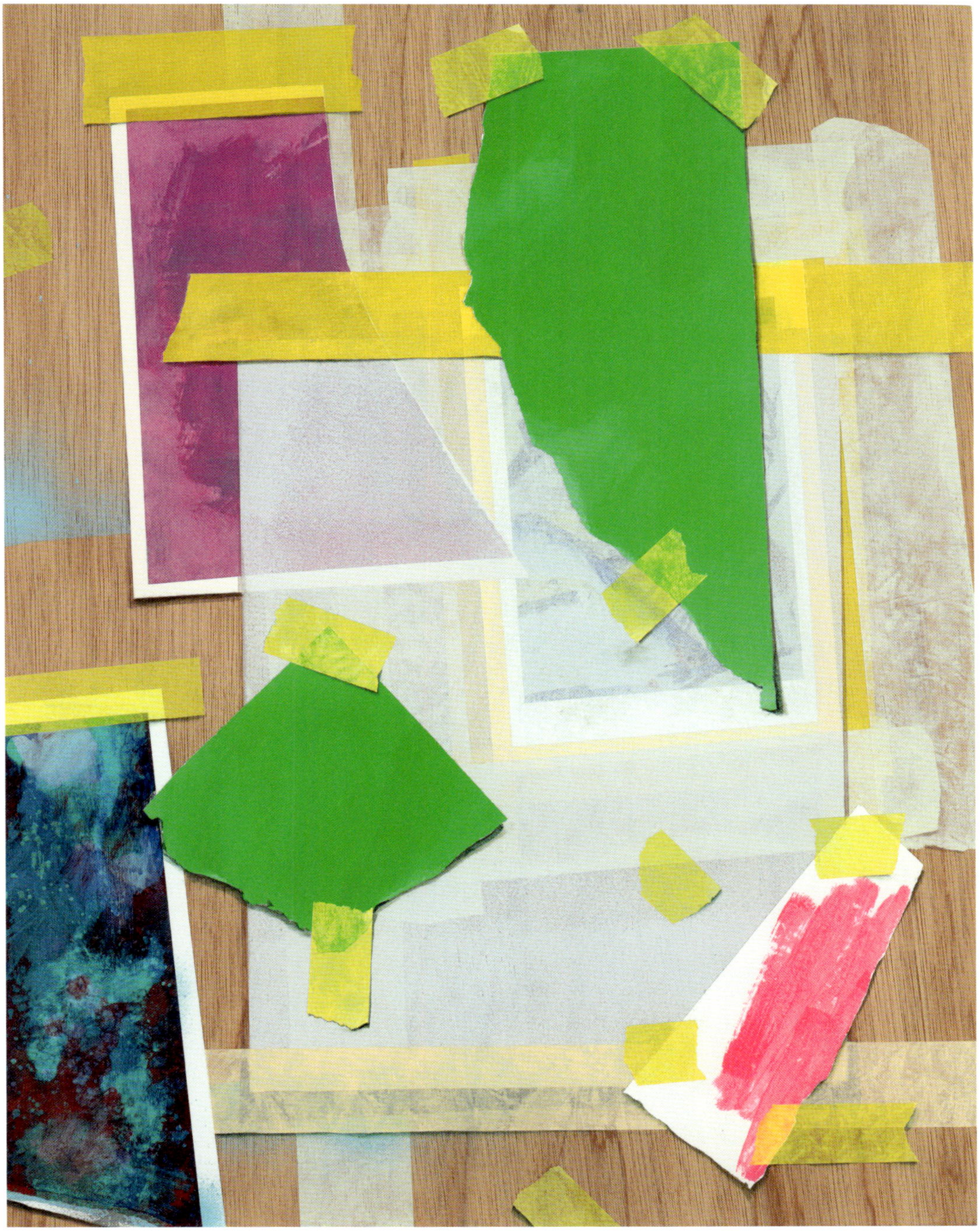

You Make Me Feel 2018 Oil on wood approx 50 × 40 cm

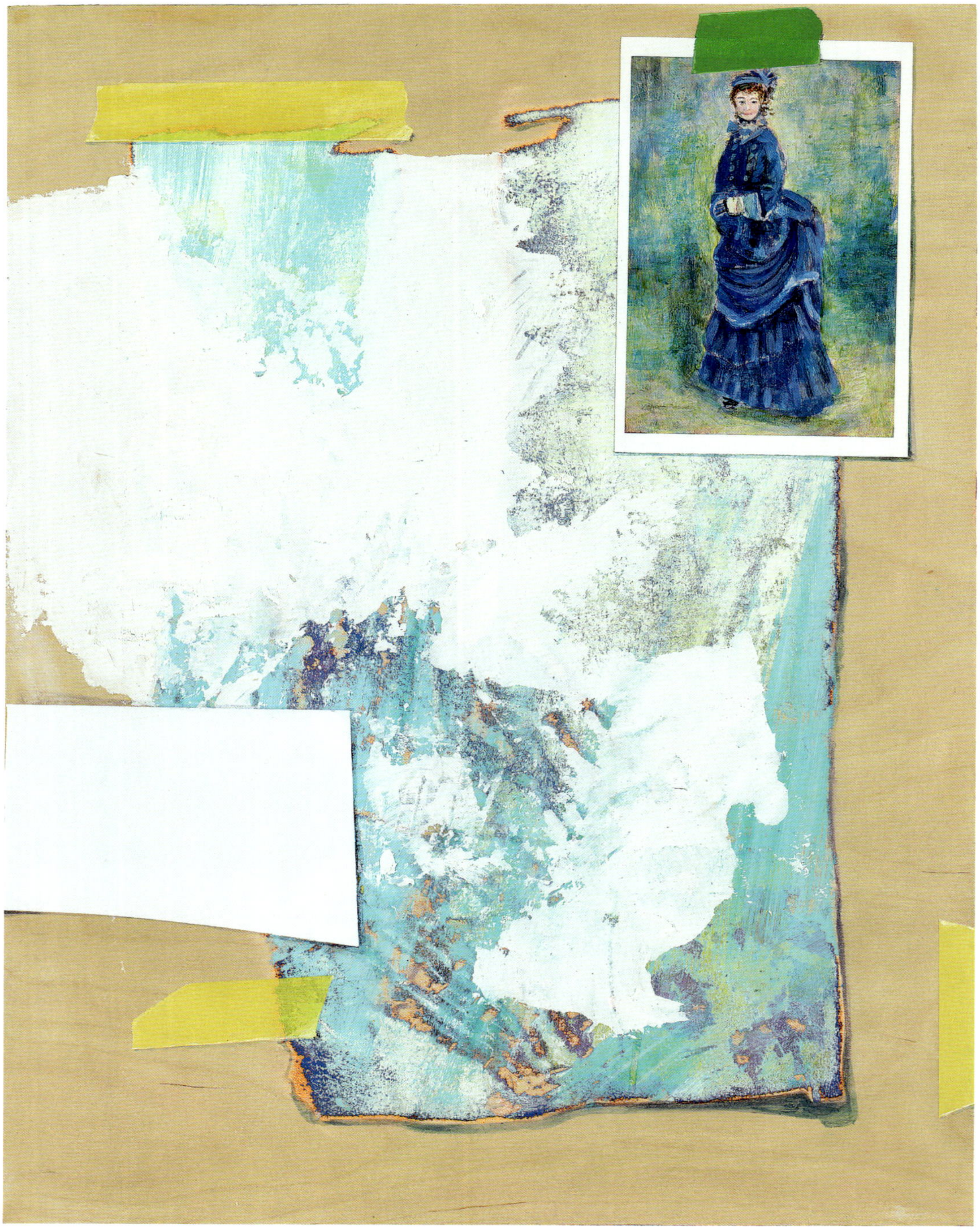

Everything We Have Chosen Has Been Granted to Us 2017 Oil and acrylic on wood 50 × 40 cm

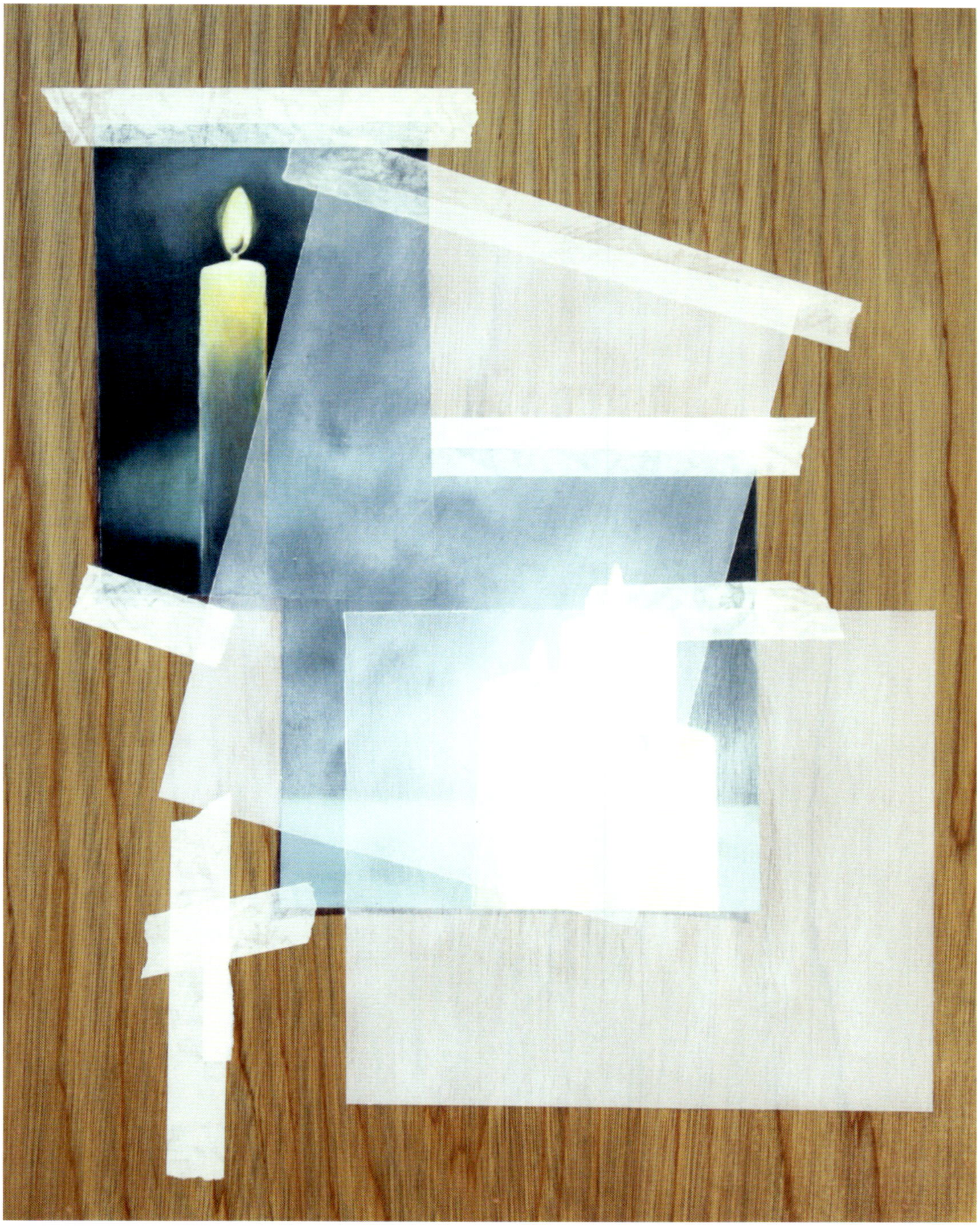

Memento Mori 2018 Oil on wood 50 × 40 cm

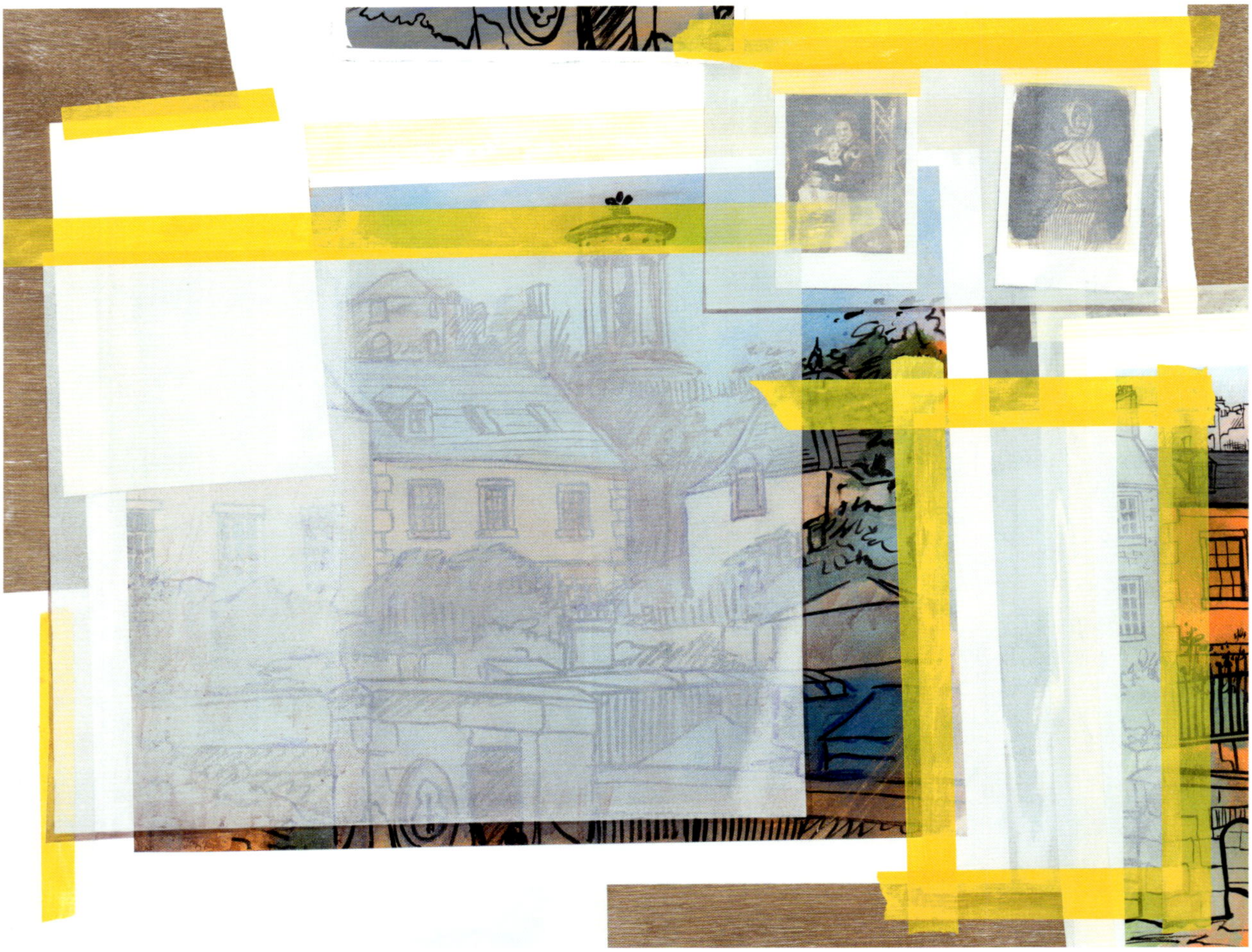

Of Rock and Salt 2018 Oil and acrylic on wood 90 × 120 cm

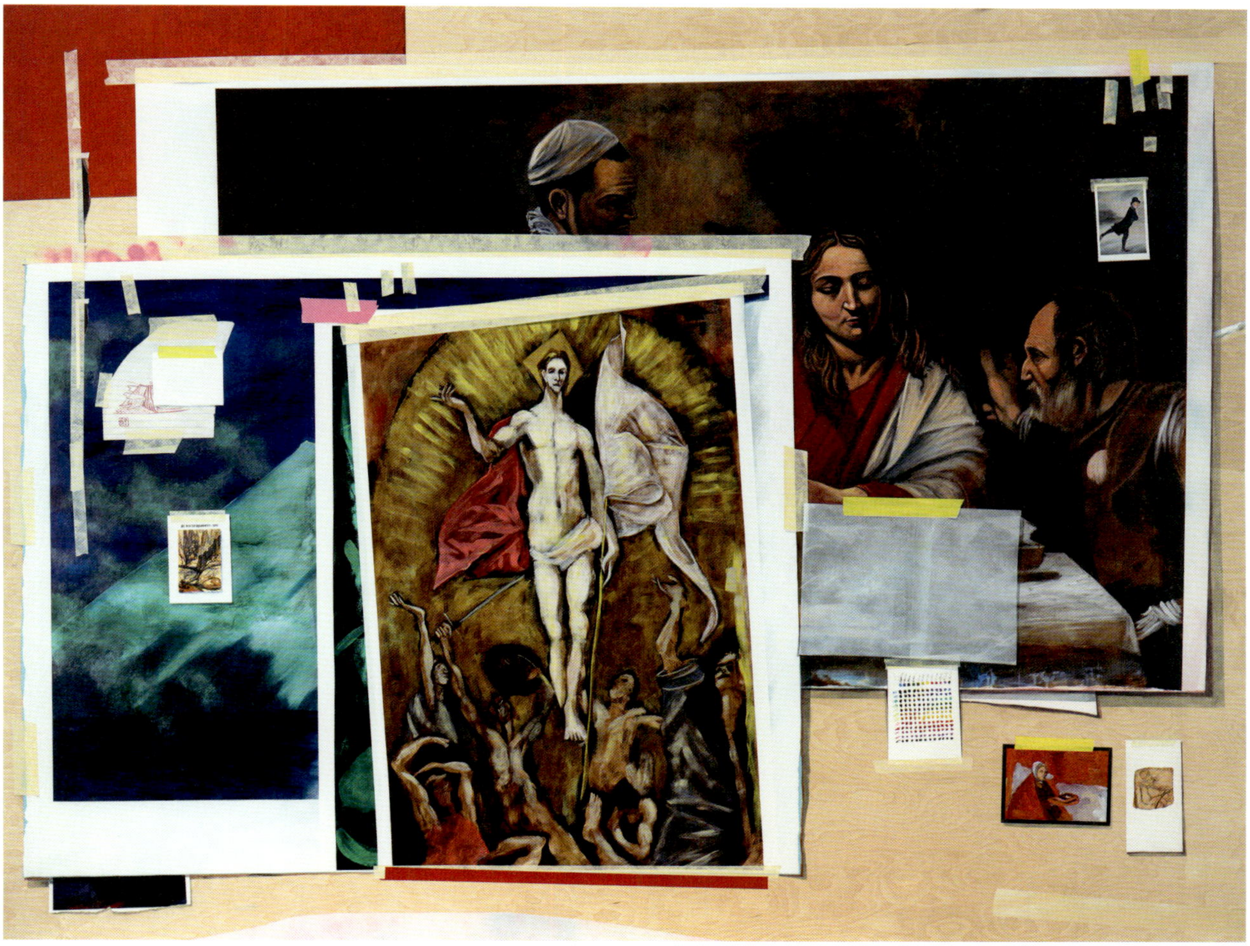

They Lying Long Shall Not Die Windily 2017 Oil and acrylic on wood 180 × 240 cm

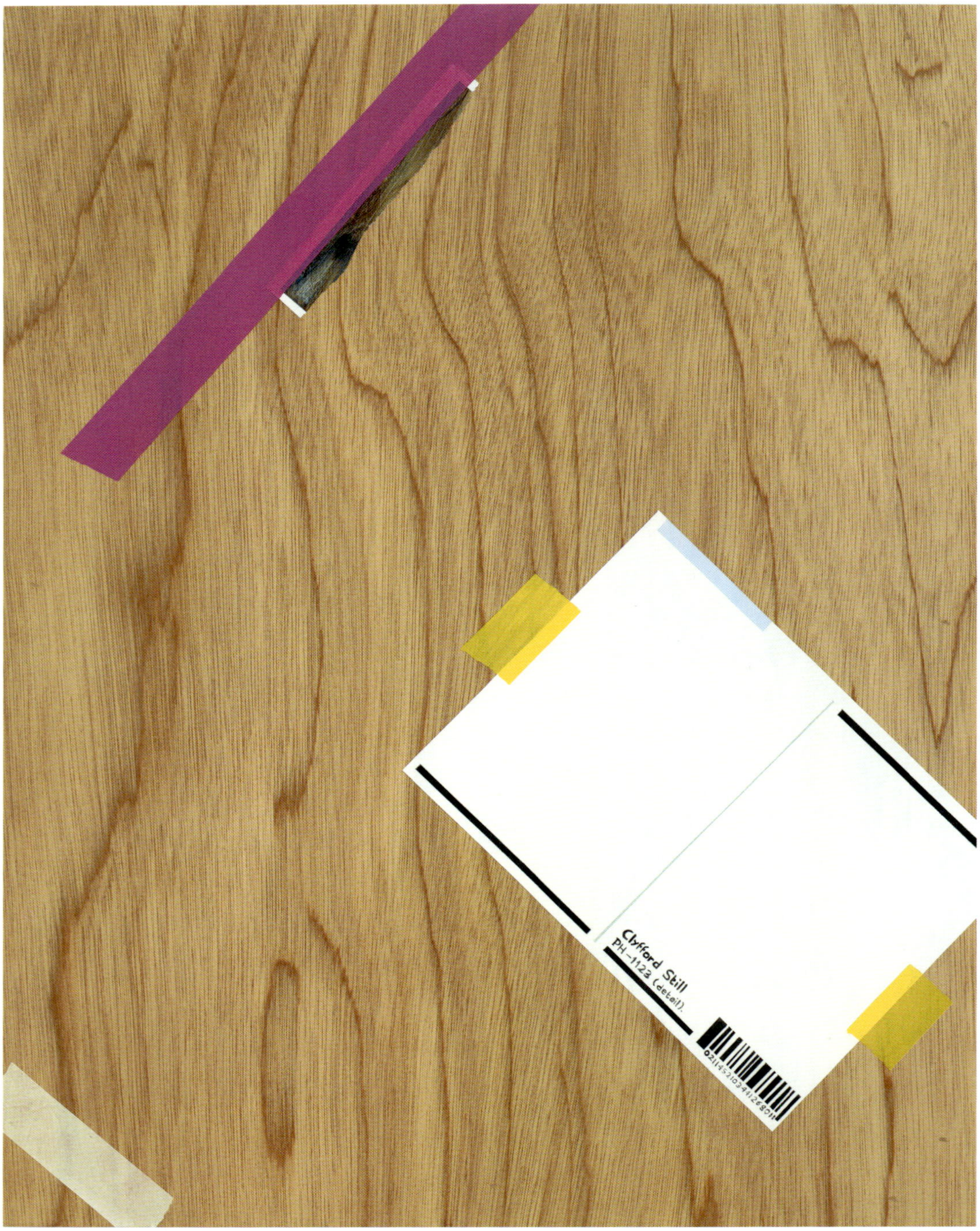

A Golden Cupidon Peeped Out 2017 Oil and acrylic on wood 50 × 40 cm

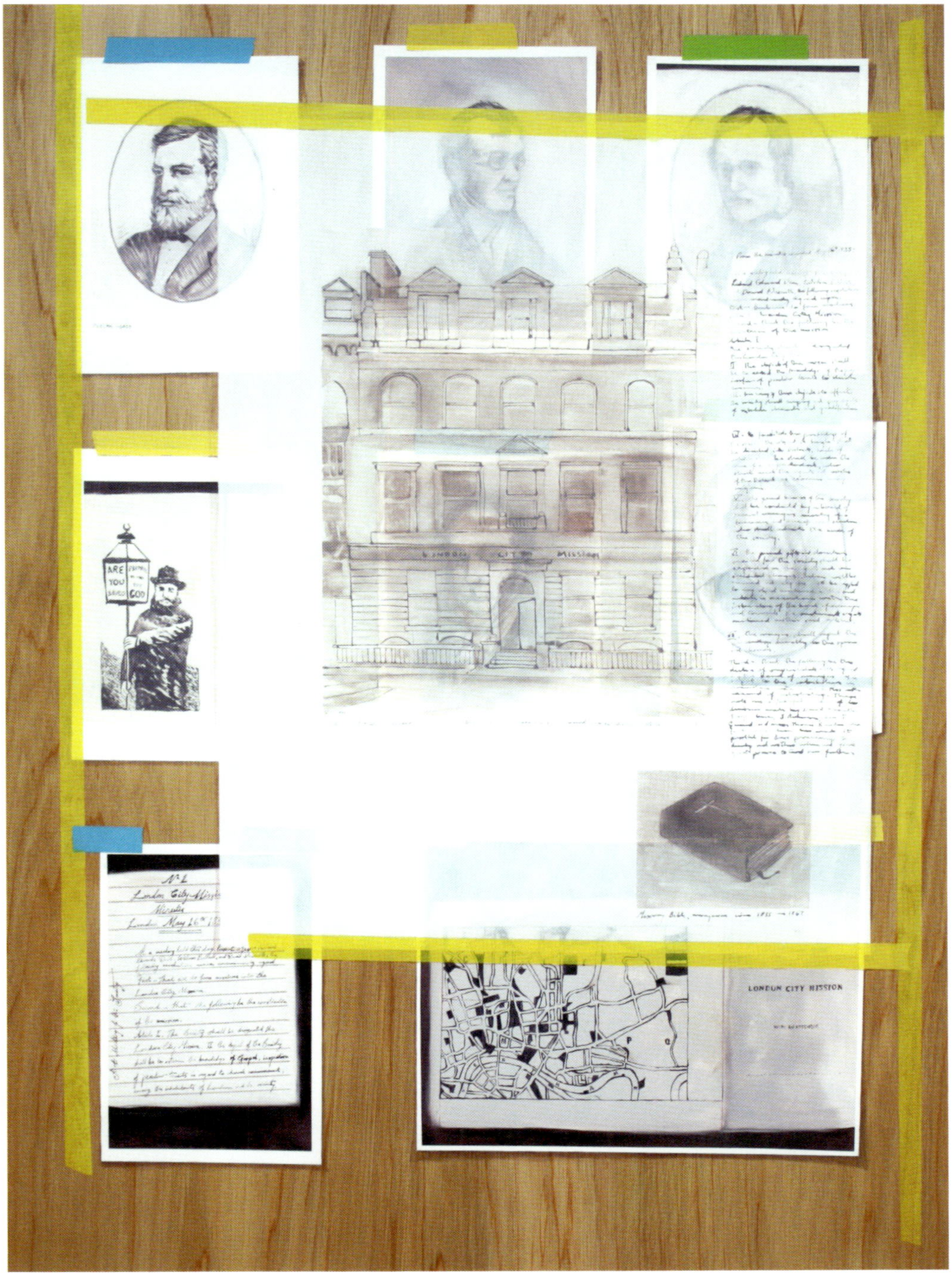

Quodlibet for LCM 2015 Oil and acrylic on wood 120 × 90 cm

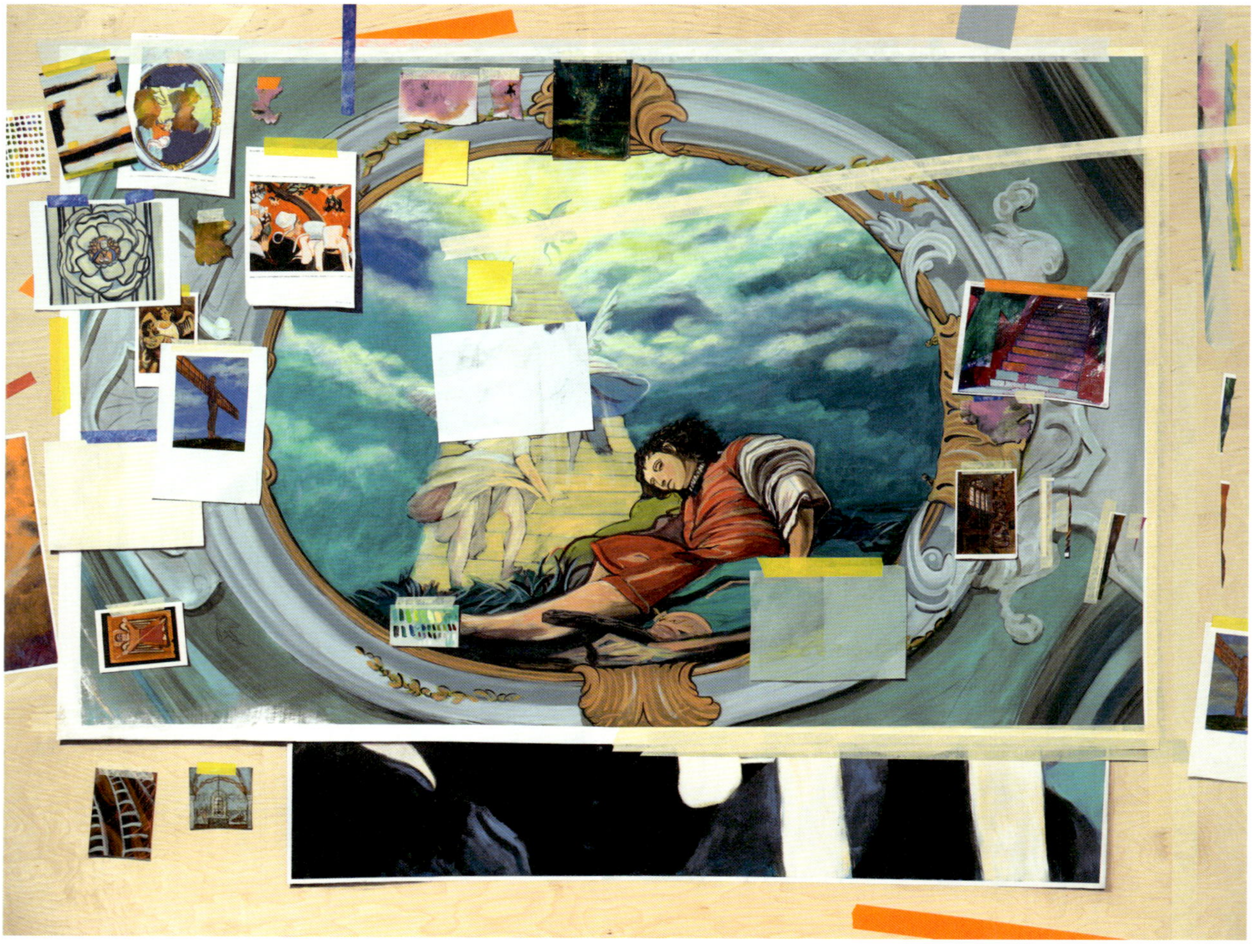

Into the Laquearia 2017 Oil and acrylic on wood 180 × 240 cm

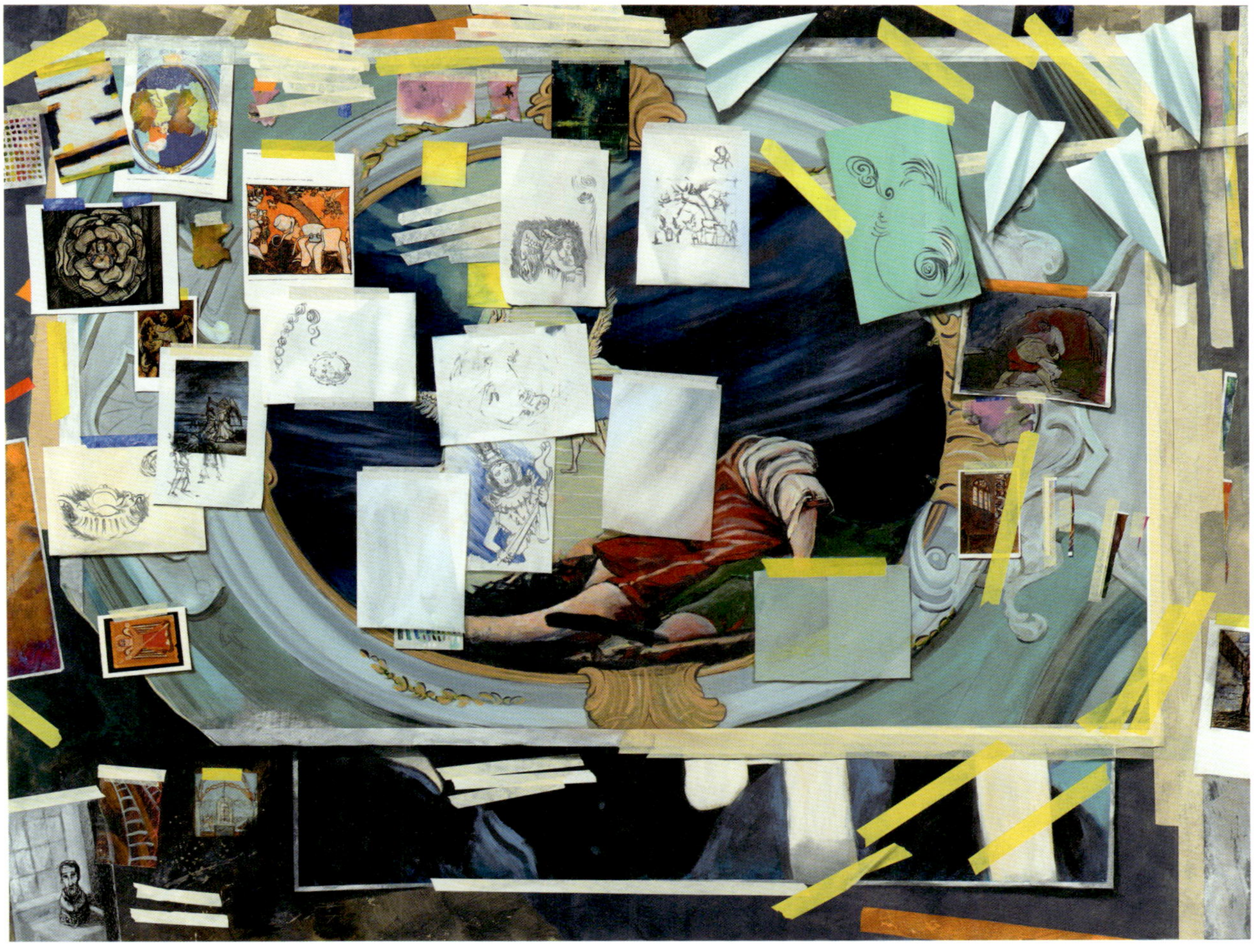

Jacob's Dream 2021 Oil and acrylic on wood 180 × 240 cm

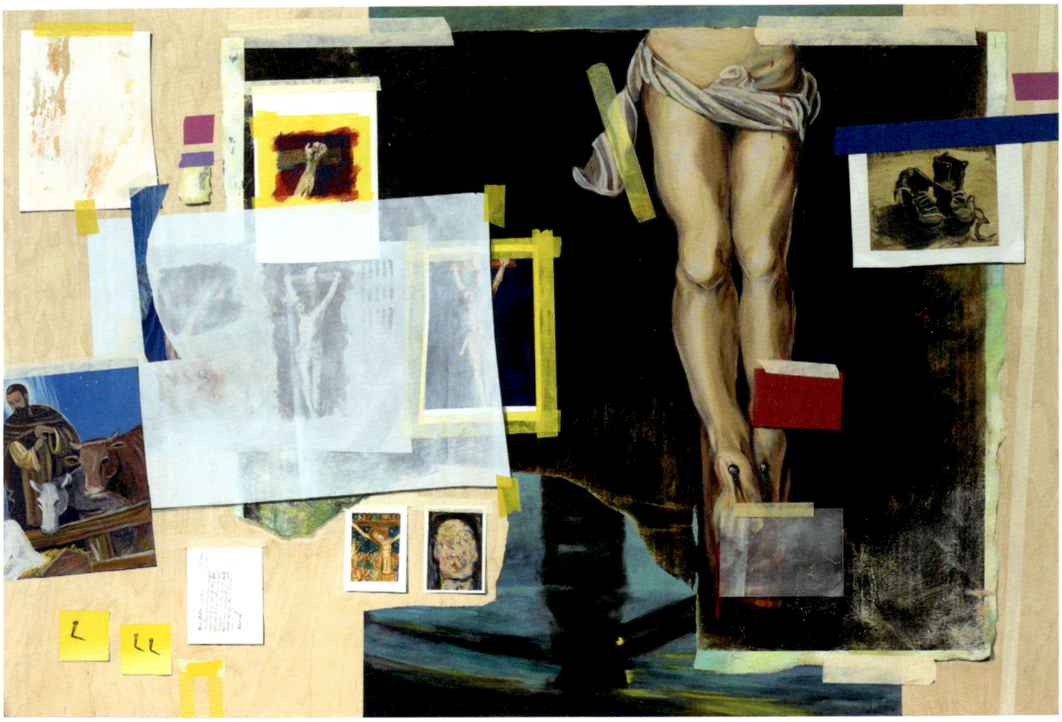

Though Lovers Be Lost Love Shall Not 2017 Oil and acrylic on wood 120 × 180 cm

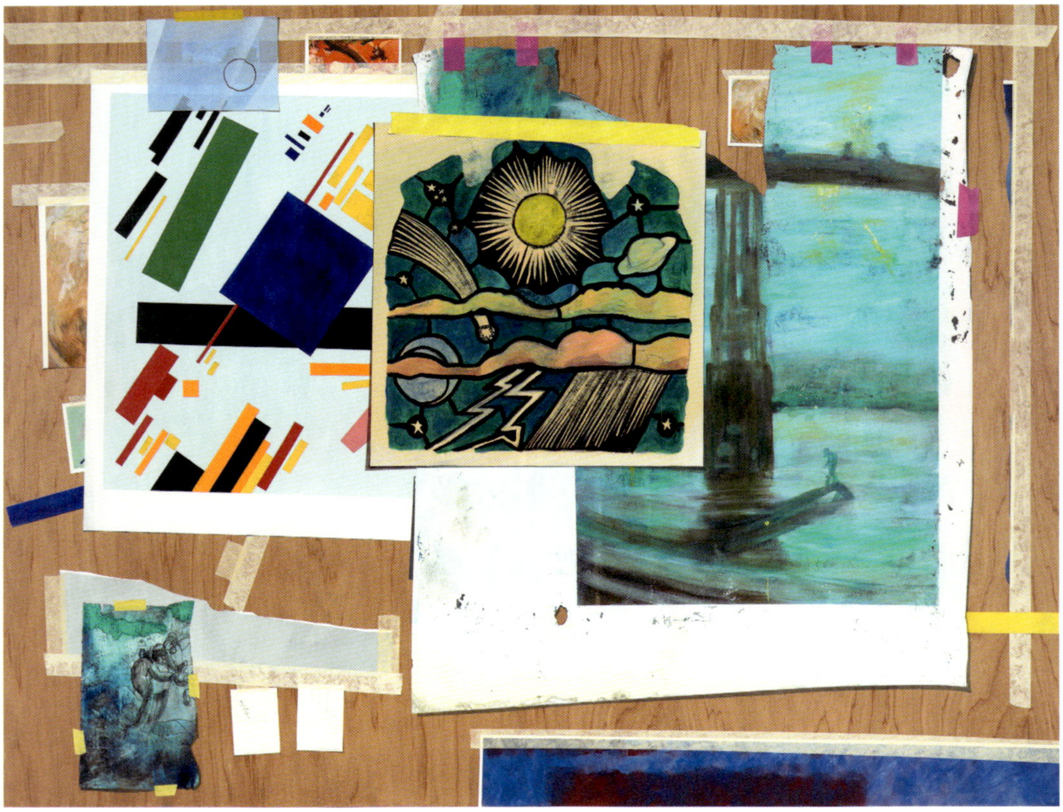

I Will Show You Fear In a Handful of Dust 2017 Oil and acrylic on wood 180 × 240 cm

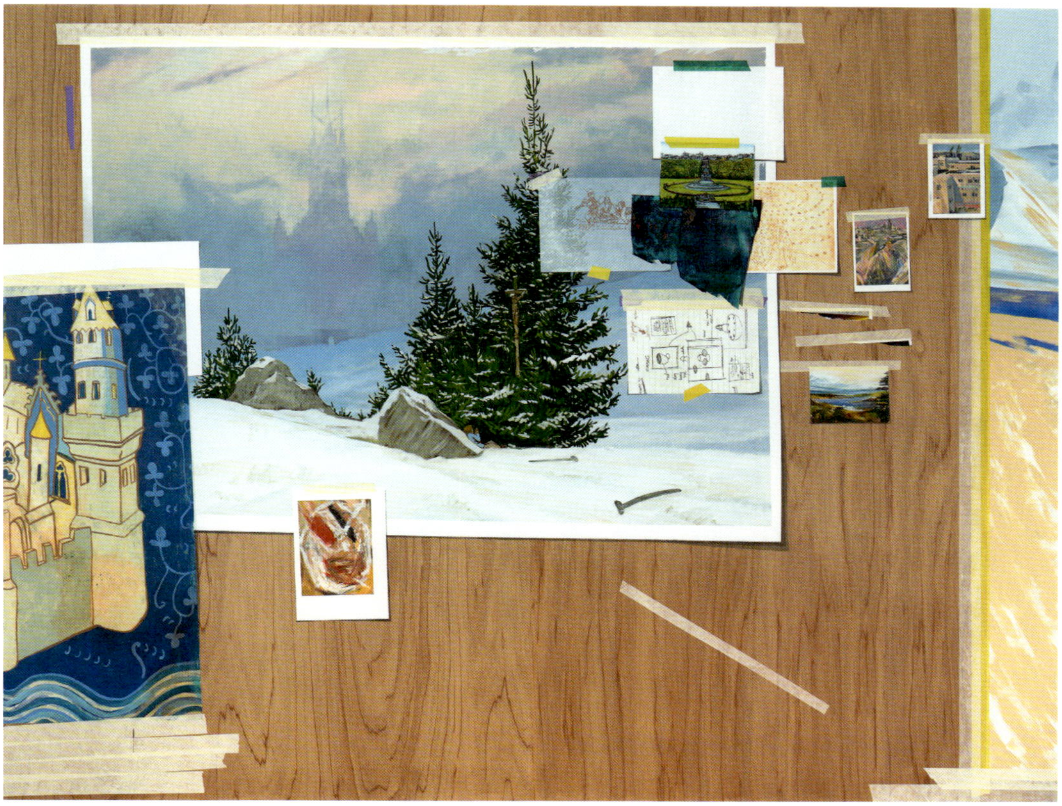

Under a Juniper Tree the Bones Sang 2017 Oil and acrylic on wood 180 × 240 cm

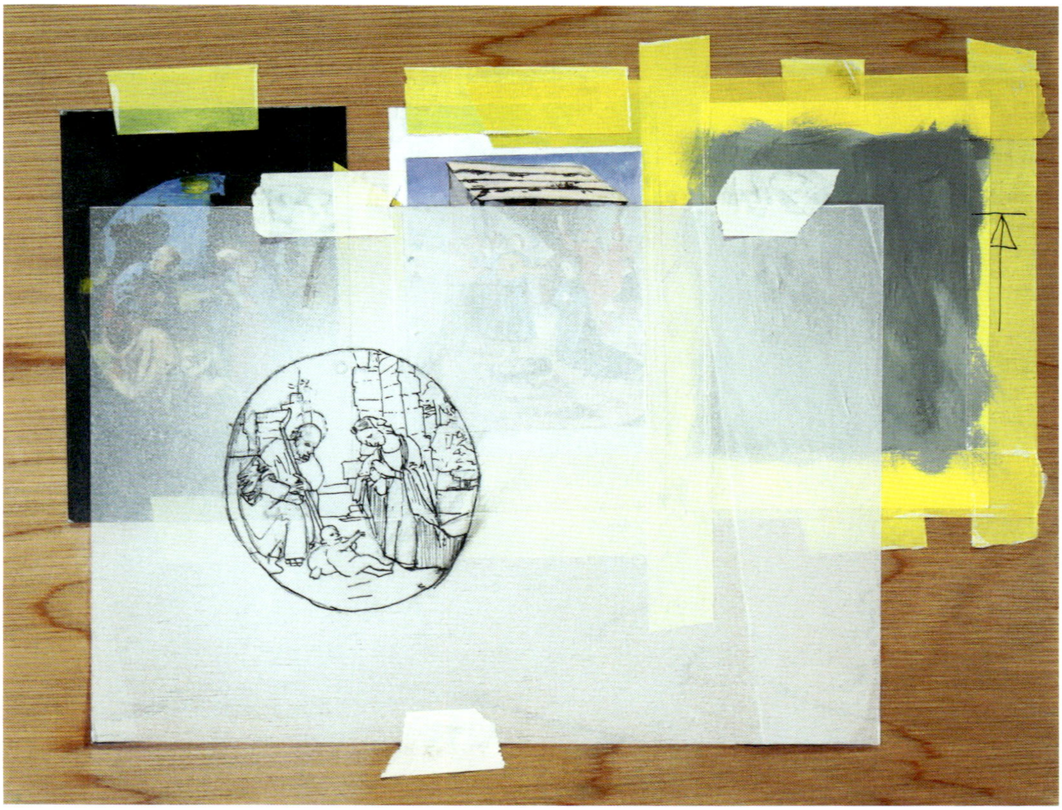

A Study of Postcards Sent From a Friend (After Fra' Bartolomeo and Piero Della Francesca) 2016
Oil and acrylic on wood 40 × 50 cm

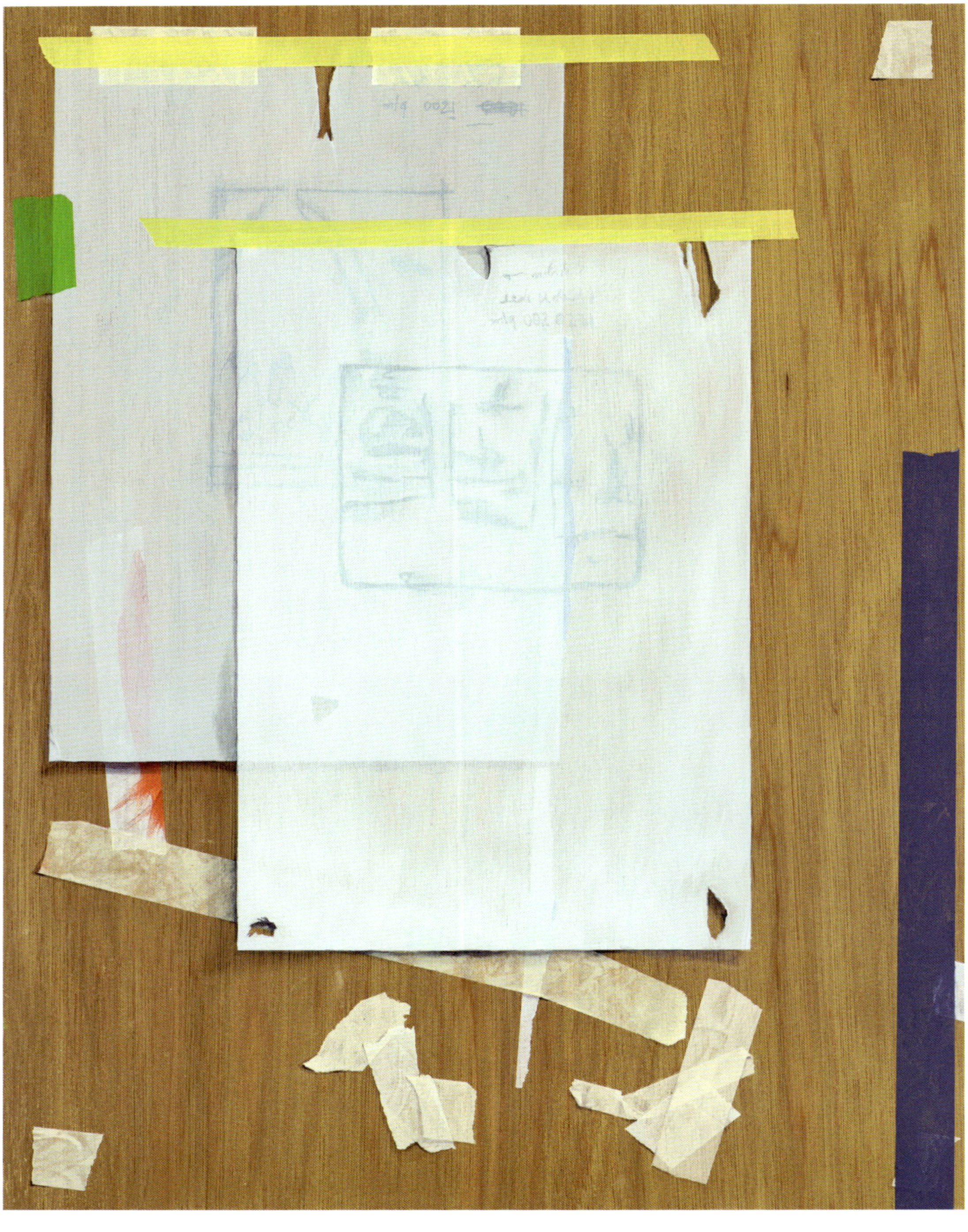

Tabula Rasa 2016 Oil and acrylic on wood 50 × 40 cm

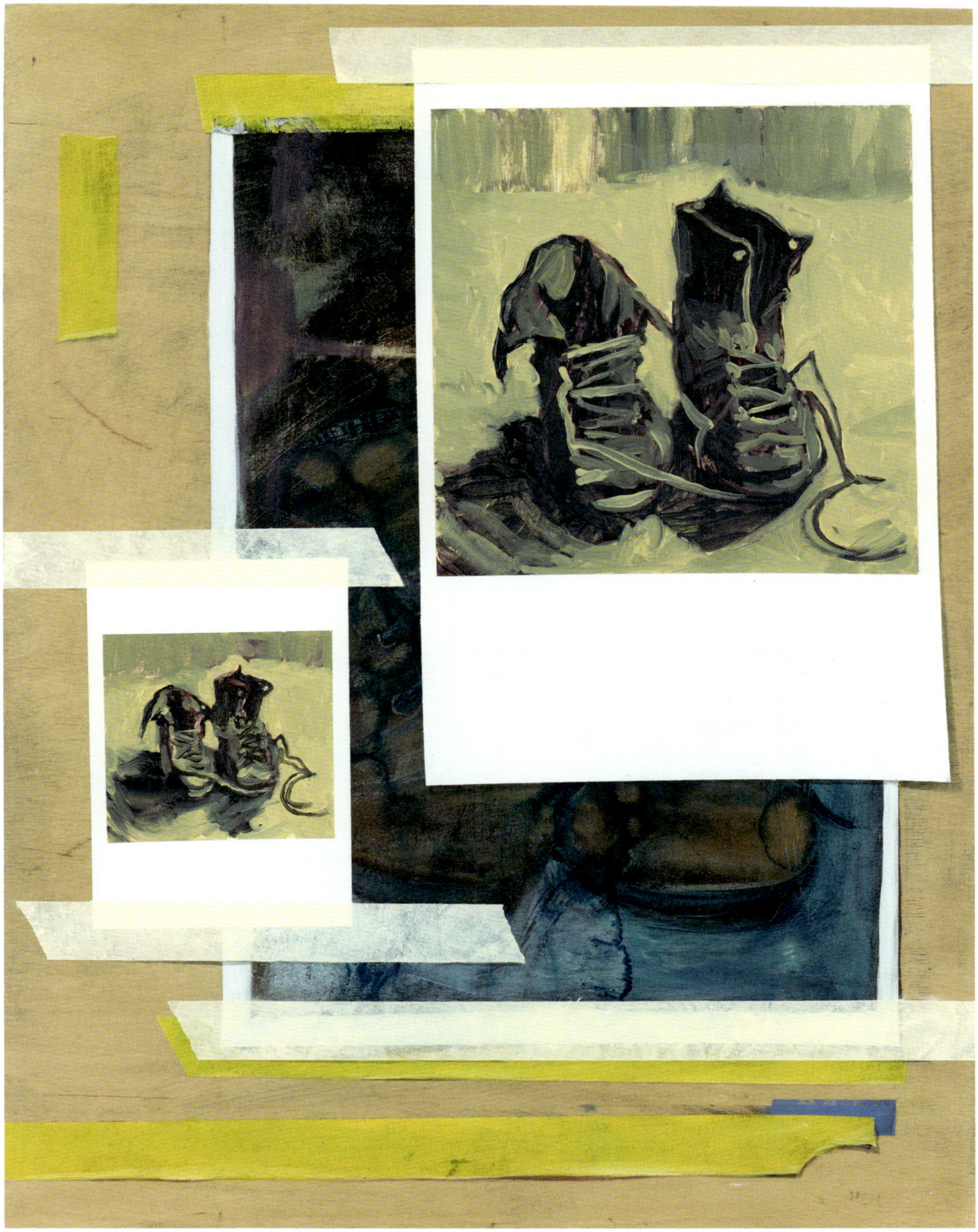

Where the Dead Men Lost Their Bones 2017 Oil and acrylic on wood 50 × 40 cm

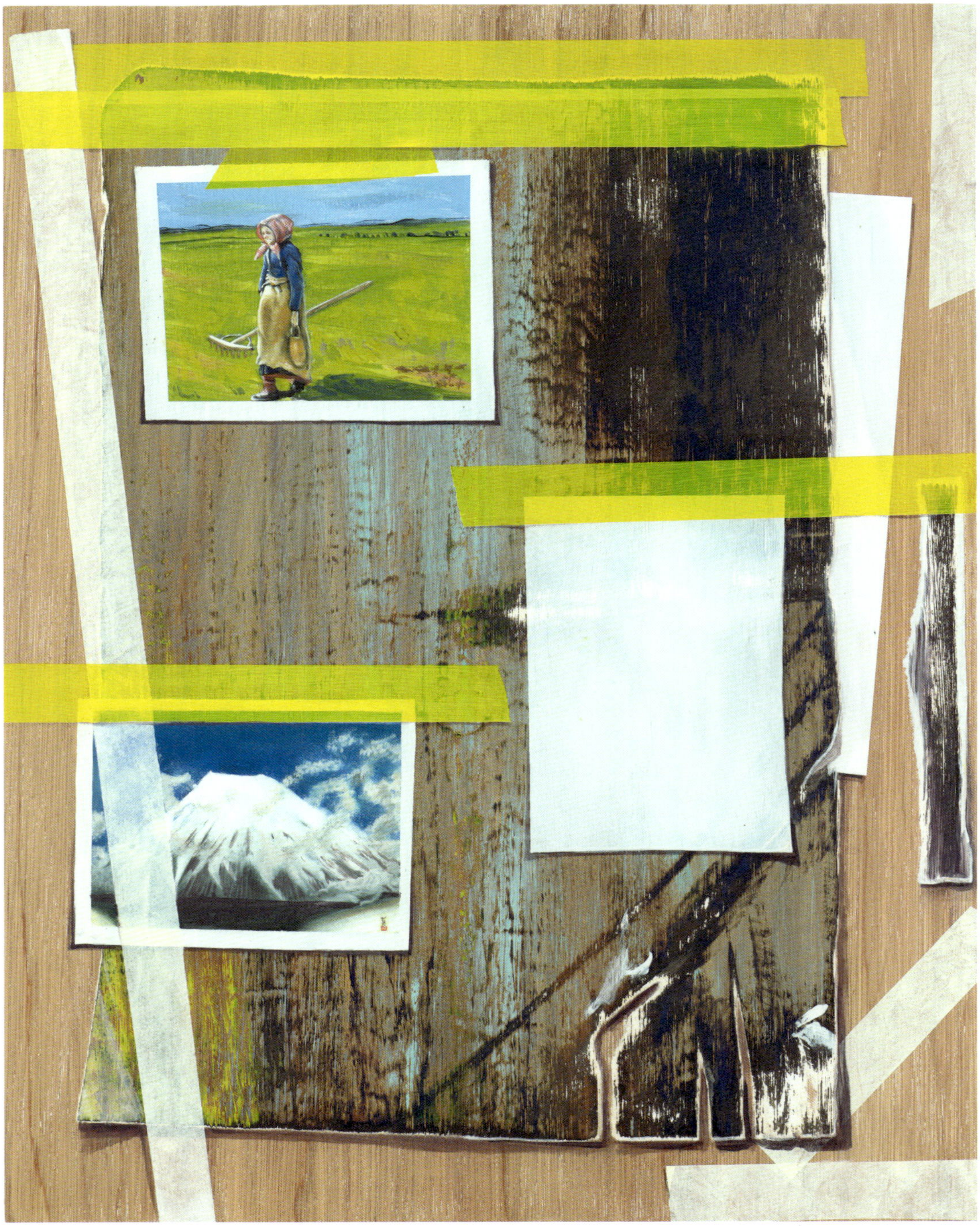

The Old That Is Strong Does Not Wither 2017 Oil and acrylic on wood 50 × 40 cm

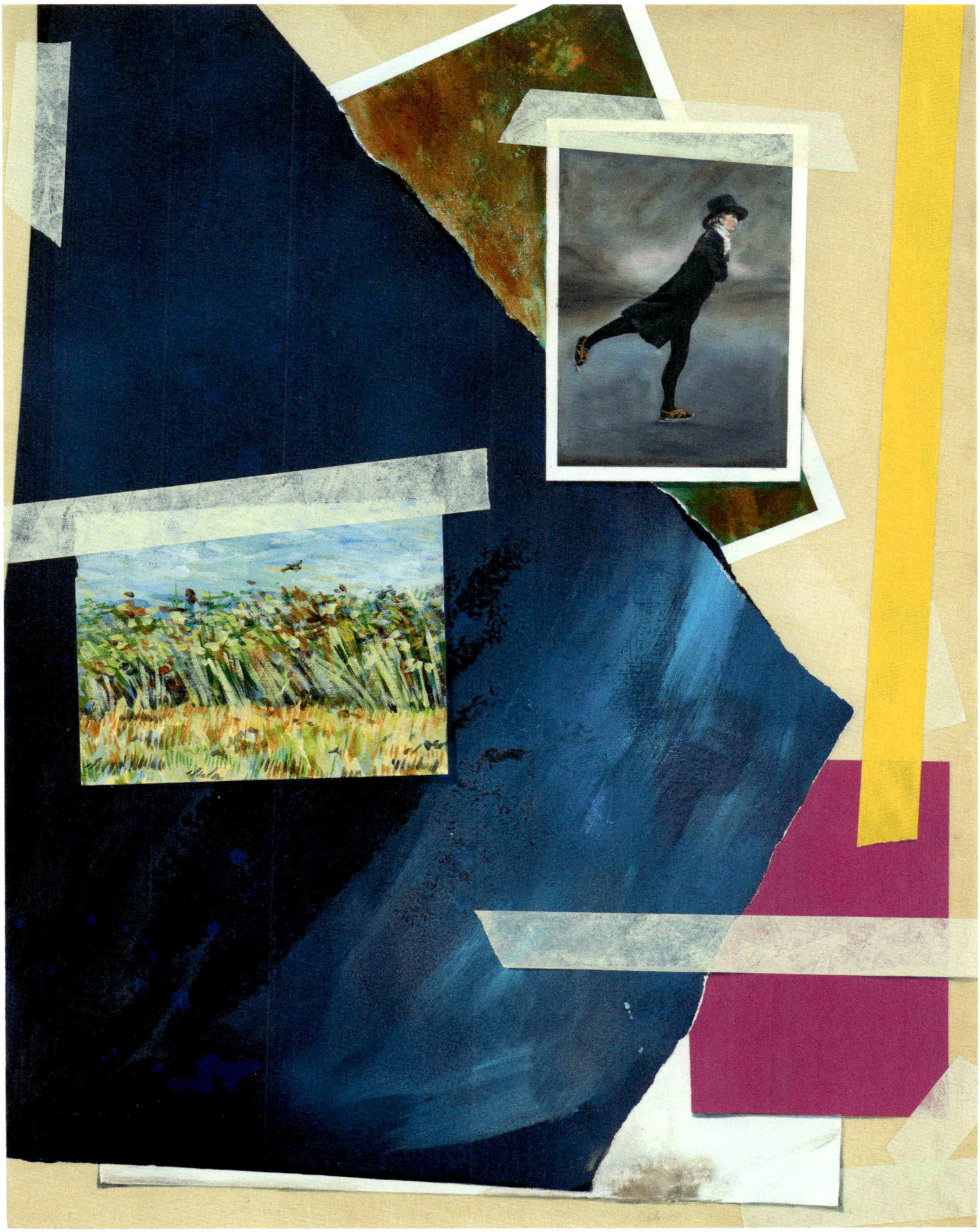

O O O O That Shakespearean Rag 2017 Oil and acrylic on wood 50 × 40 cm

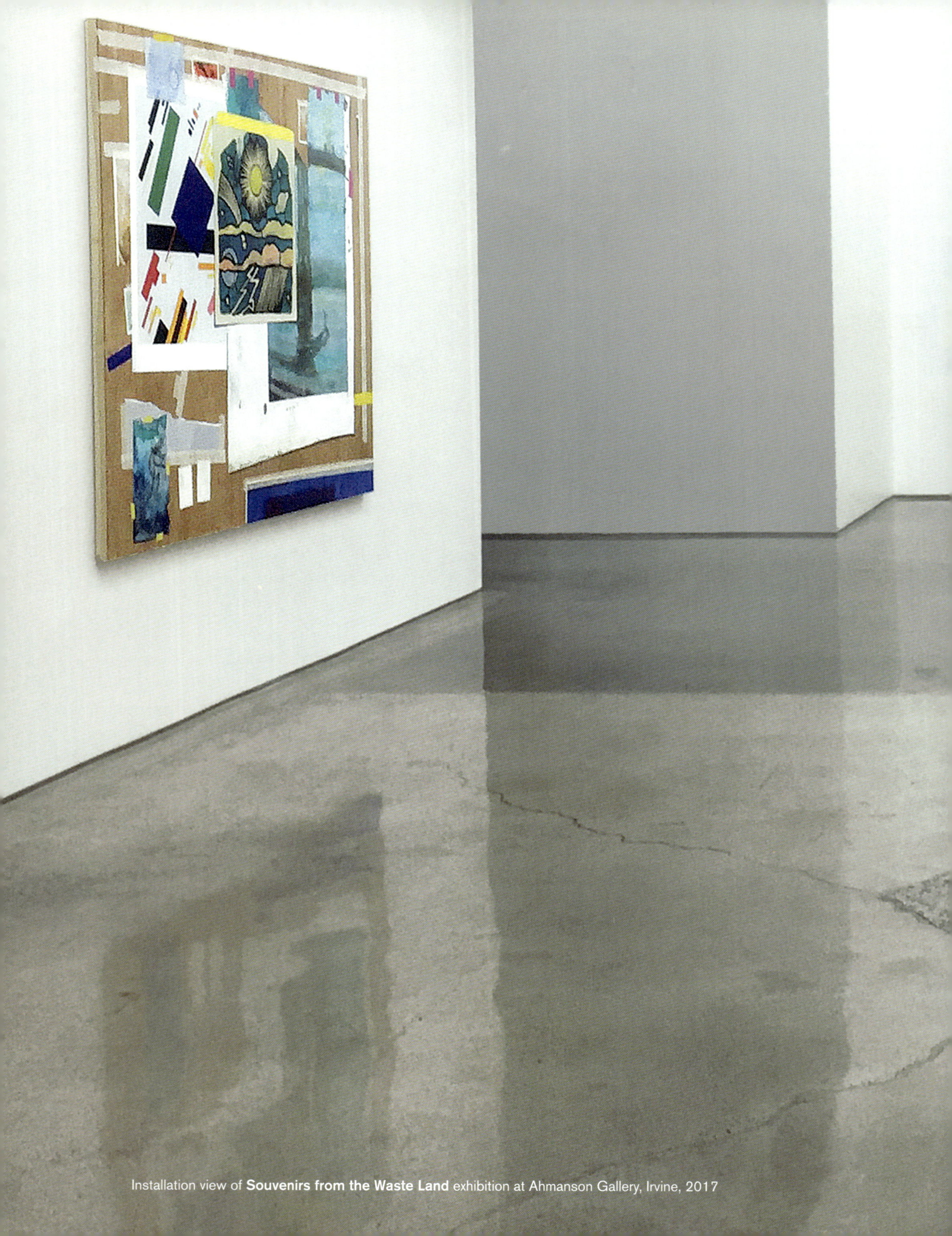

Installation view of **Souvenirs from the Waste Land** exhibition at Ahmanson Gallery, Irvine, 2017

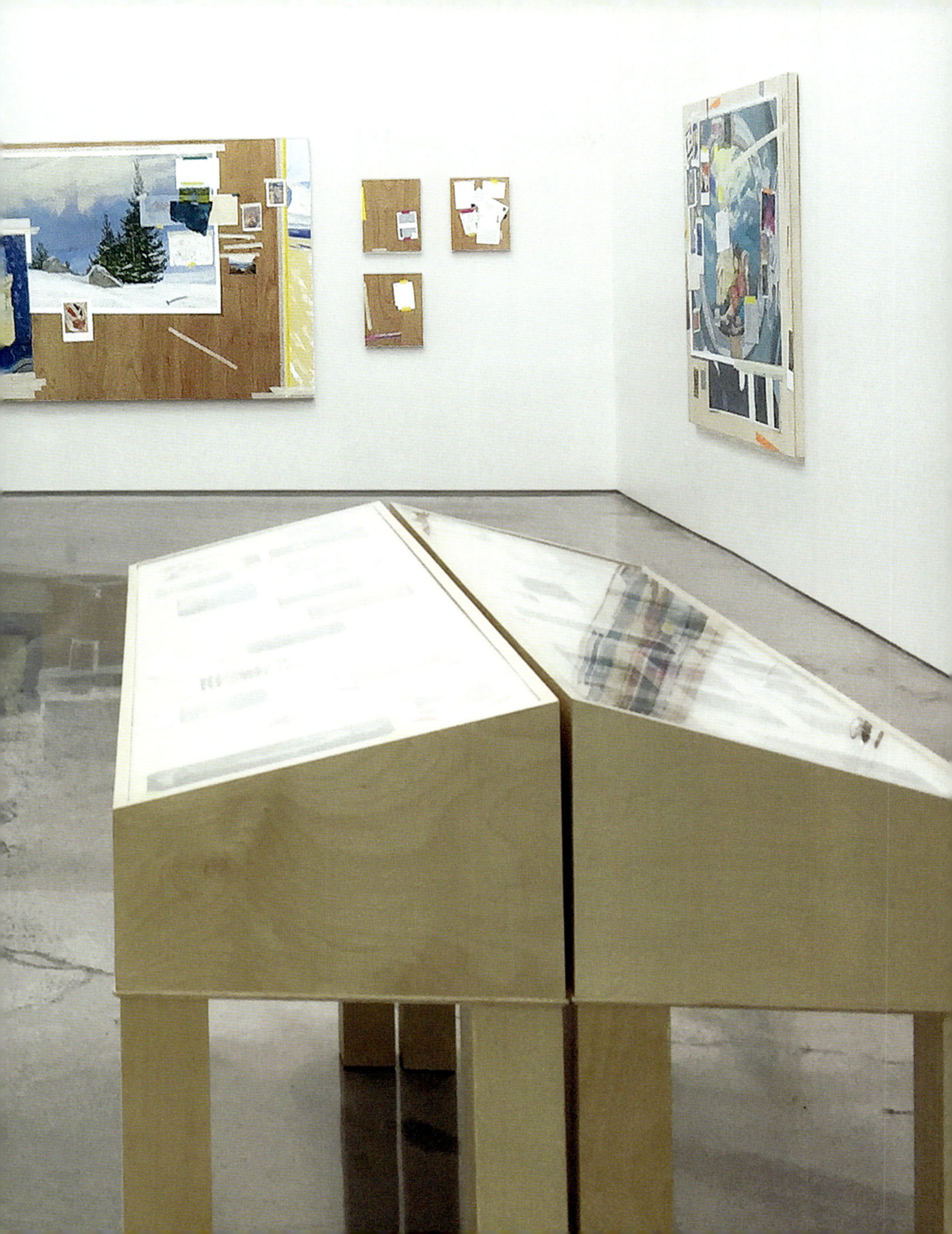

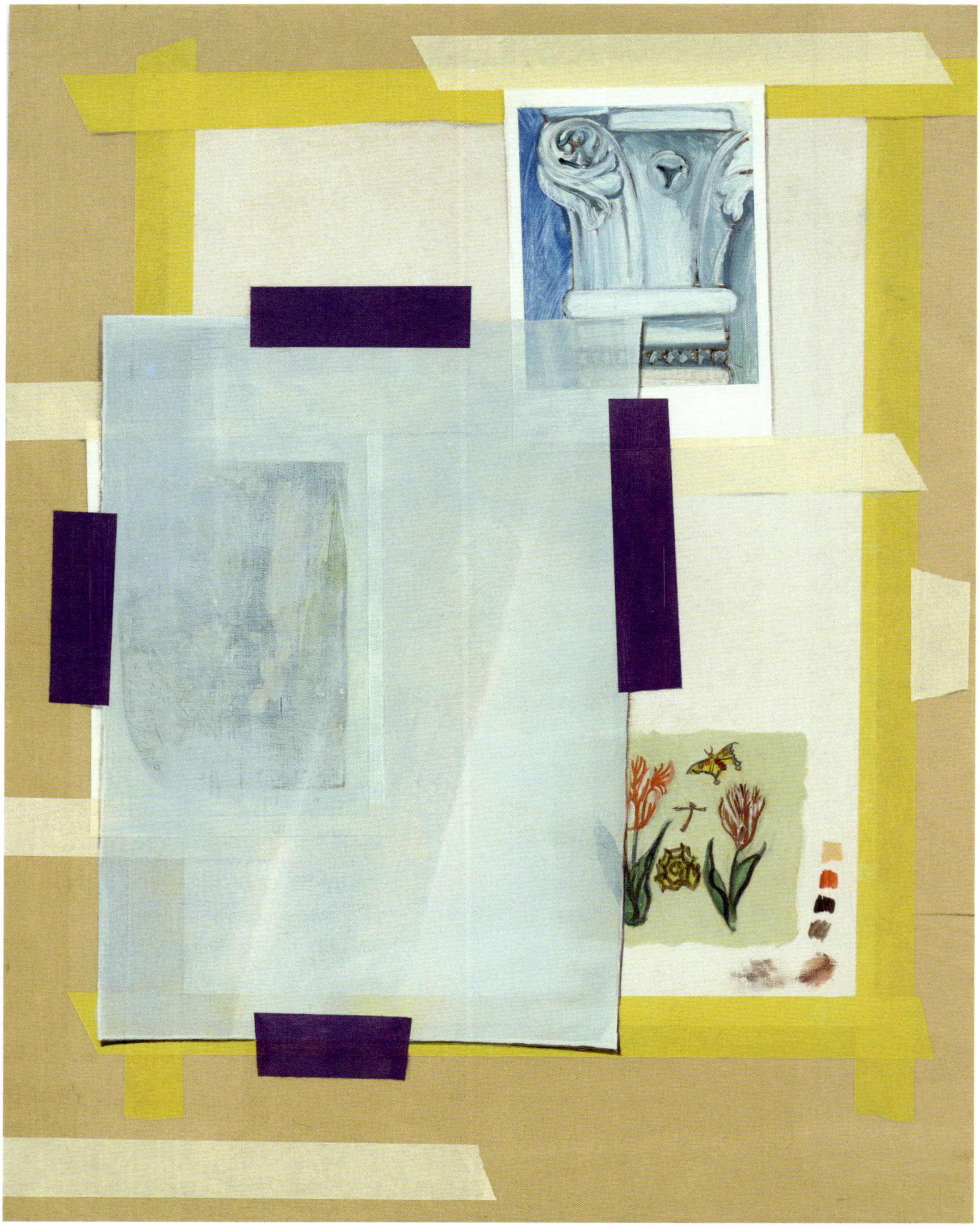

Old Man With Wrinkled Dugs 2017 Oil on wood 50 × 40 cm

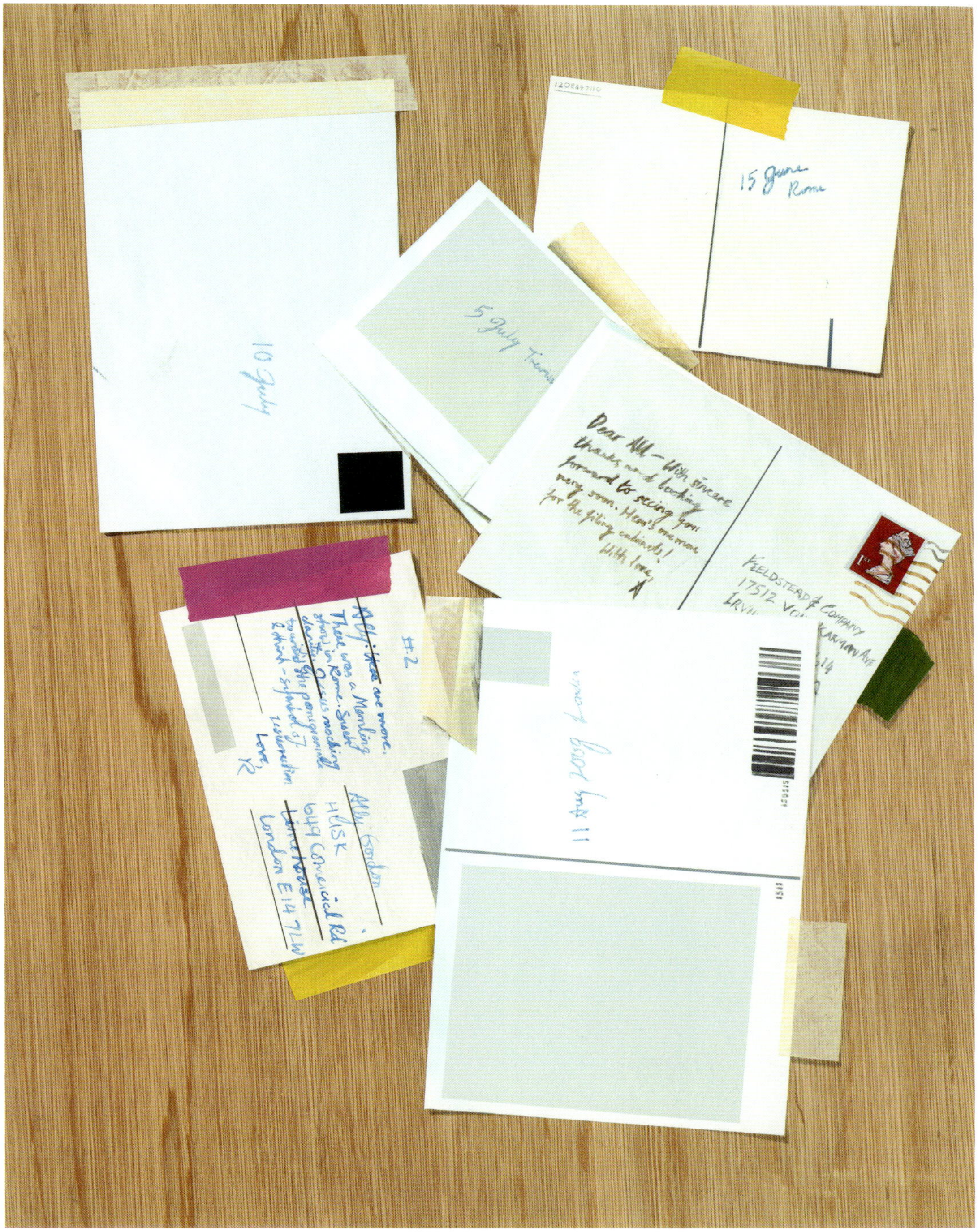

In the Deserts of the West, Still Today 2017 Oil and acrylic on wood 50 × 40 cm

He Dreams of Being an Honest Coward 2017 Oil and acrylic on wood 50 × 40 cm

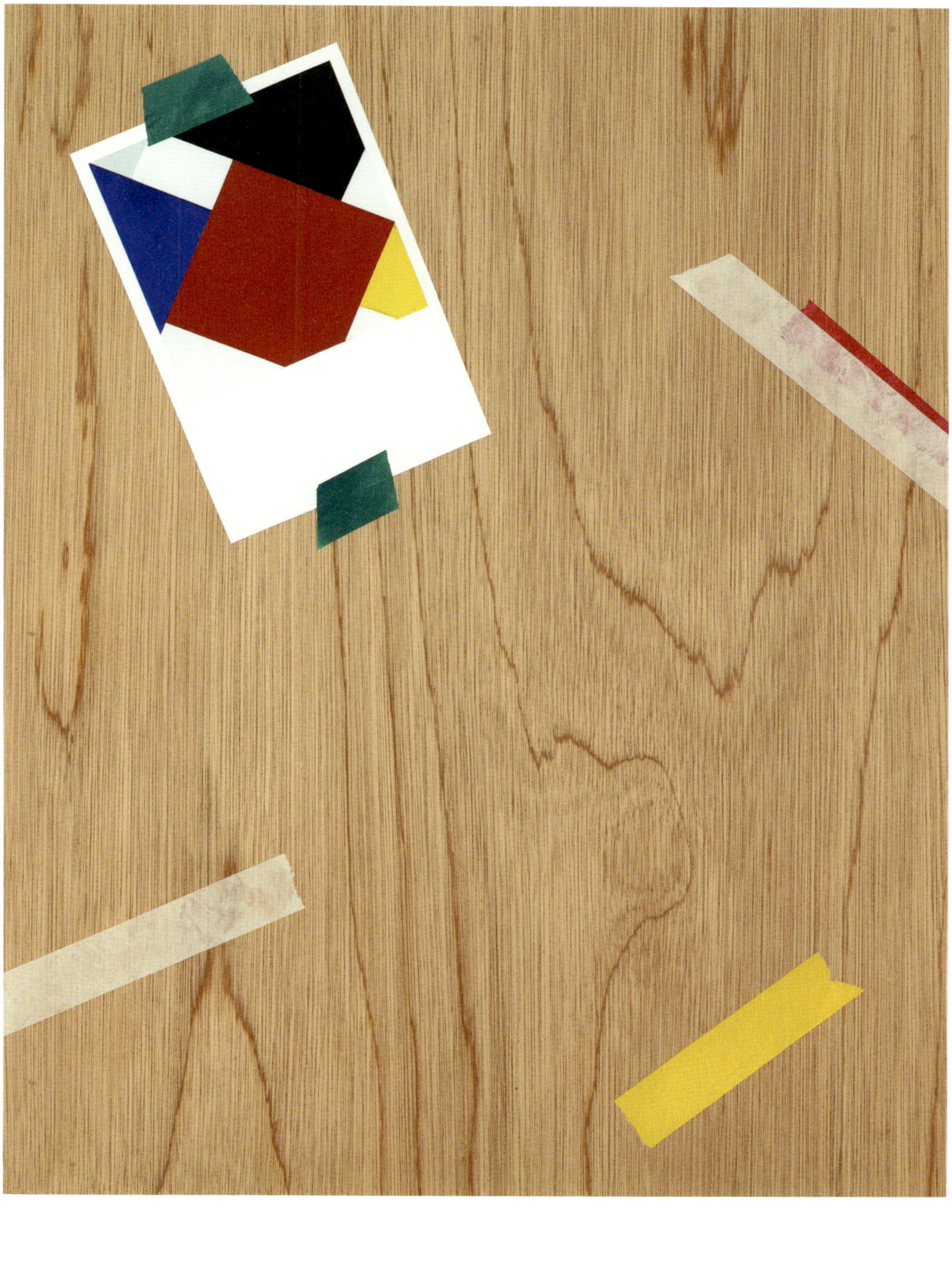

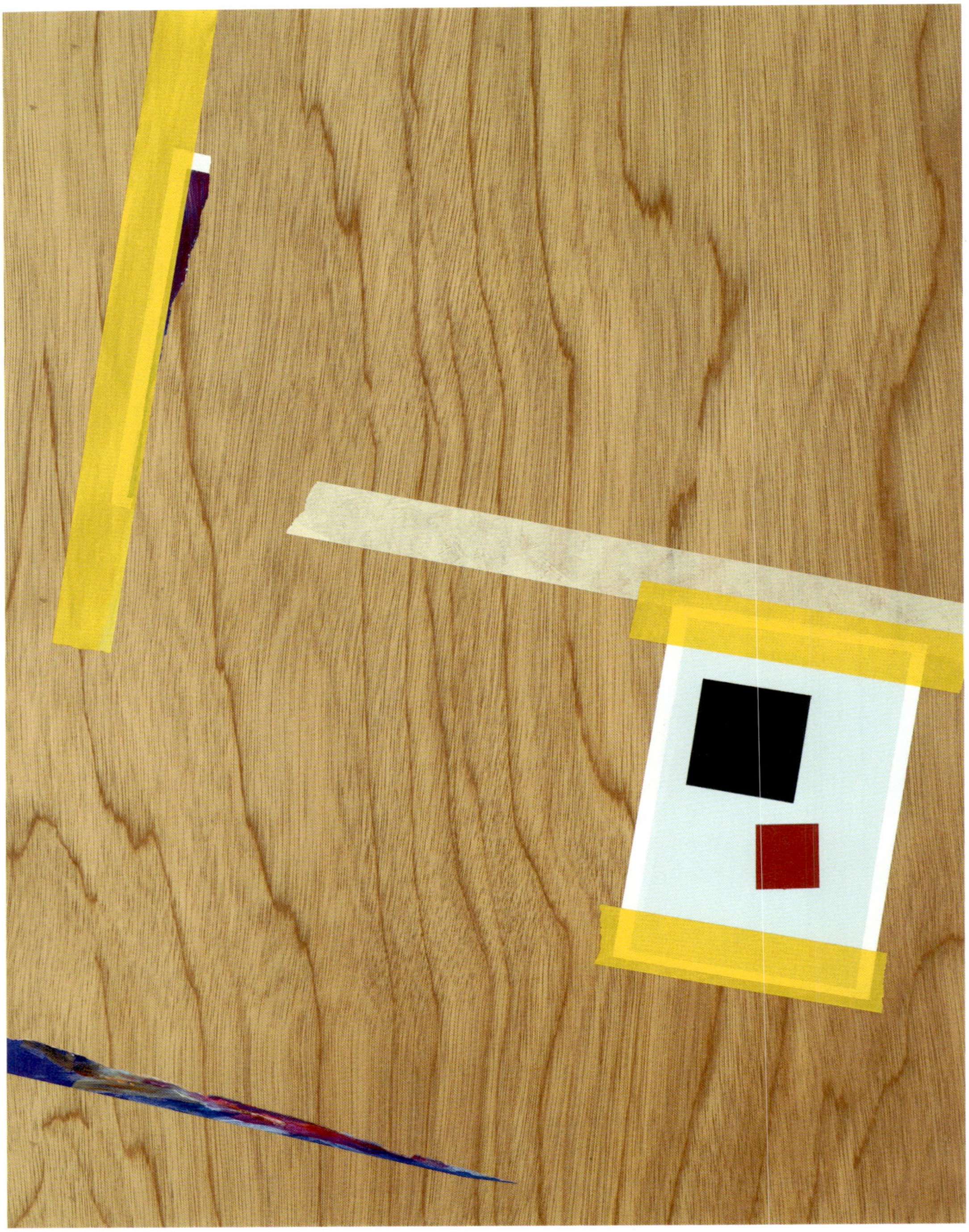

Righteousness and Bliss Shall Kiss One Another 2017 Oil and acrylic on wood 50 × 40 cm

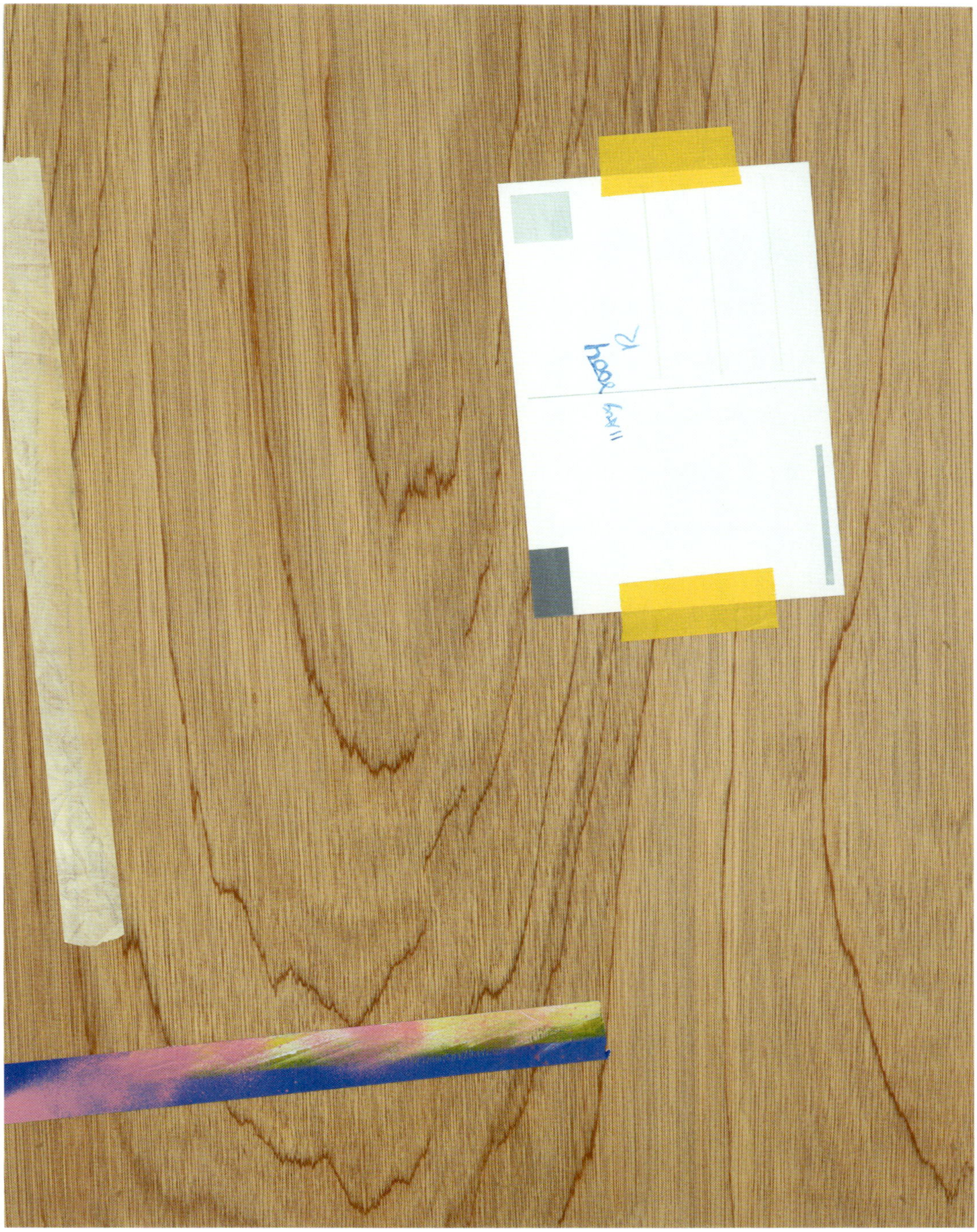

They Delivered It Up to the Inclemencies of Sun and Winters 2017 Oil and acrylic on wood 50 × 40 cm

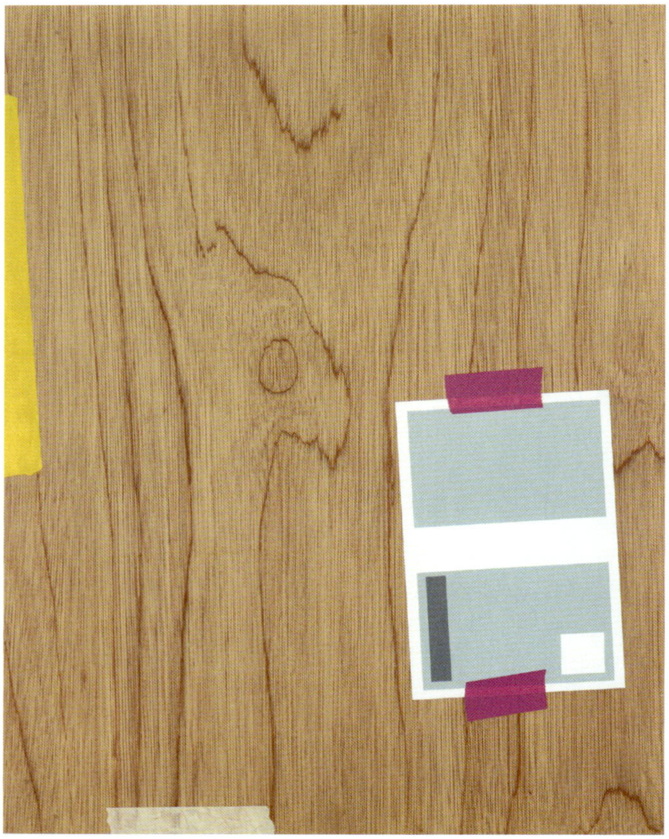

Vanity, Vanity. All is Vanity. 2017
Oil and acrylic on wood 50 × 40 cm

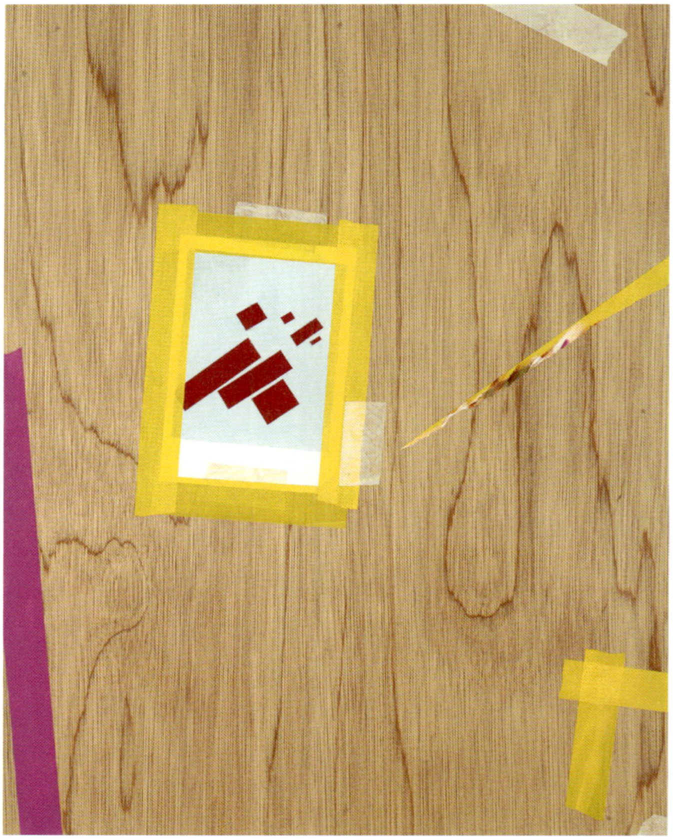

And What We Discover Must Not Be Concealed 2017
Oil and acrylic on wood 50 × 40 cm

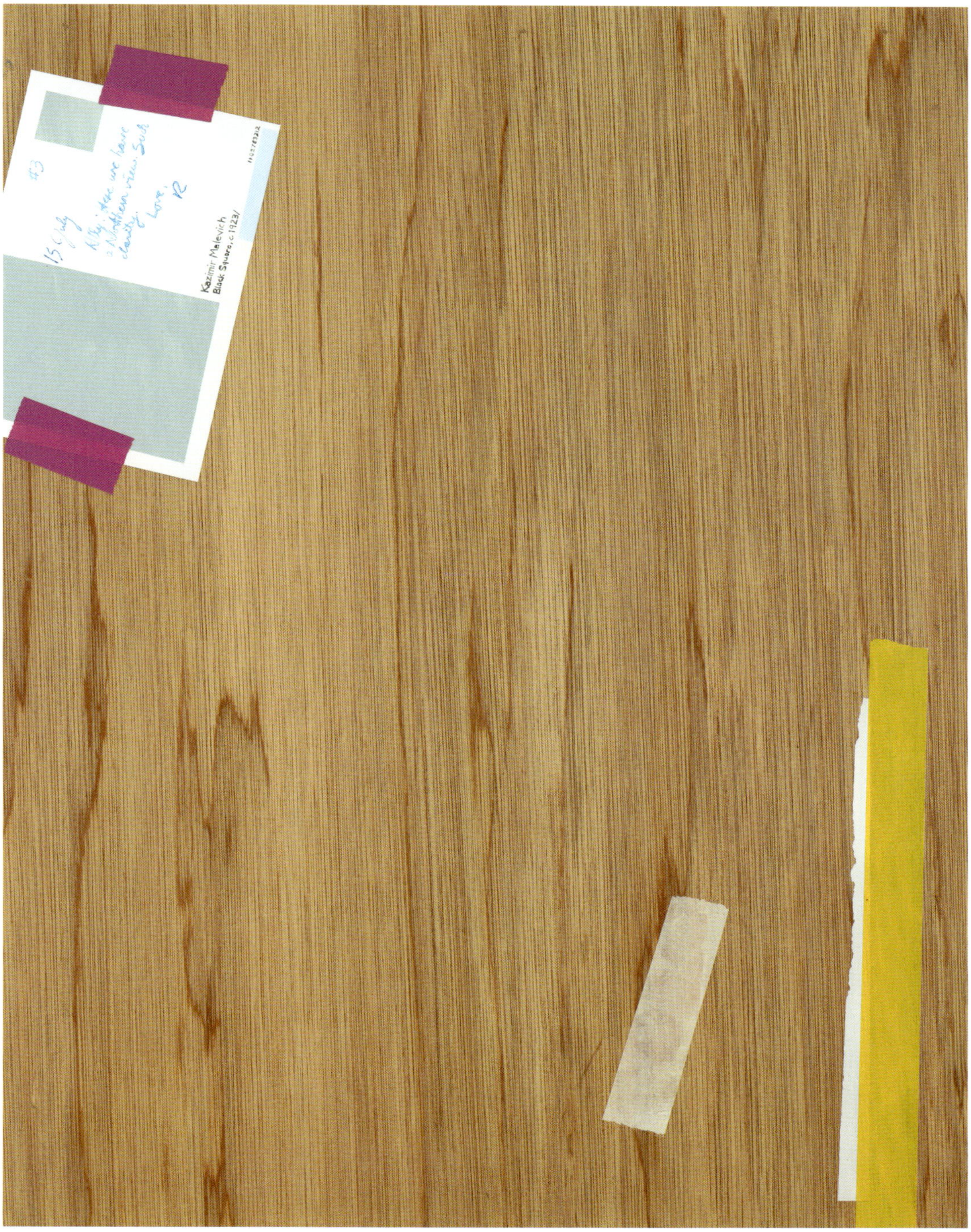

It Can Exist, In and for Itself, Without Things 2017 Oil and acrylic on wood 50 × 40 cm

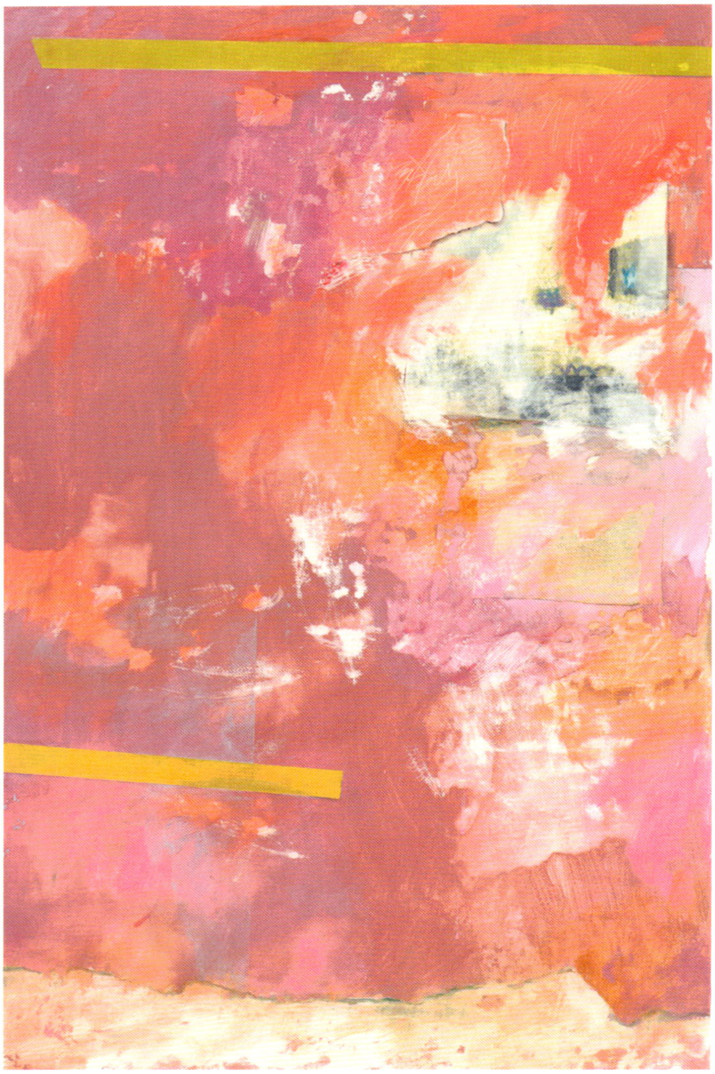

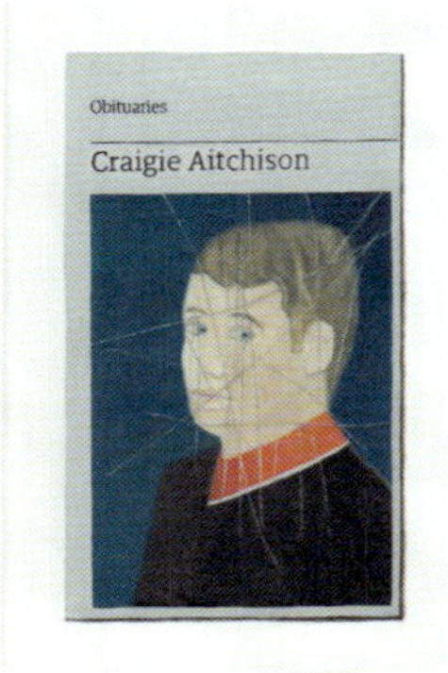

As Long As the World Exists One Should Attempt To Record That
2017 Oil on gesso panel 90 × 60 cm

Hugh Mendes
Obituary: Craigie Aitchison
2017
Oil on linen 30 × 20 cm

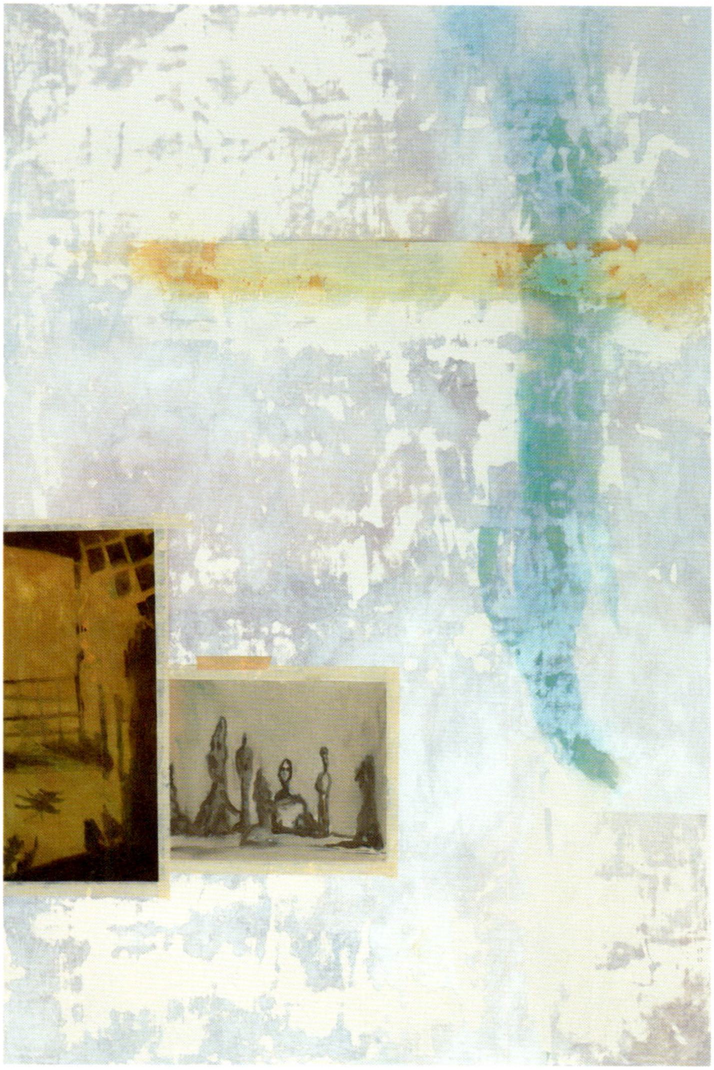

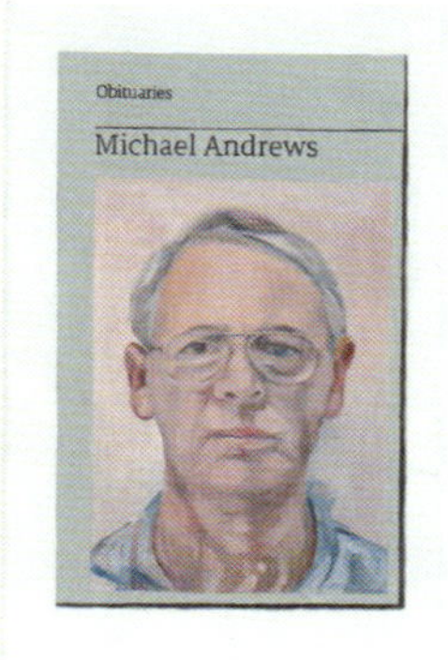

A Fraction of Landscape at the Edge of Water 2017
Oil on gesso panel 90 × 60 cm

Hugh Mendes
Obituary: Michael Andrews
2017
Oil on linen 30 × 20 cm

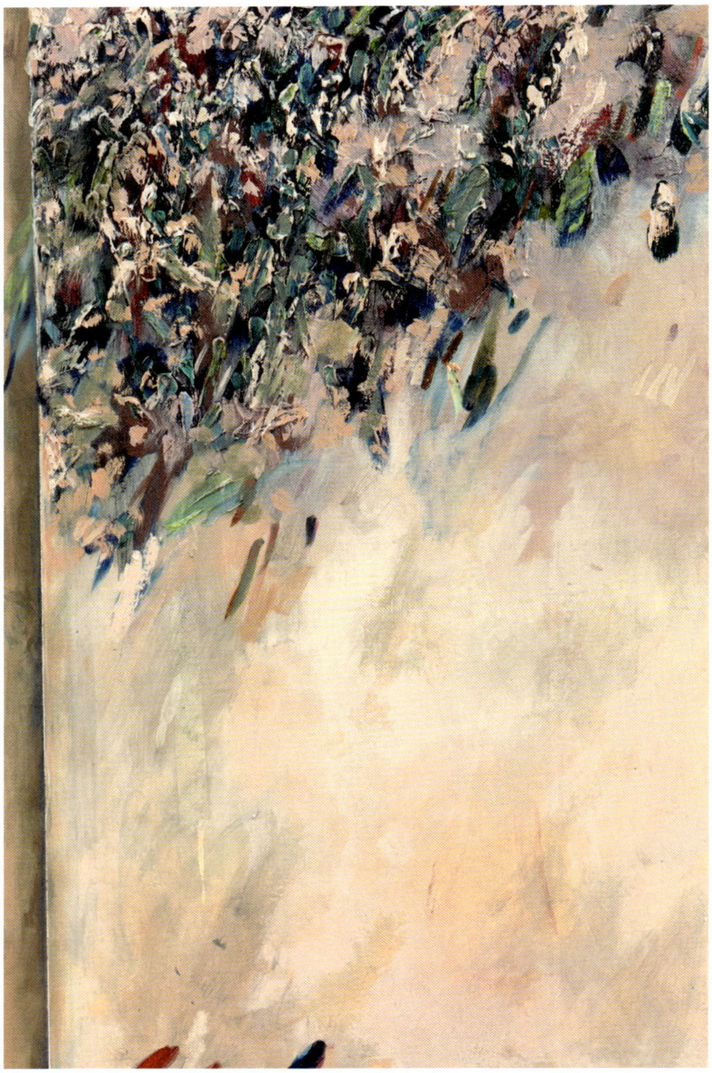

I'm Only Trying To Do What I Can't 2017
Oil on gesso panel 90 × 60 cm

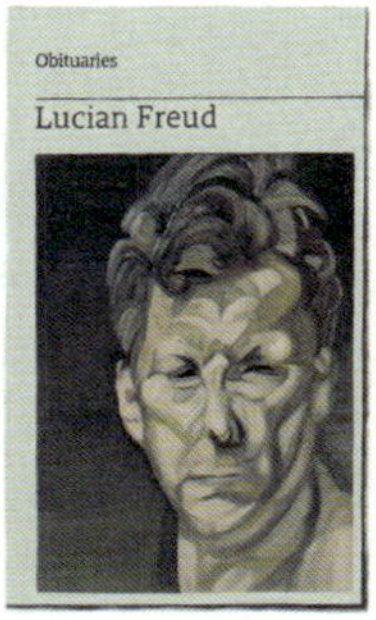

Hugh Mendes
Obituary: Lucian Freud
2017
Oil on linen 30 × 20 cm

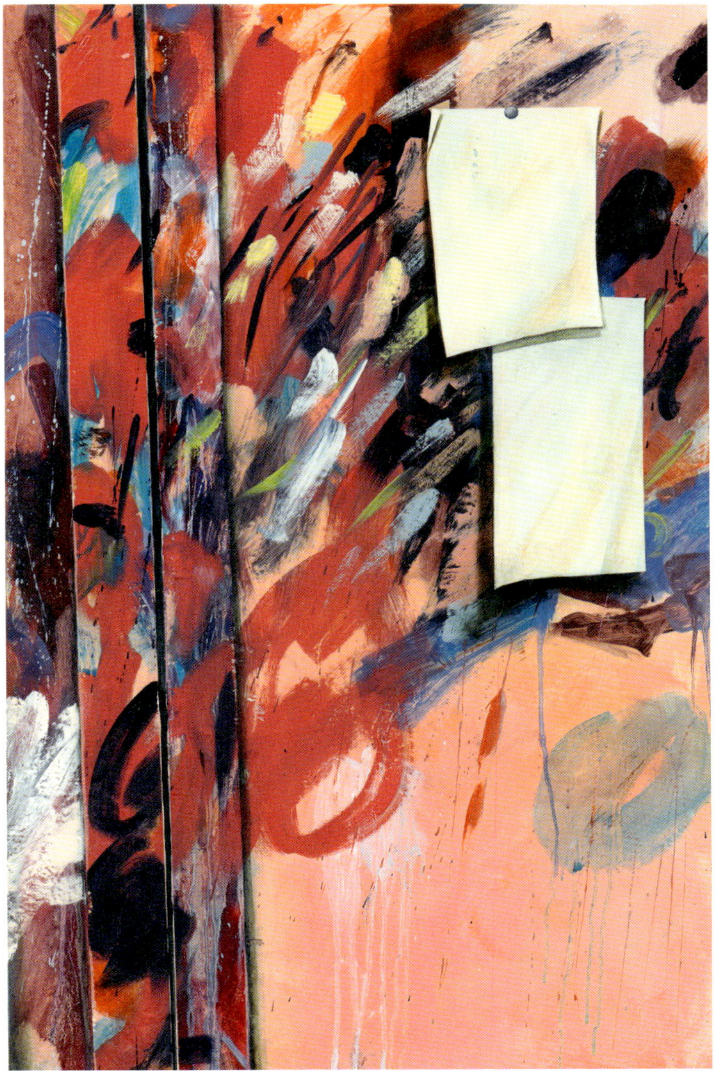

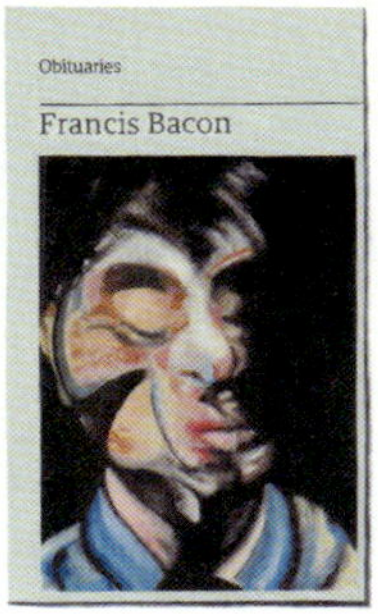

One Must Select What Part of the Accident One Chooses To Preserve
2017 Oil on gesso panel 90 × 60 cm

Hugh Mendes
Obituary: Francis Bacon
2017
Oil on linen 30 × 20 cm

Thirty Feathers and a Mouse 2019 Oil and acrylic on paper 94 × 72 cm

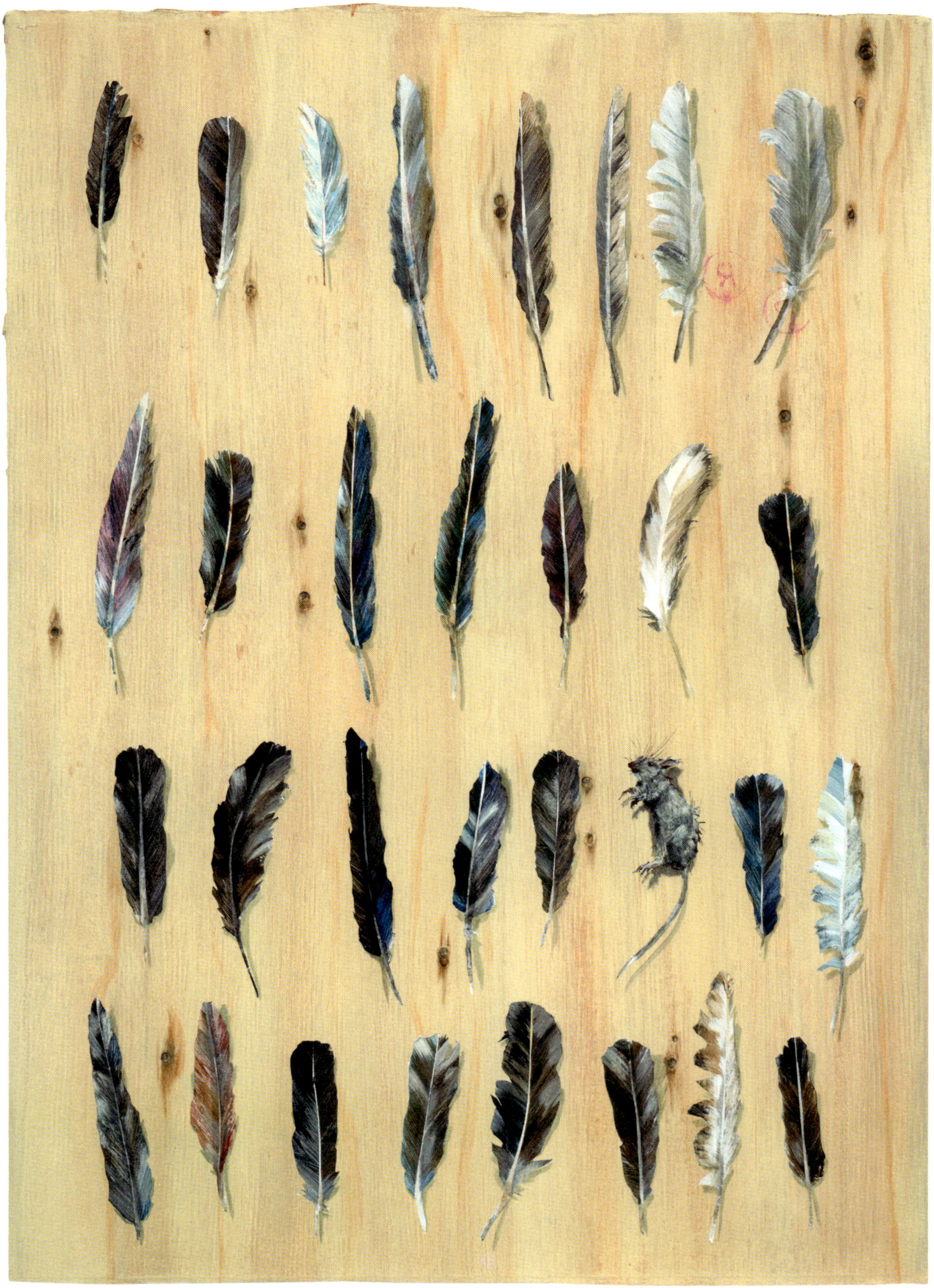

Desk Quodlibet 2020 Oil and acrylic on paper 94 × 72 cm

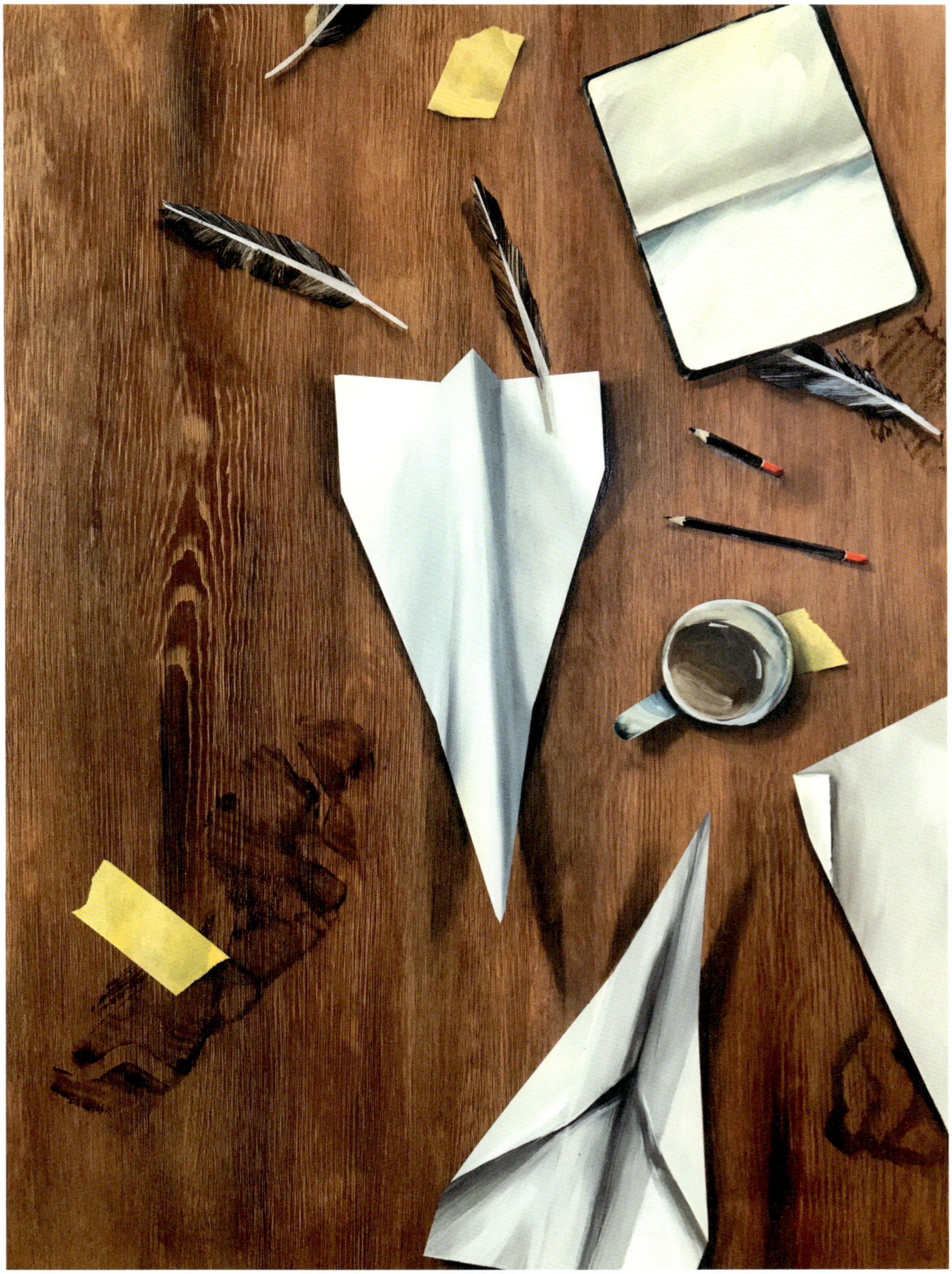

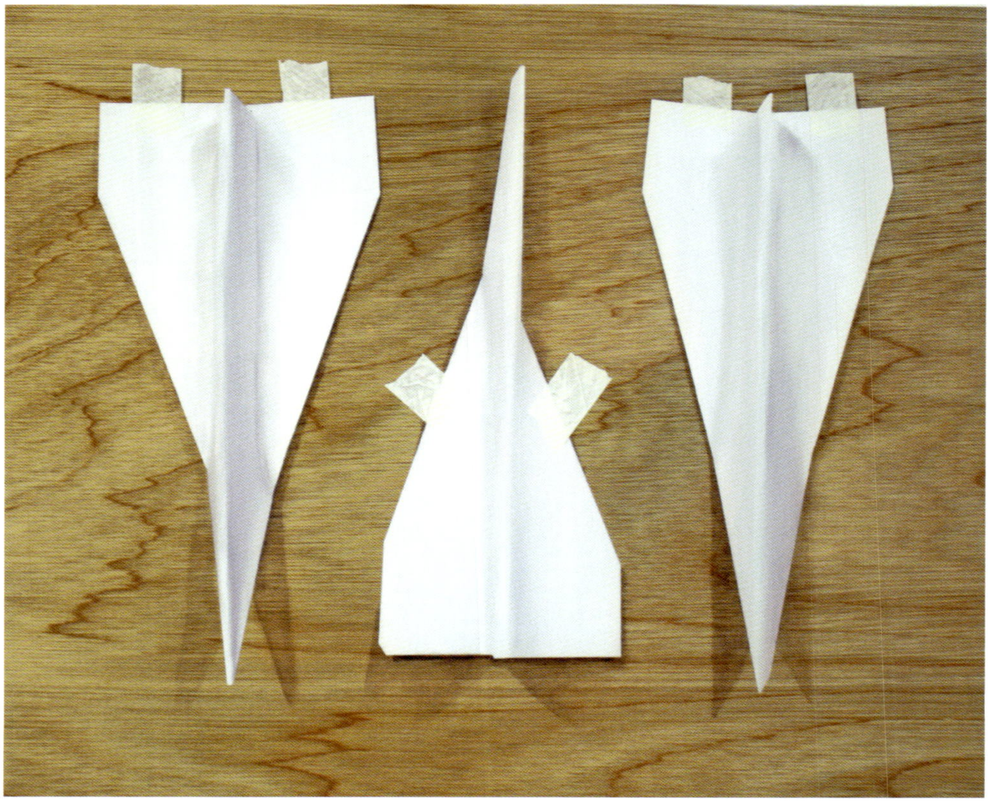

Paper Planes 2014 Oil on wood 40 × 50 cm

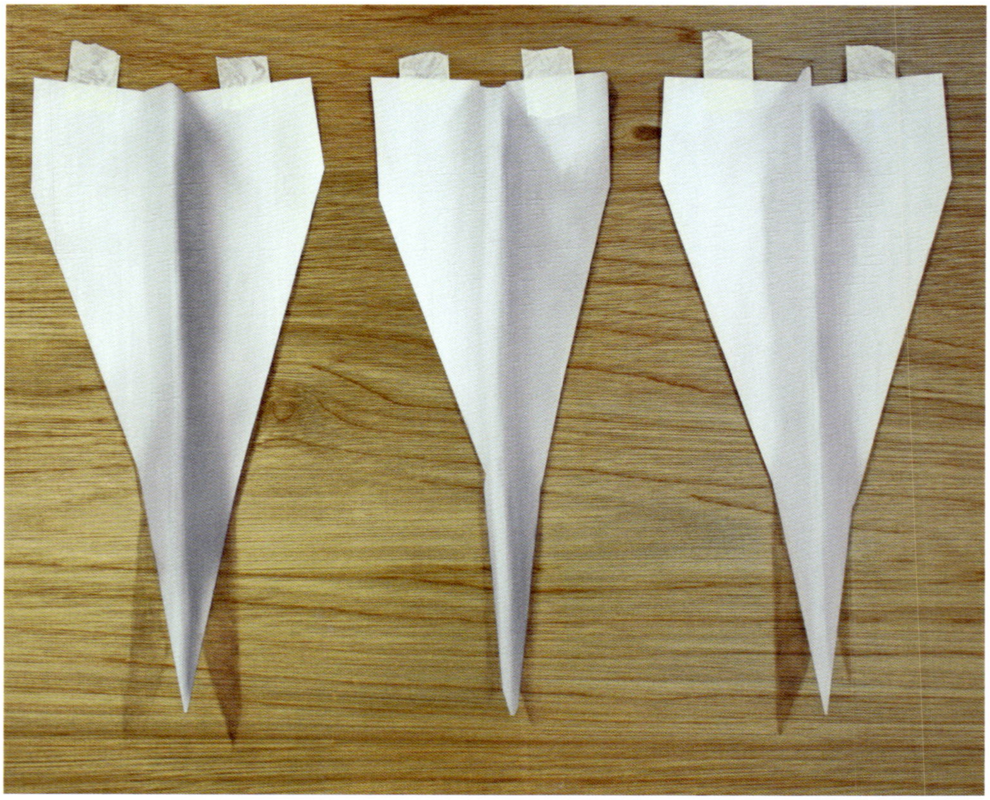

Three Paper Planes 2014 Oil on wood 40 × 50 cm

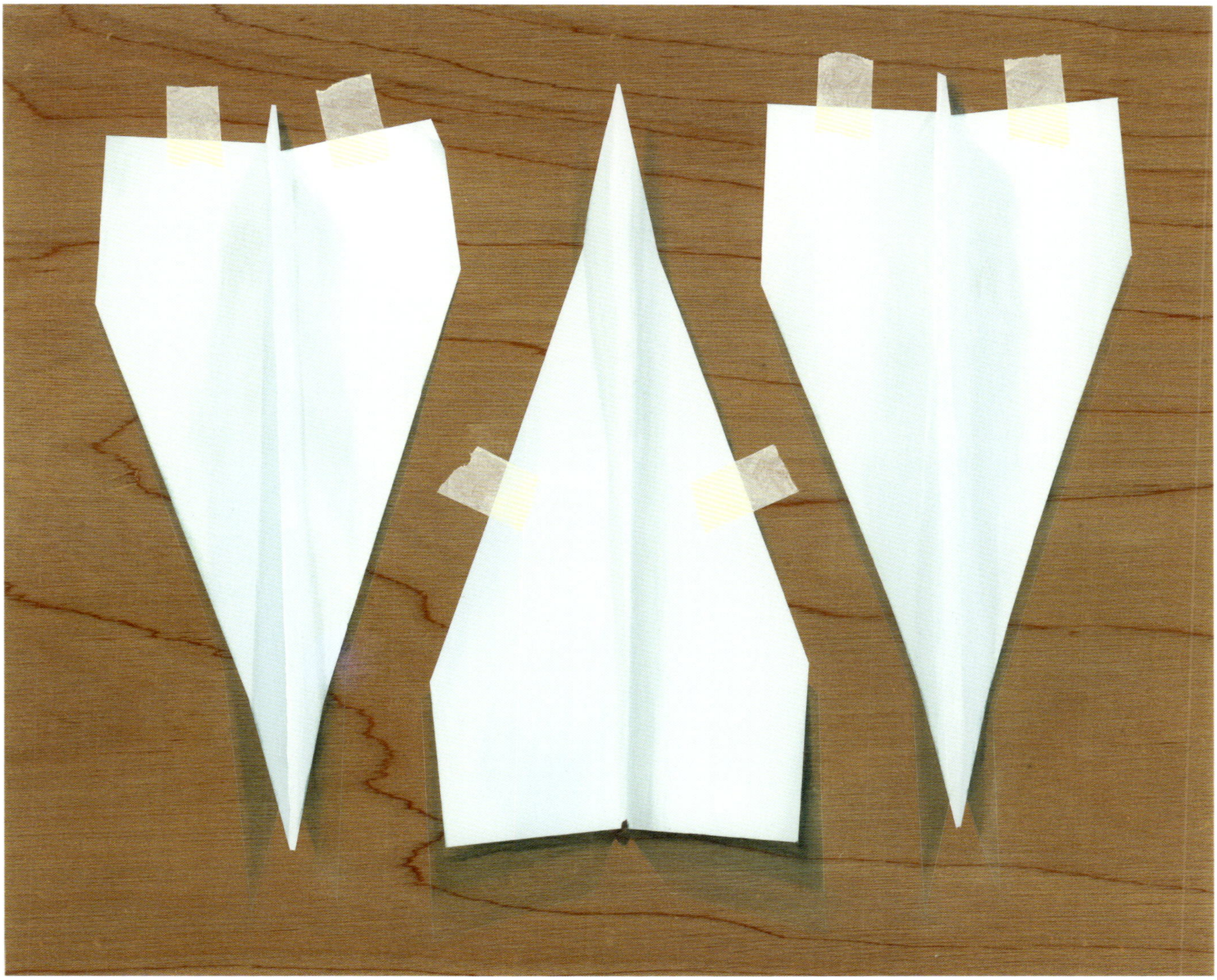

Three Paper Darts 2020 Oil on wood 40 × 50 cm

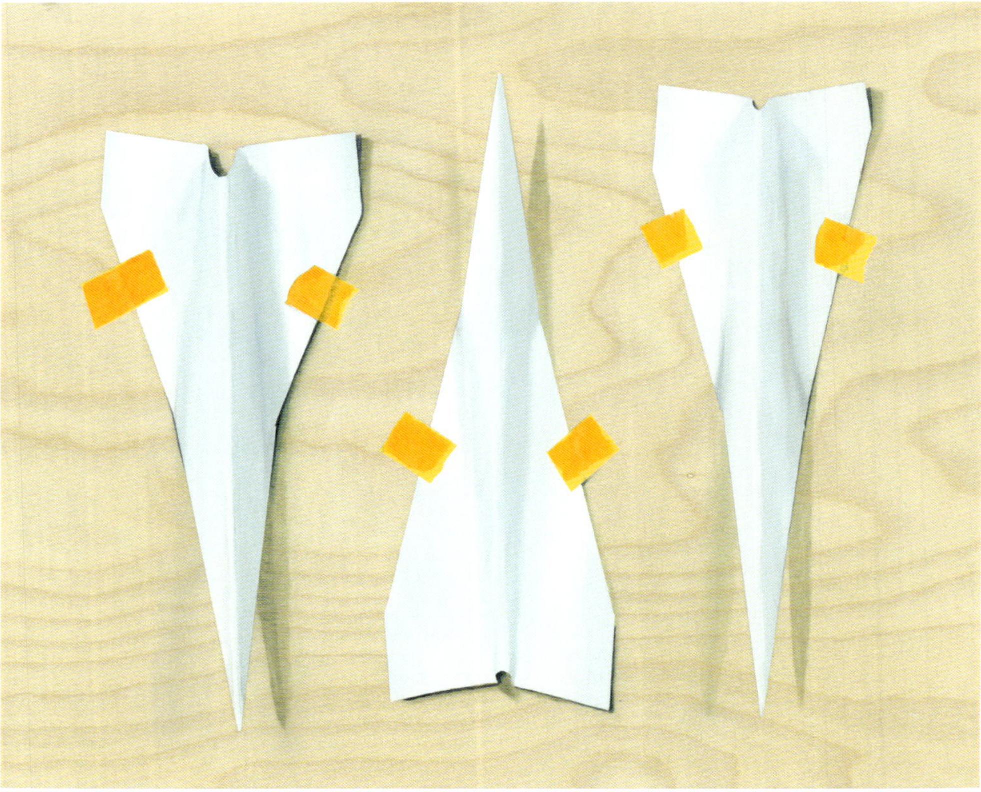

Paper Darts (Yellow Tape I) 2018 Oil on wood 40 × 50 cm

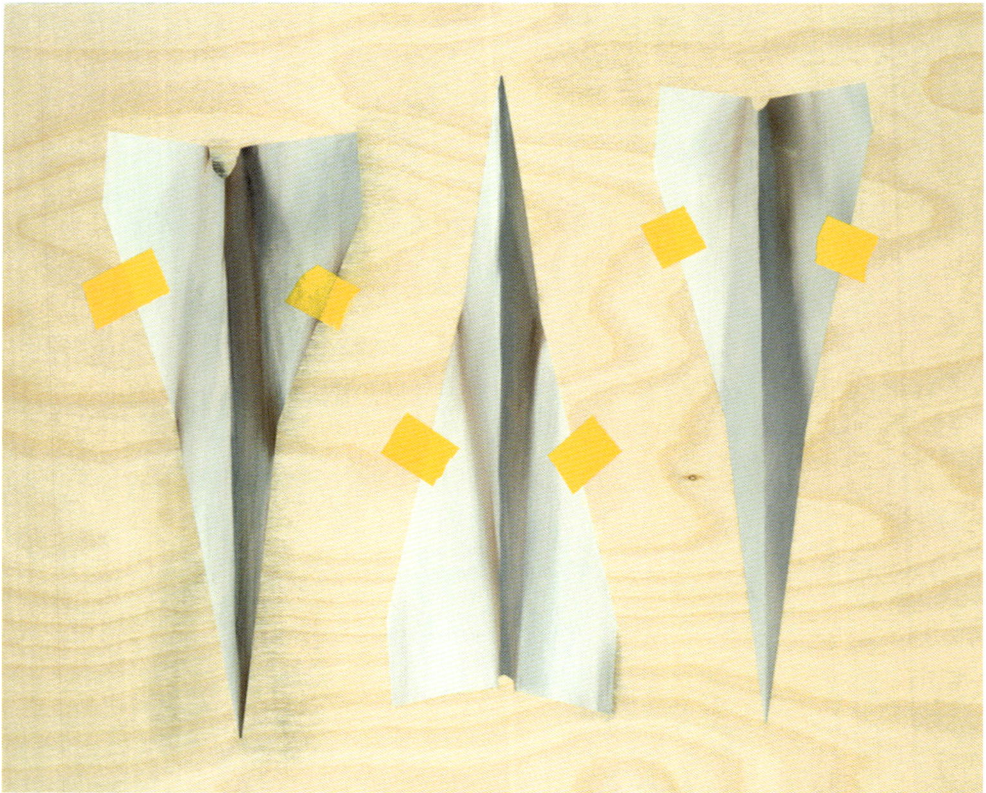

Paper Darts (Yellow Tape II) 2018 Oil on wood 40 × 50 cm

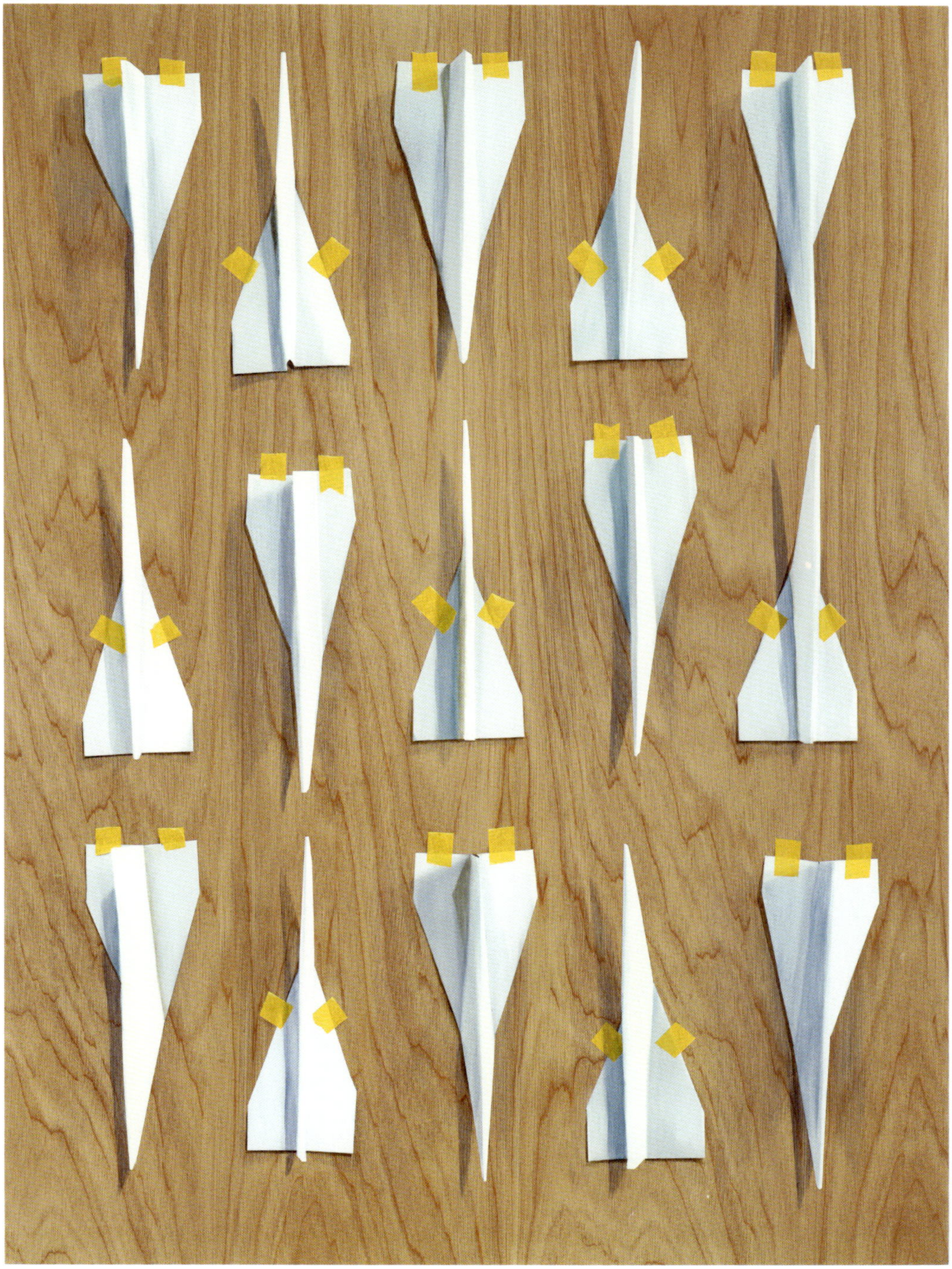

Fifteen Paper Planes 2016 Oil and acrylic on wood 120 × 90 cm

And We Give It To You, The People 2018 Oil on wood 180 × 240 cm

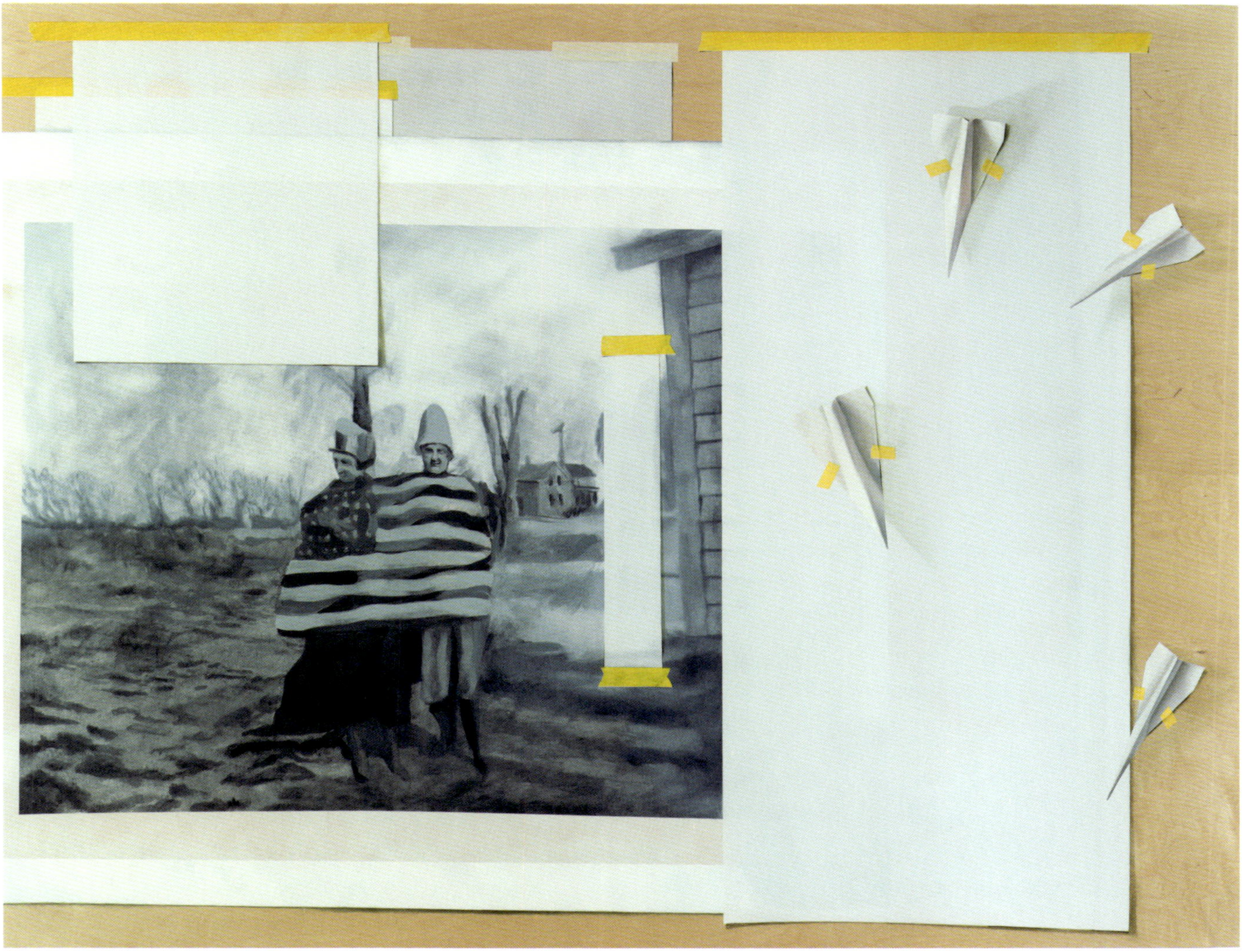

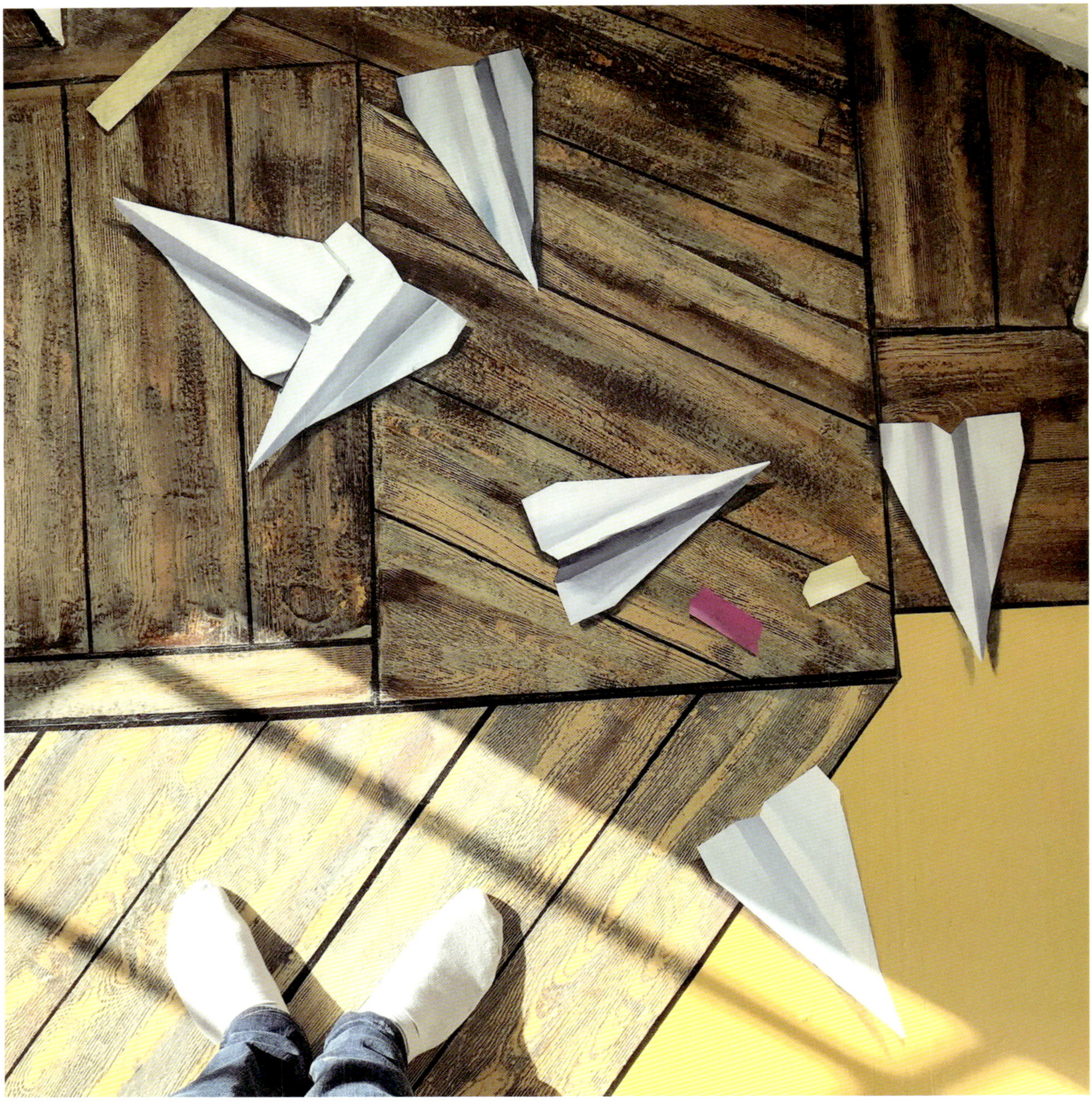

All That Remains Detail from floor painting at City & Guilds of London Art School 2019

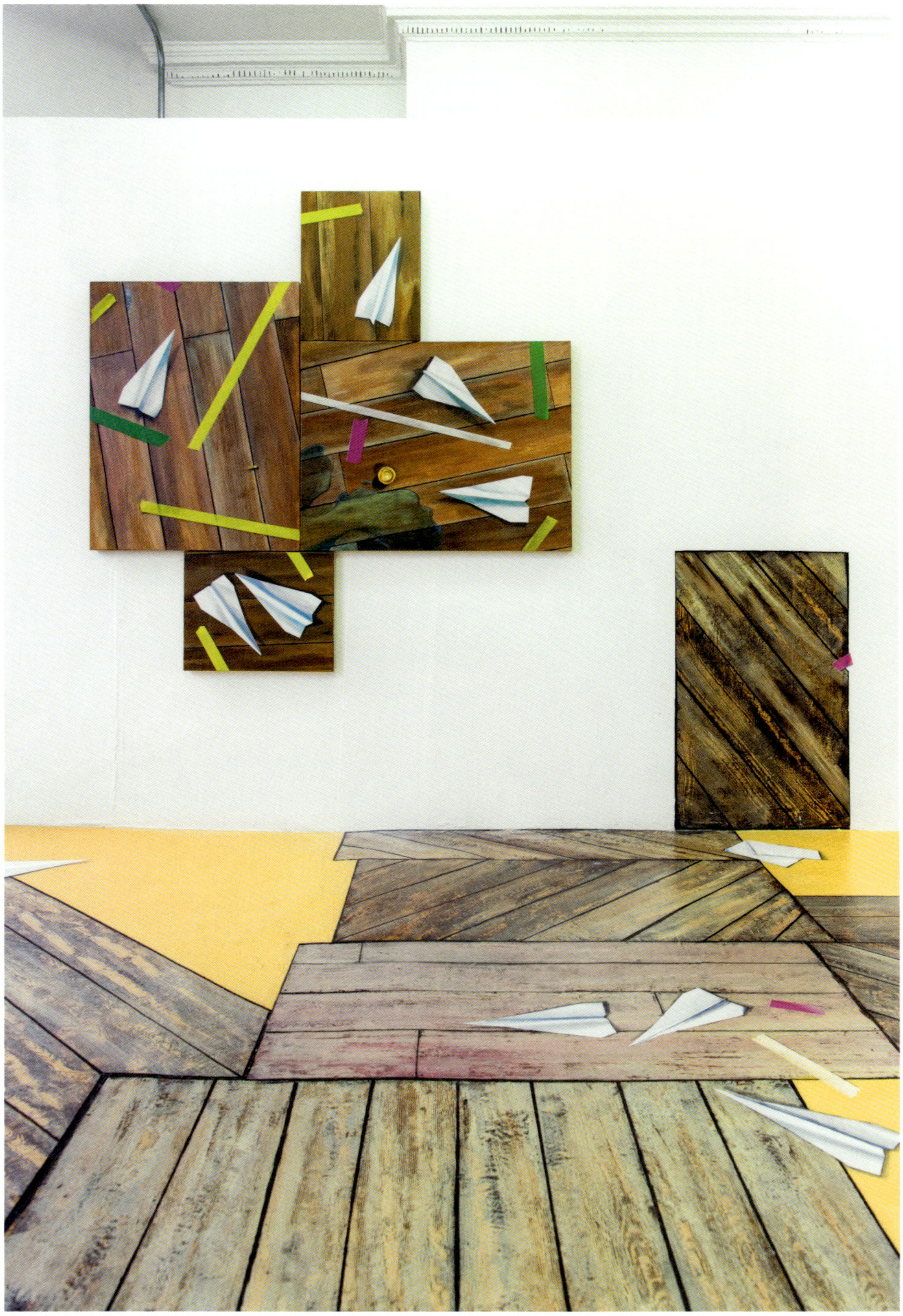

All That Remains Installation view of residency exhibition at City & Guilds of London Art School 2019

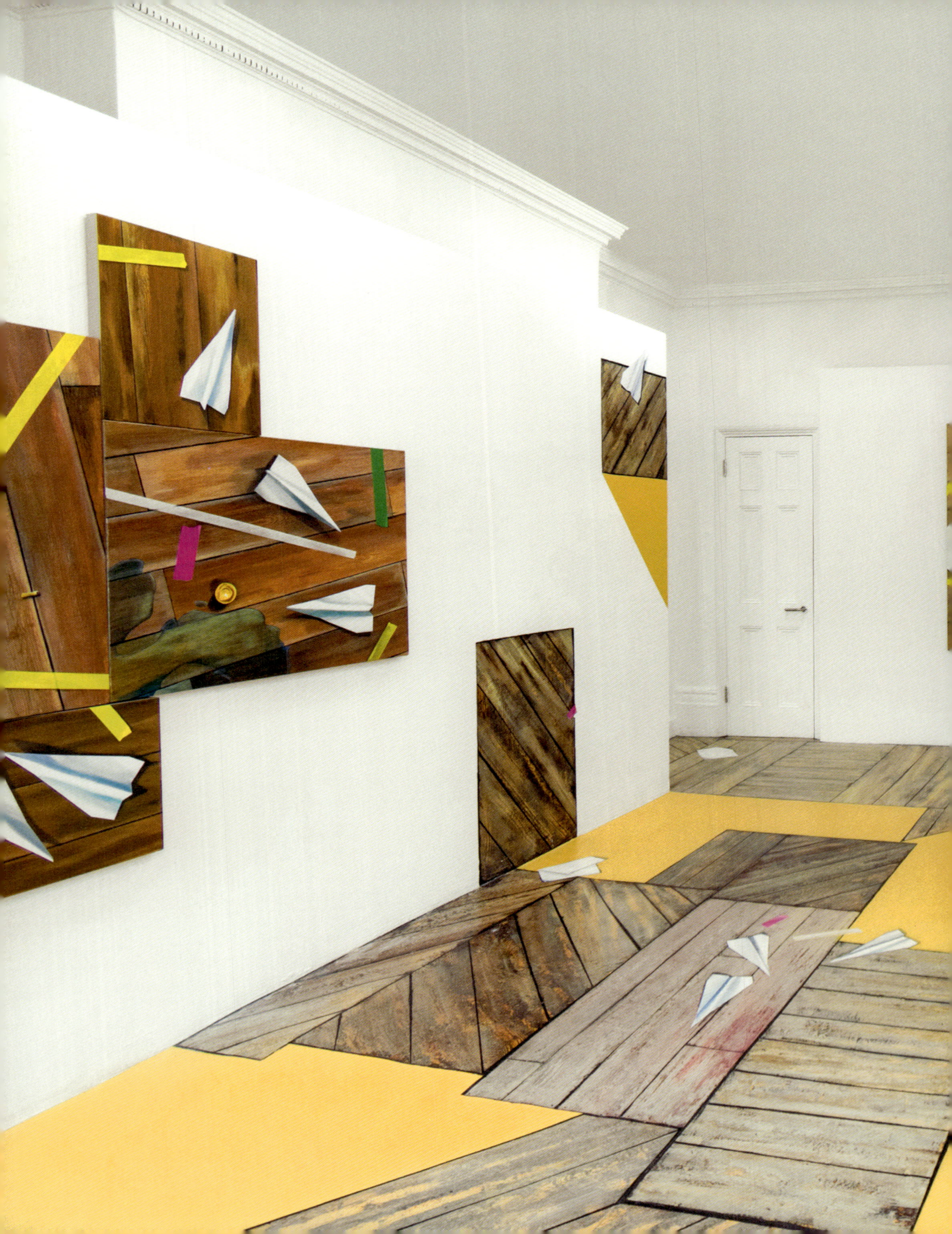

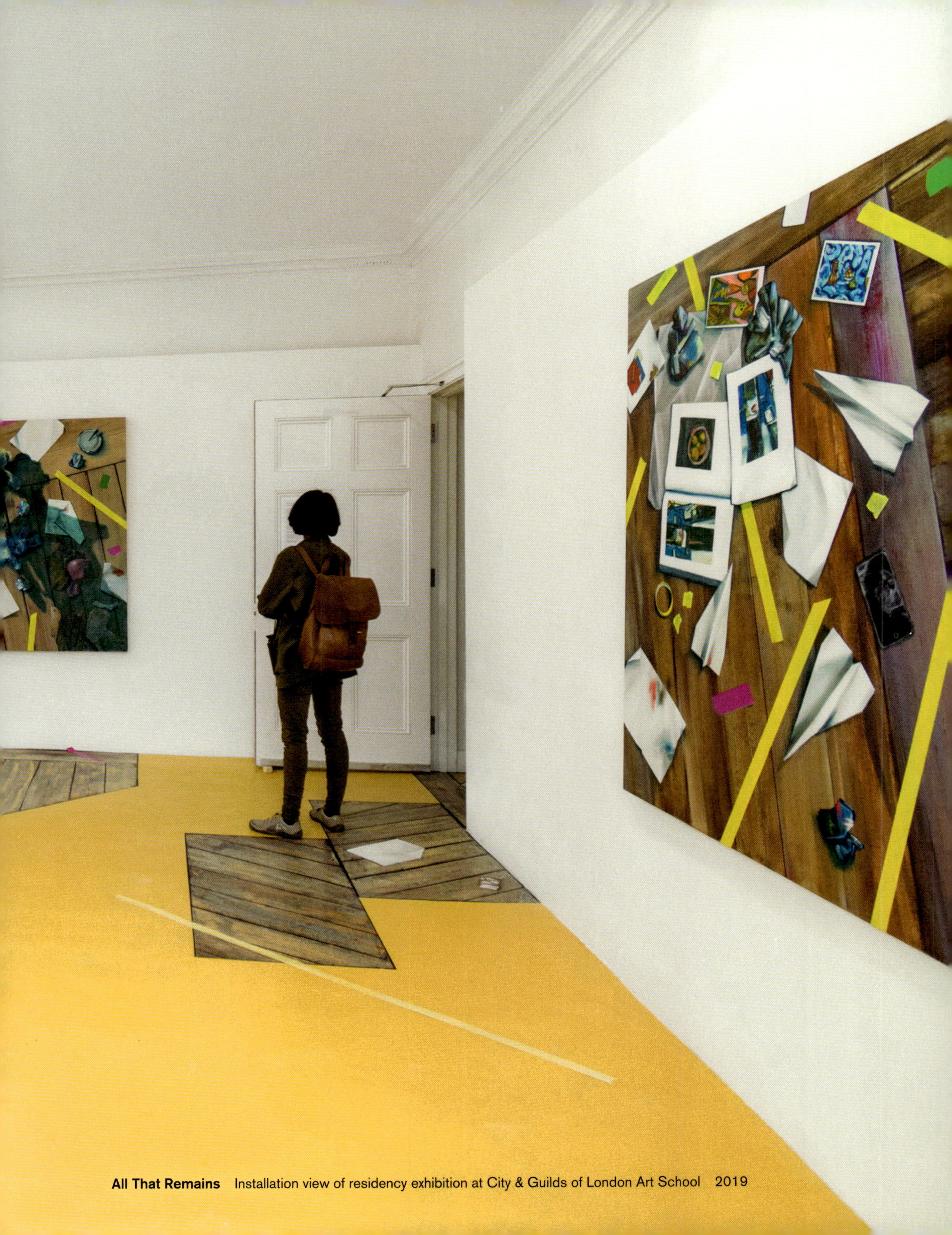

All That Remains Installation view of residency exhibition at City & Guilds of London Art School 2019

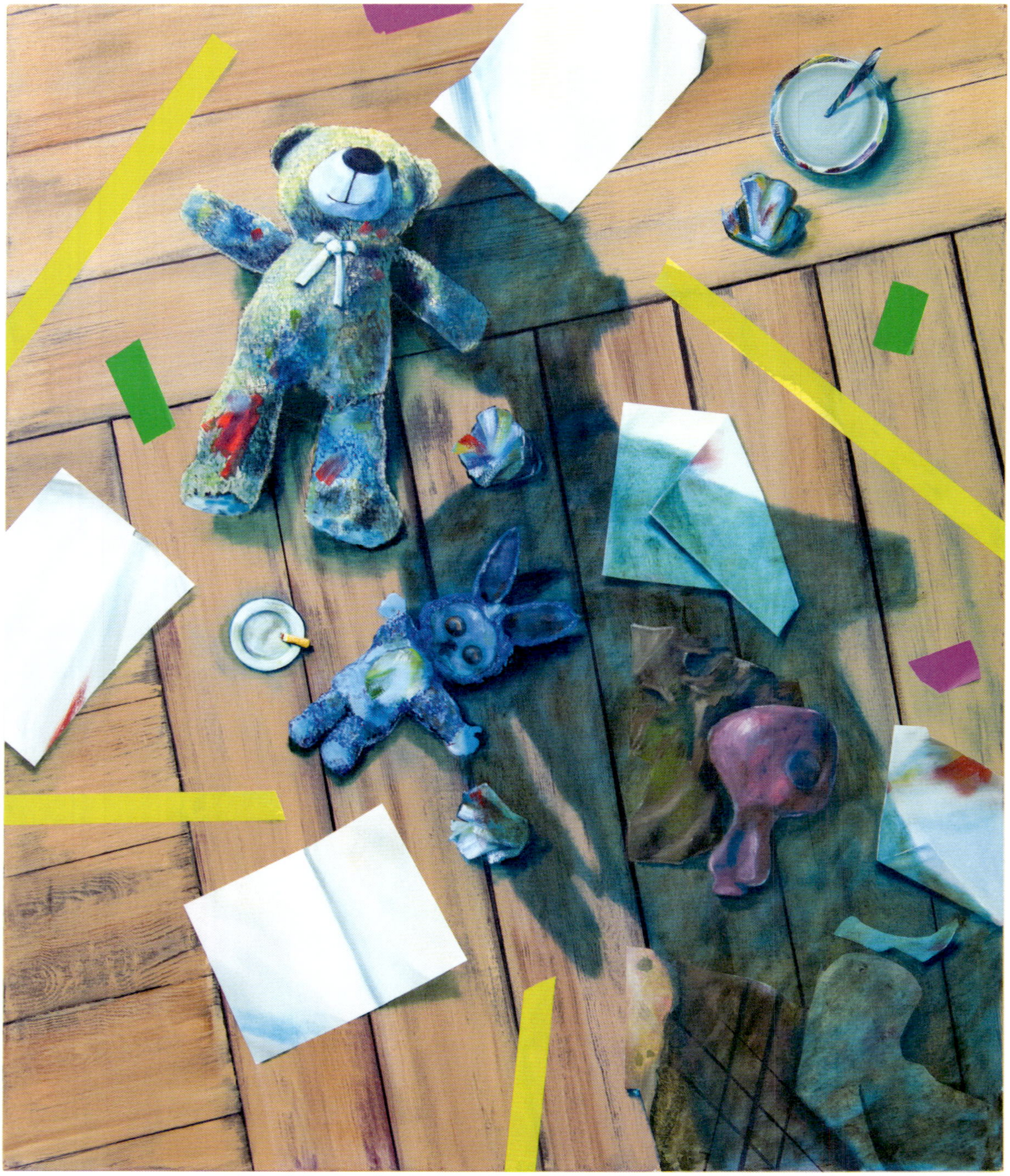

The Ones We Lost 2019 Oil and acrylic on canvas 120 × 98 cm

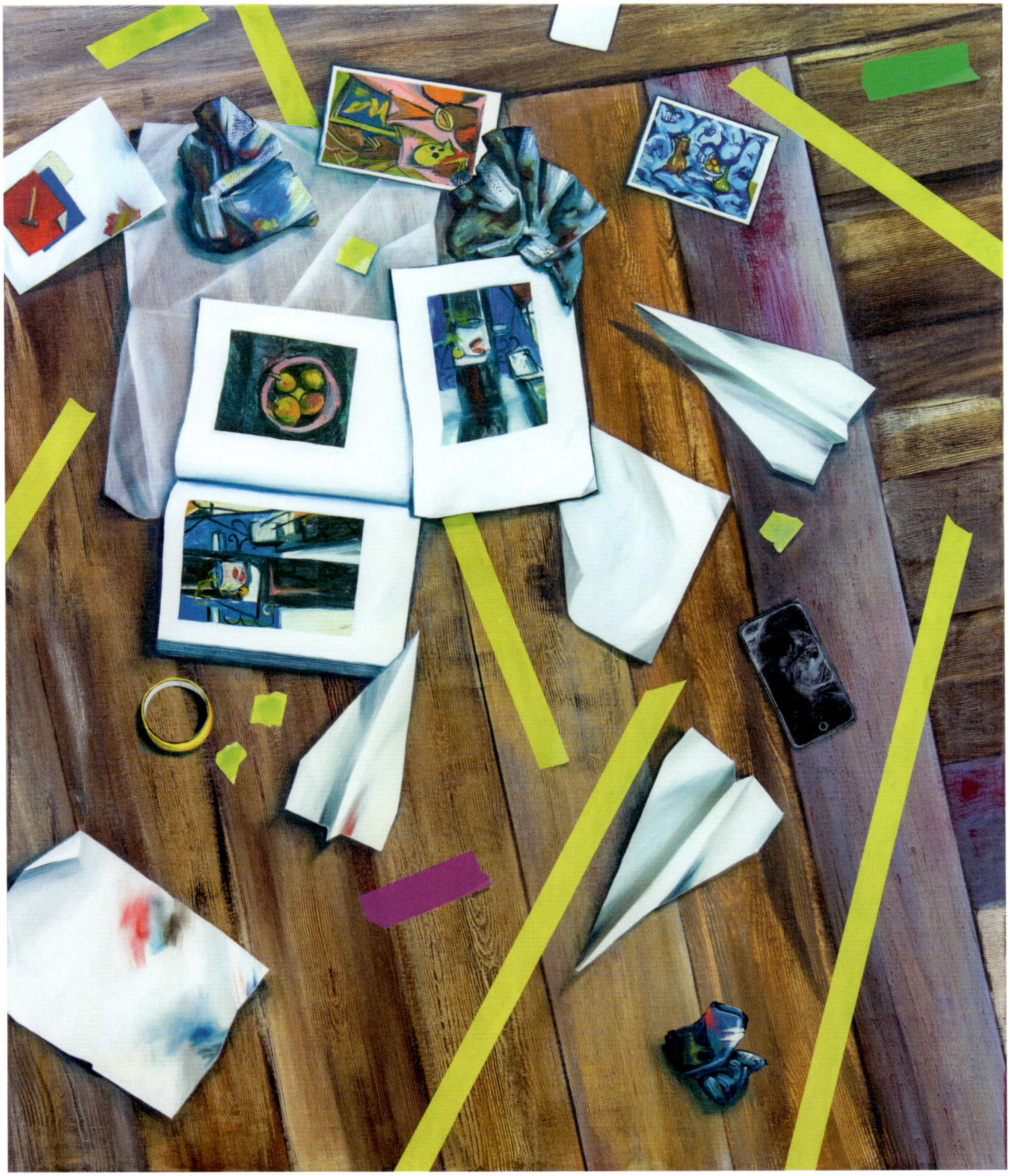

Remains of the Day 2019 Oil and acrylic on canvas 120 × 98 cm

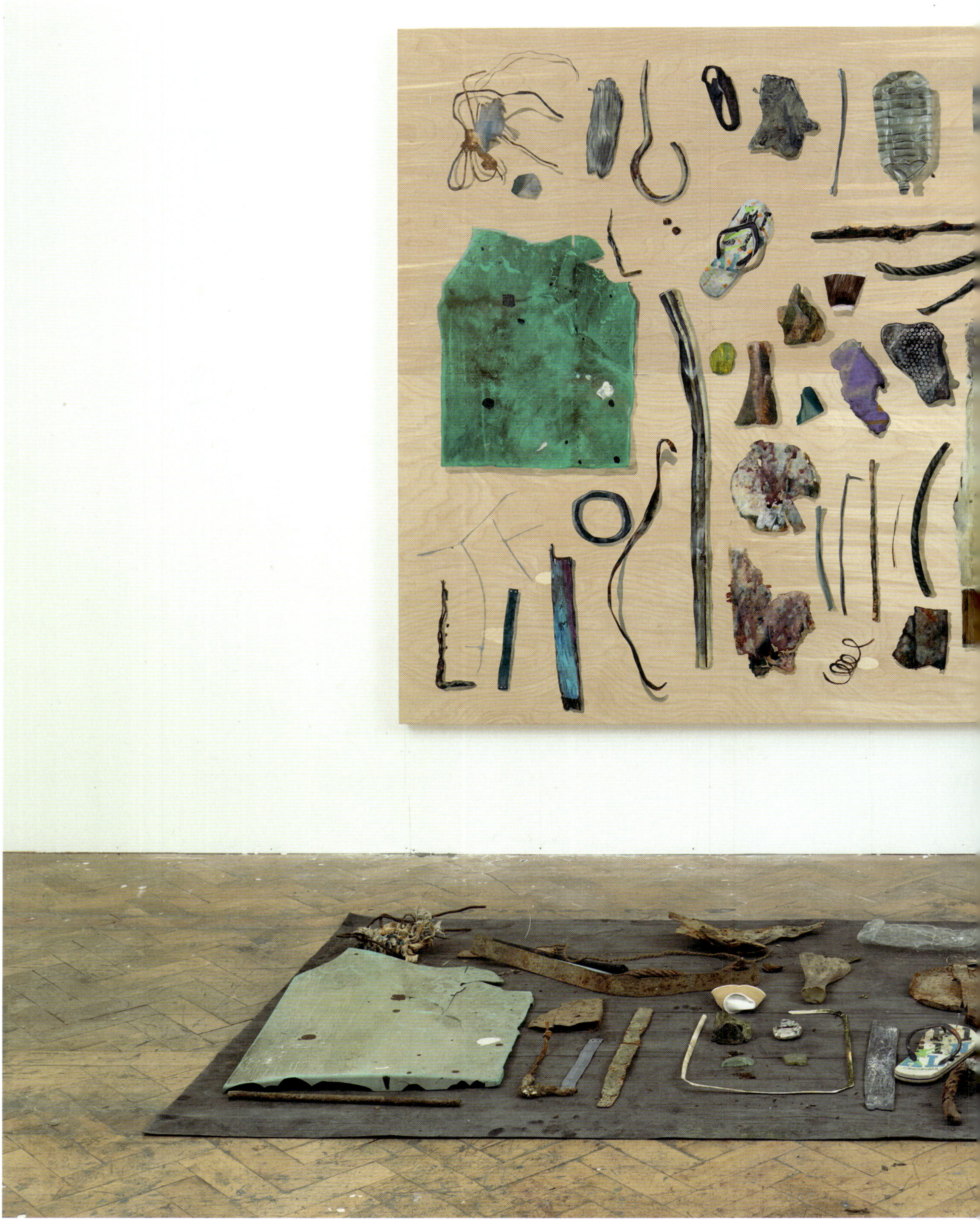

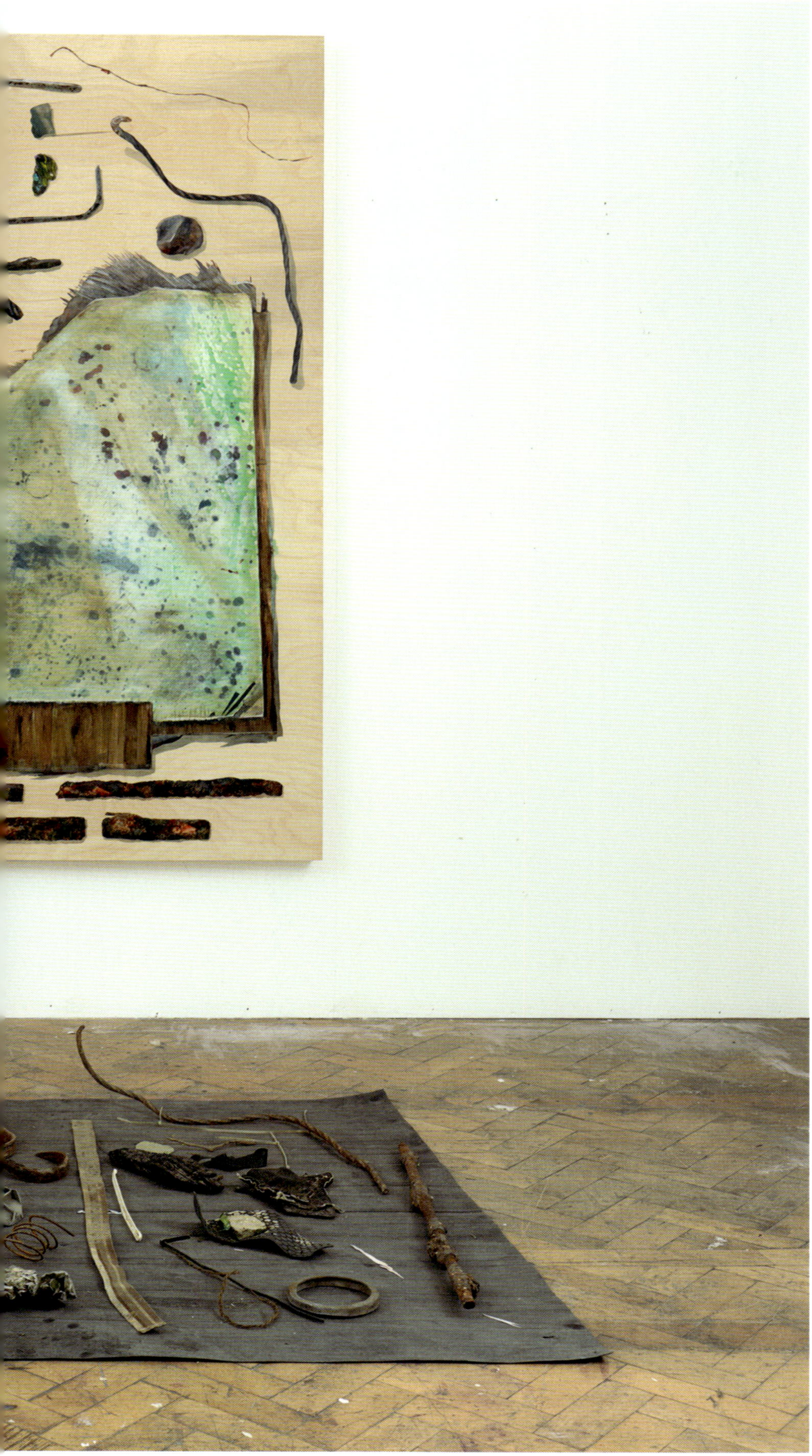

River Wasteland 2019
Oil and acrylic on wood with found objects
Painting: 180 × 240 cm
Objects: sizes variable

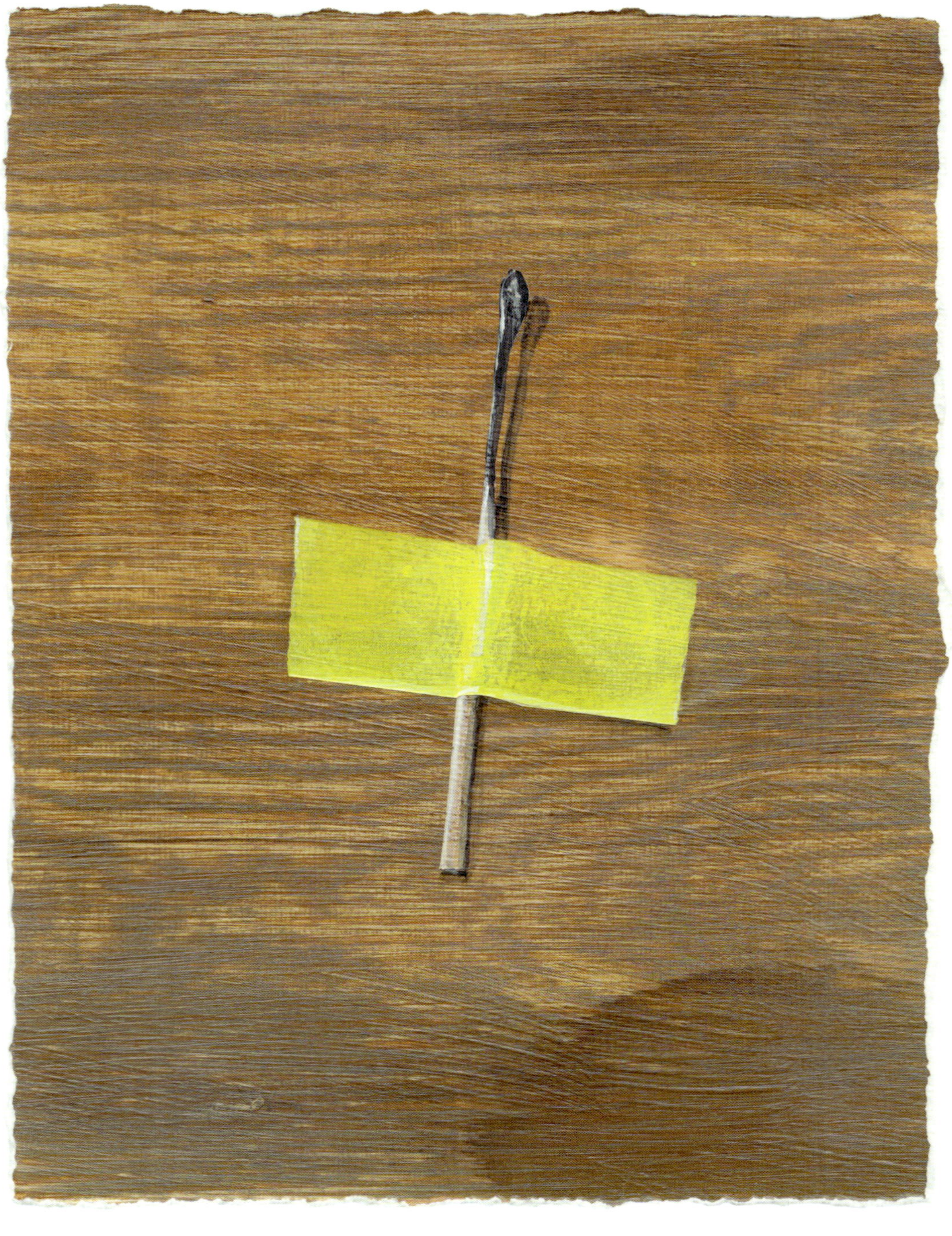

A Prayer for Connie 2020 Oil and acrylic on paper approx 20 × 14 cm

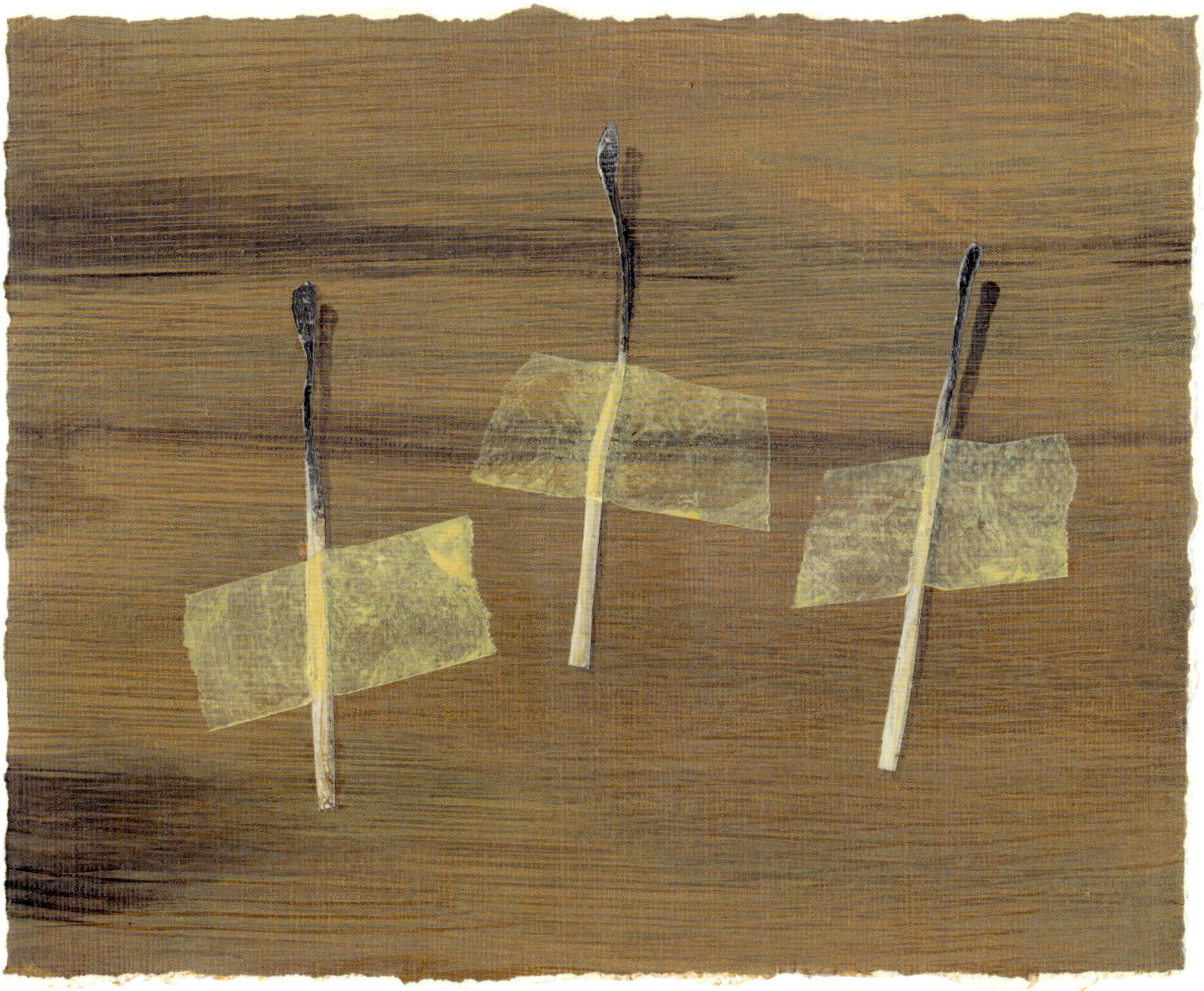

Prayer Matches, Day 114 2020 Oil and acrylic on paper approx 14 × 20 cm

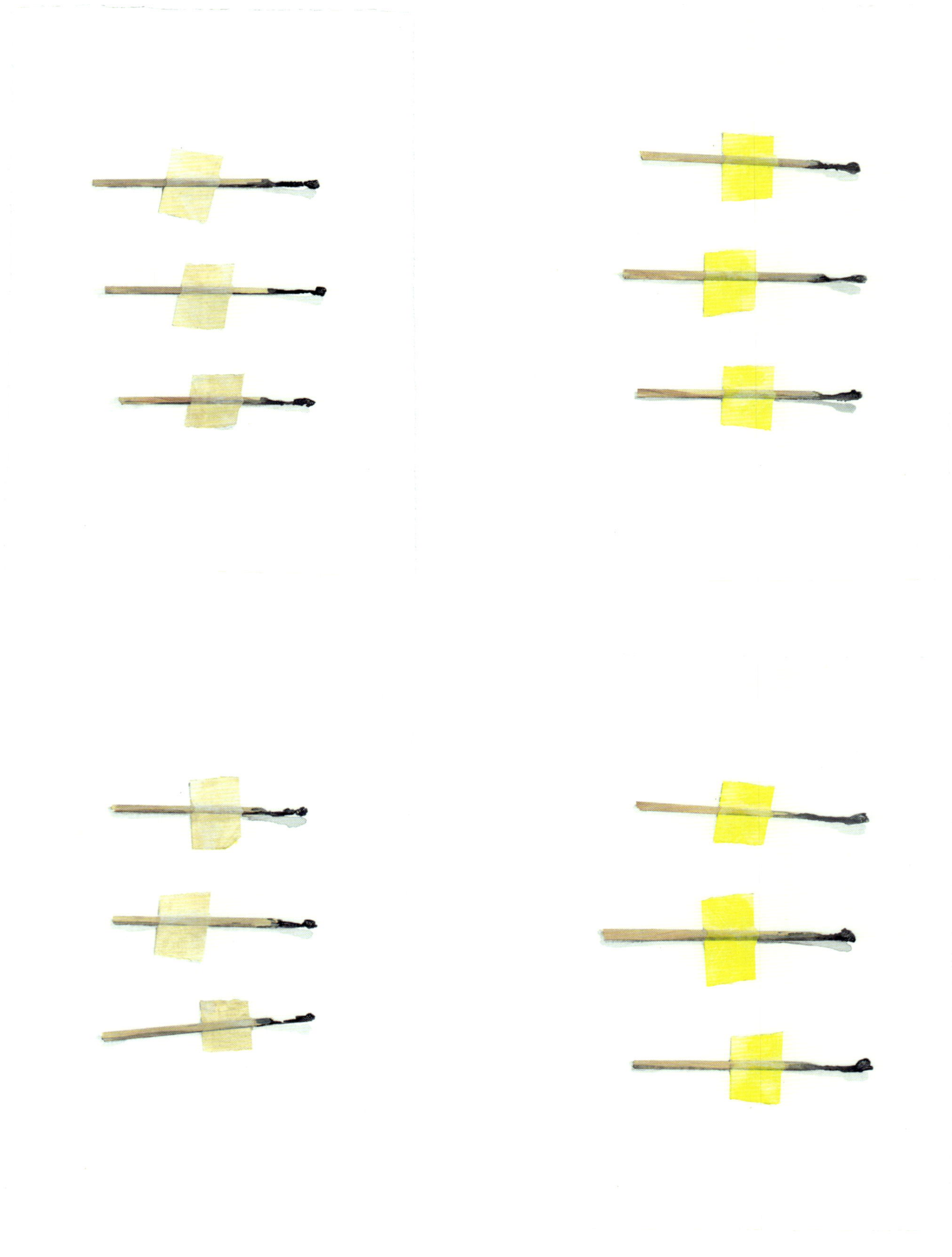

Selection of works from the **Prayer Match** series   2020   Oil and acrylic on paper   each approx 20 × 14 cm

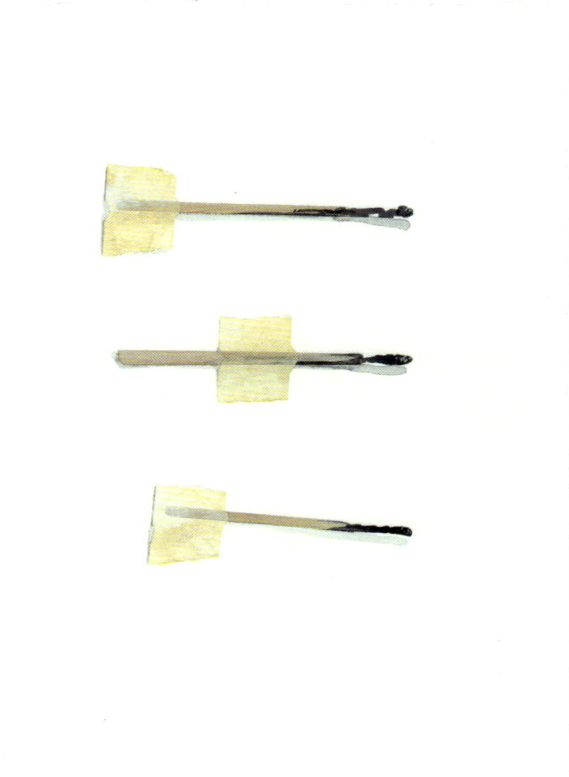
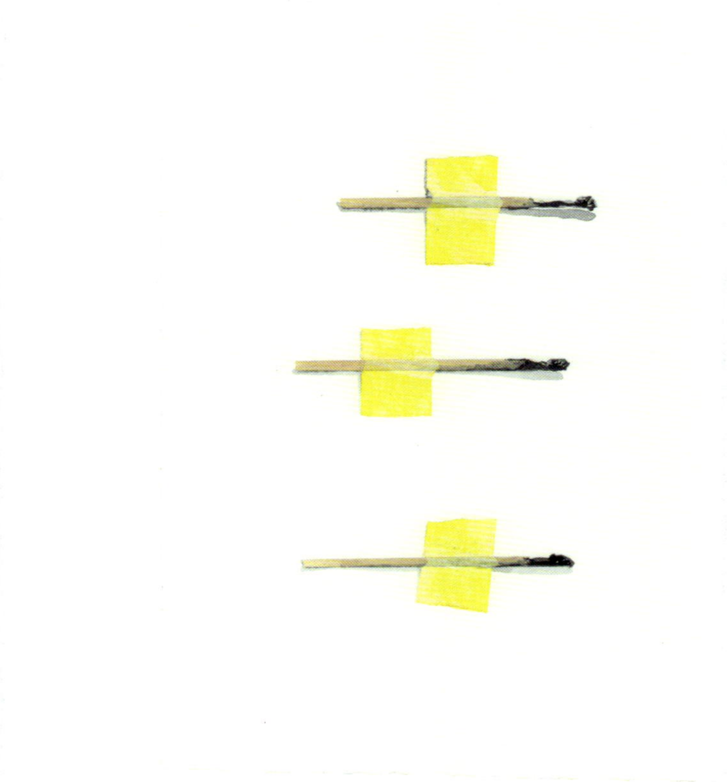

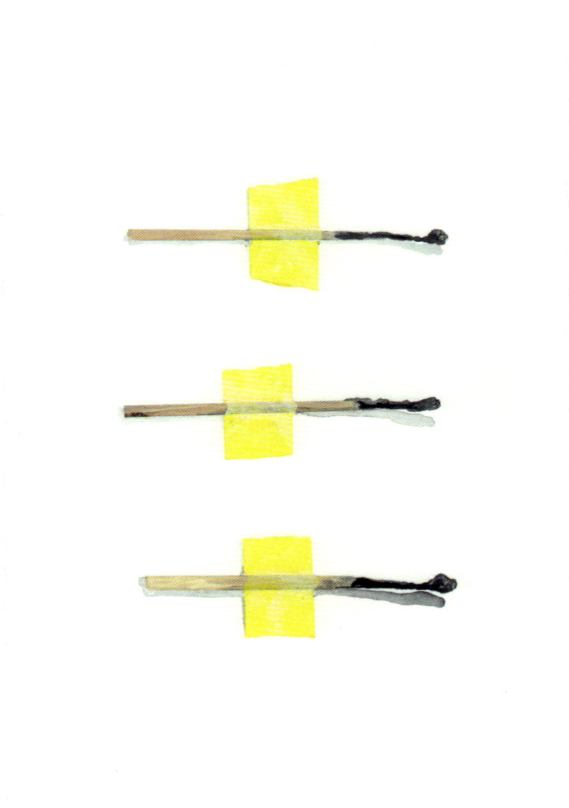
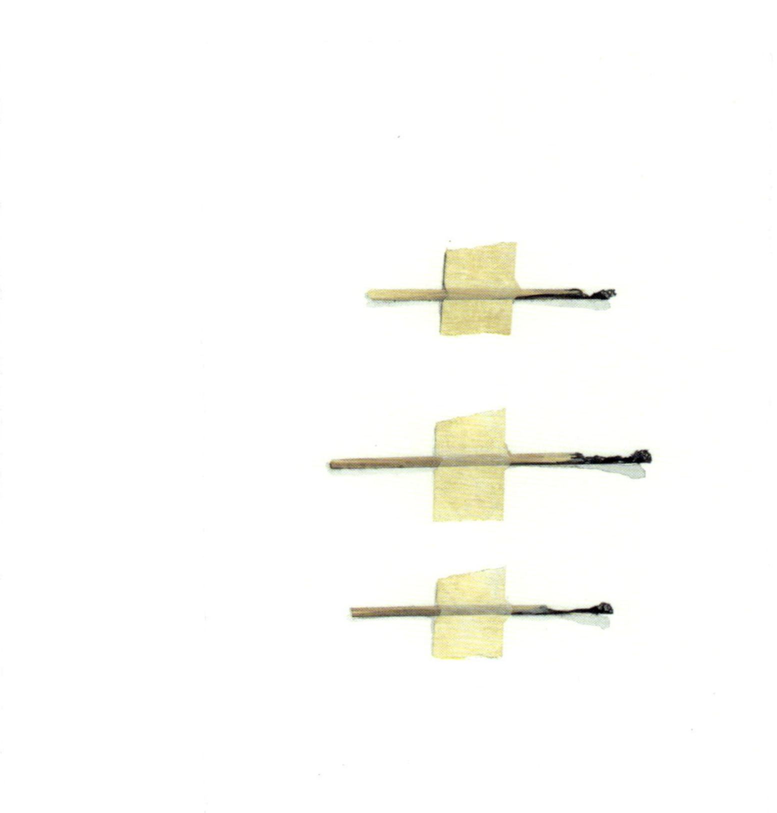

142

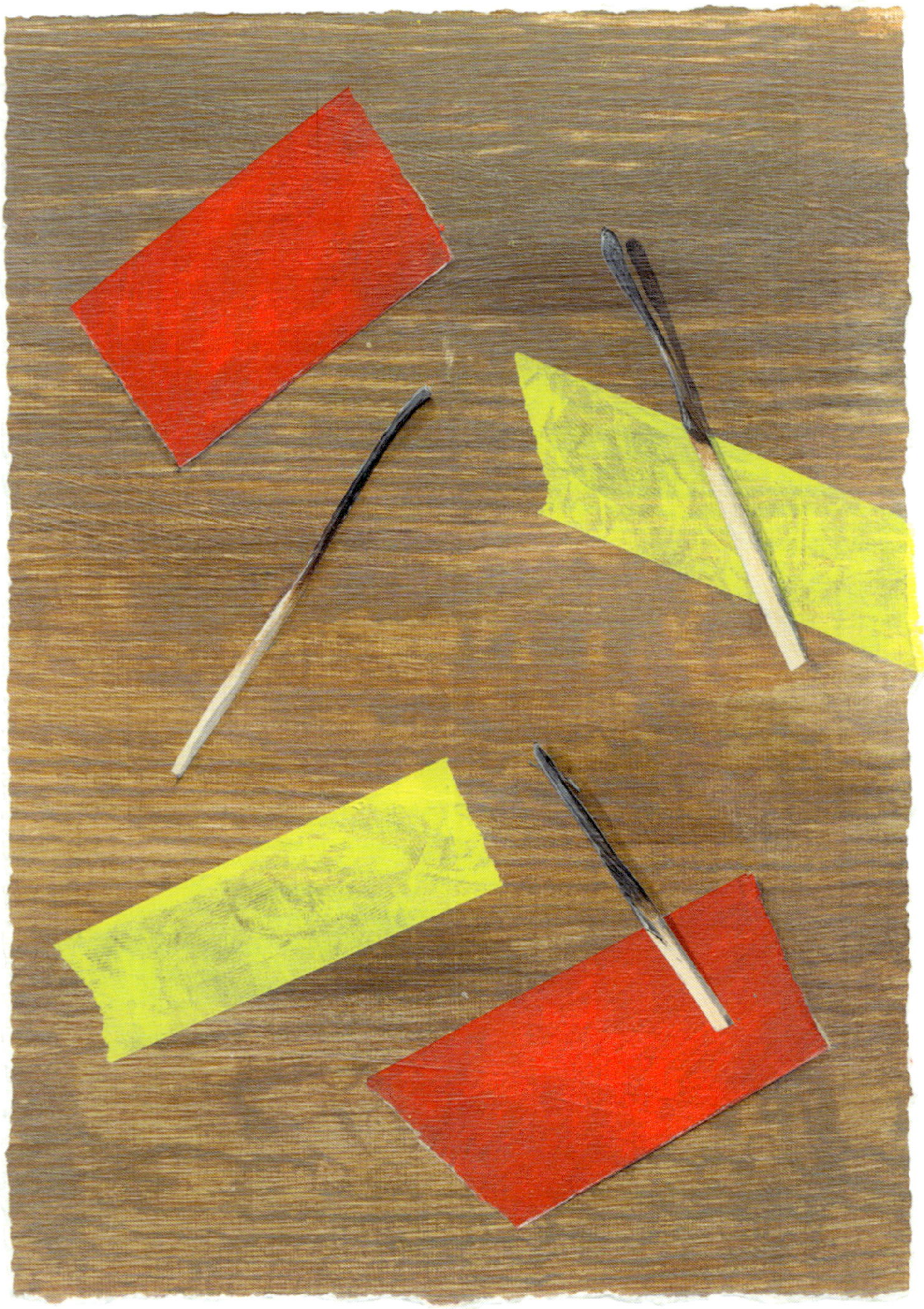

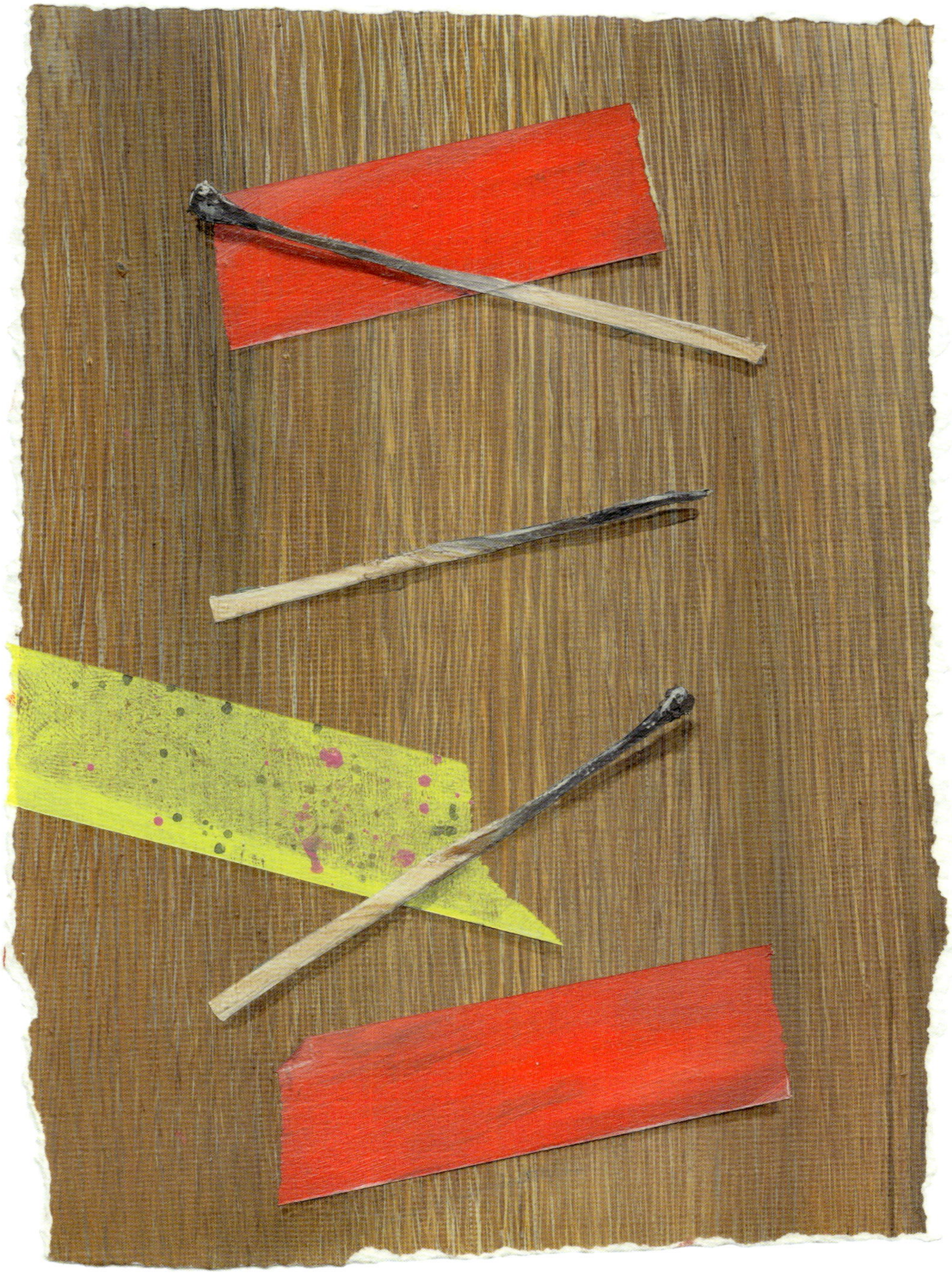

I have always enjoyed sketching outdoors. There's something about trying to capture a sense of place while working in the landscape itself. More recently, these outdoor escapades have found their way into the studio, and secret sketchbook drawings have found their way into paintings. When I work outside, I'm not trying to replicate the landscape, but to evoke a sense of place. To borrow from Cézanne, it's not about copying what I see, but realising my sensibilities towards it.

Writing in 1938, the painter Paul Nash spoke of the 'unseen landscapes' of England,[1] unseen simply because they were overlooked rather than hidden; landscapes that exist somewhere on the periphery of our collective vision. He wrote about the edge-lands or interzones between town and country, hedgerows, industrial estates, metal scrapyards and city bypasses. The kind of places businesses go to die or be reborn. Where artists find cheap rent and set up studios.

I have always found such places fascinating, and teach at an art school located in one. Leith School of Art was established thirty-eight years ago in the heart of the Edinburgh docklands. Housed in a converted Norwegian church, this remarkable little community of artists is dwarfed by the architectural flotsam of a derelict industry; rusting cranes, empty wharfs, mountainous metal scrapyards, and all the detritus of a once-thriving shipping industry. Like many post-industrial landscapes, Leith has undergone a process of regeneration, and the art school has stood vigil as wharfs have turned into apartments for city workers and greasy-spoon cafés have made way for wine bars and artisan coffee shops.

Incidental Landscapes

Last year, my family and I were invited to stay at a friend's home, perched in isolation on the rolling peat bogs of Caithness, another kind of edgeland, but more rugged and wild. Somewhere between sky and ground, land and sea, bog and ocean, a border between above and below, heaven and Earth, or an *axis mundi*. Many of my new paintings were born from the peat of that bog. When I returned to the studio, my subsequent works became a re-telling or evocation of those moments in the landscape. They become a collage of elements, a still life from the landscape, at times involving objects collected from the Flows,[2] pigments from moss and earth, integrated into the painting itself. In this way, the material of the landscape became part of the painting. I made paintings of paintings and drawings of sketches I had made in the landscape. The nature of quodlibet allows for such fragmentation of meaning, the process itself a kind of ancillary incident.

Growing up in rural Scotland, I enjoyed a different sort of peripheral vision. For me, the mountains were both seen and unseen. Those heather-clad hills and quiet brooks of Deeside were both a familiar backdrop to the mundanity of daily life and a window of possibility, promising great adventure and untamed wilderness. We ate breakfast with a view of the mountains. My walk to school was often flanked by granite and snow. The wilderness was ever present in the domestic routines of life. The land, people, agriculture and creative culture so intertwined they became ingrained in my imagination, and I find myself returning to these wild places of Scotland as a source for painting. If my work involves everyday moments of wonder, here is a landscape so inveterate to Scottish culture it is both domestic and sublime. This shift in focus presents a new way of working for me. I am grateful to Aleph Contemporary and Cynthia Corbett Gallery, who have exhibited some of these fledgling works.

Back in the studio, I look over sketches and studies made in the landscape. They flitter on my worktop and nestle down among the paint pots, paper scraps, matches, moss and collaged cuttings. The intention remains the same: to look at the overlooked, see moments of wonder, and learn again how to see. The candle flickers and the papers flit.

1 Paul Nash, 'Unseen Landscapes', *Country Life*, 21 May 1938, 526–27.

2 The Flow Country is the common name for the vast peat bogs of Caithness and Sutherland – mainland Scotland's most northern counties.

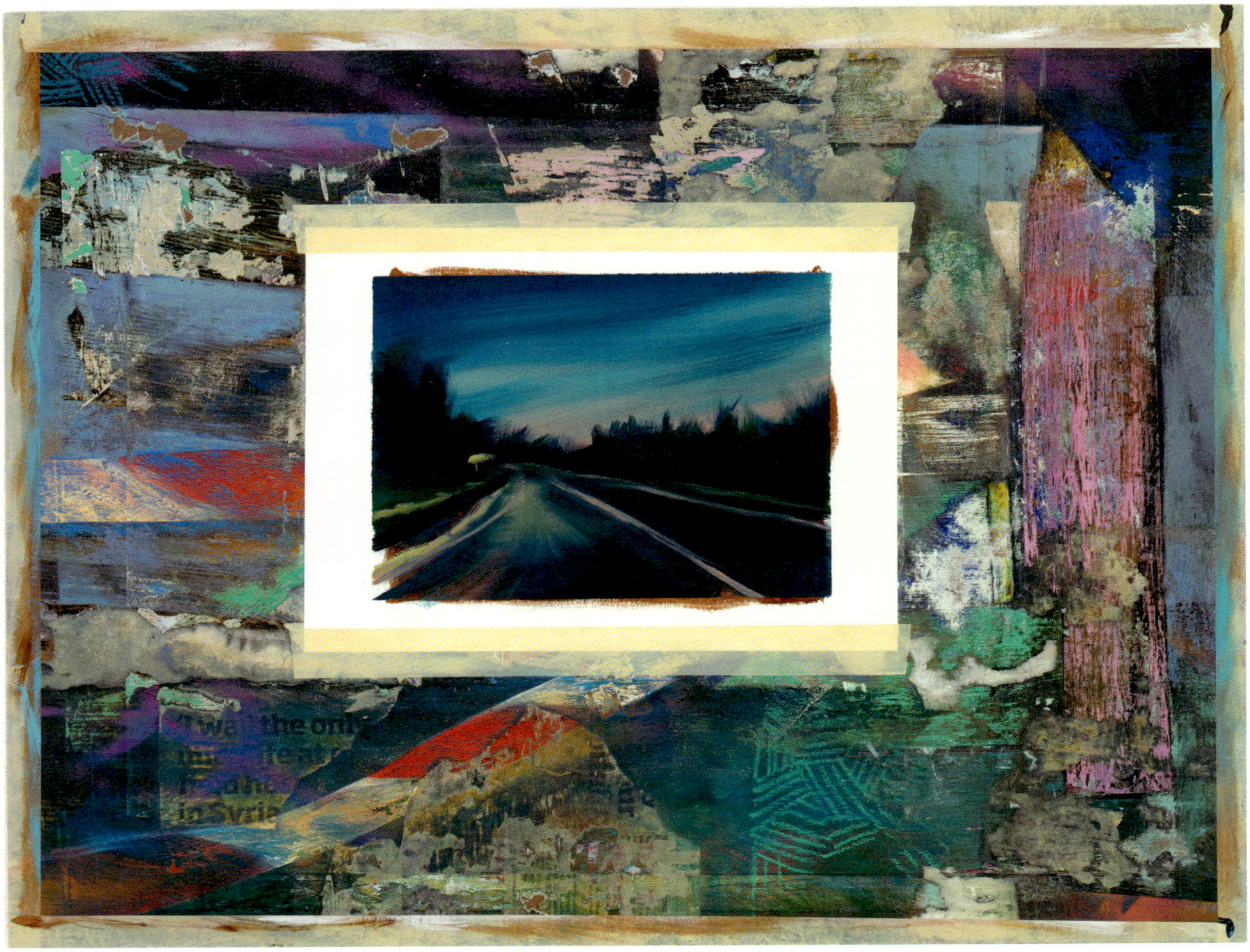

Through a Glass Darkly 2021 Oil, acrylic and mixed media on wood 68 × 90 cm

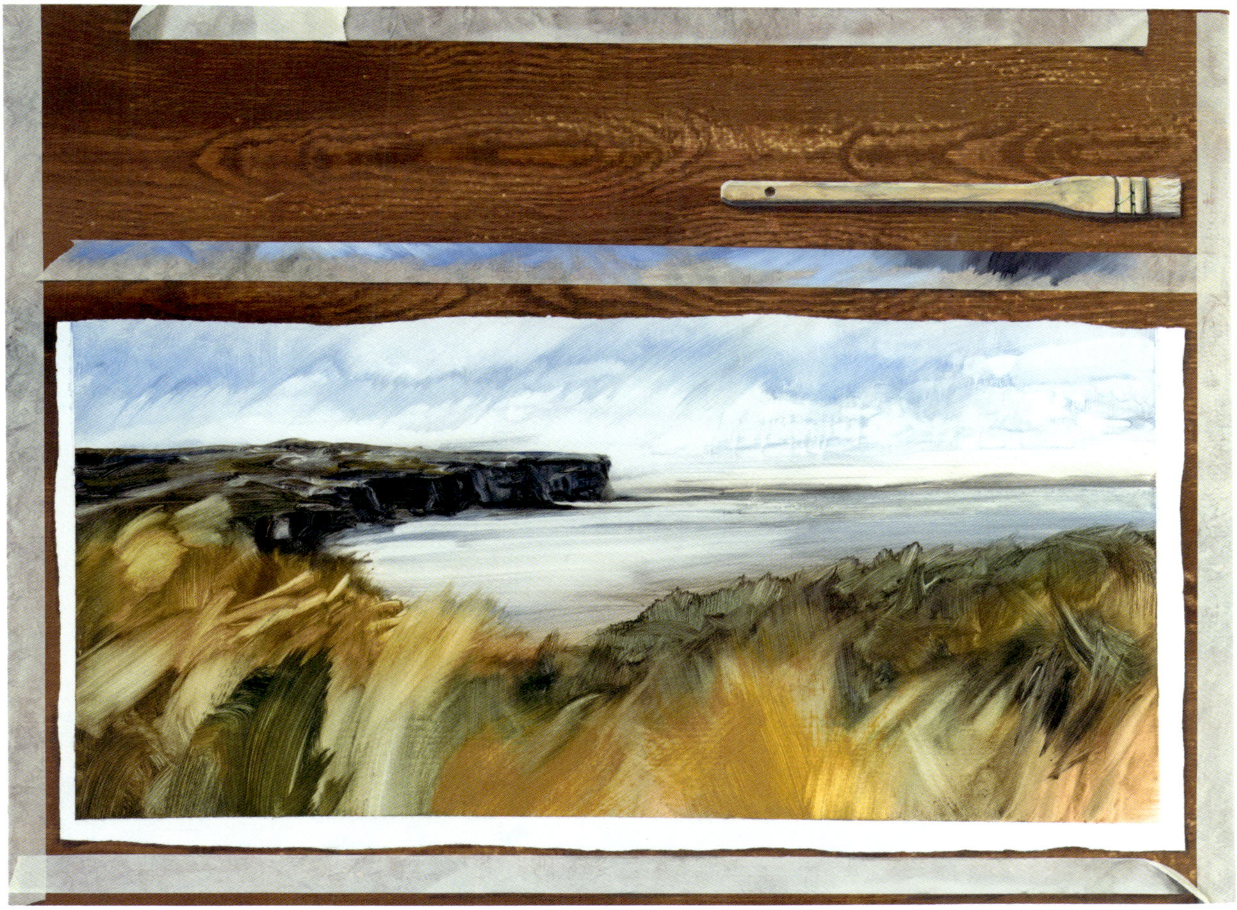

What Comes With the Wind Will Go With the Rain 2022 Oil and acrylic on canvas 56 × 76 cm

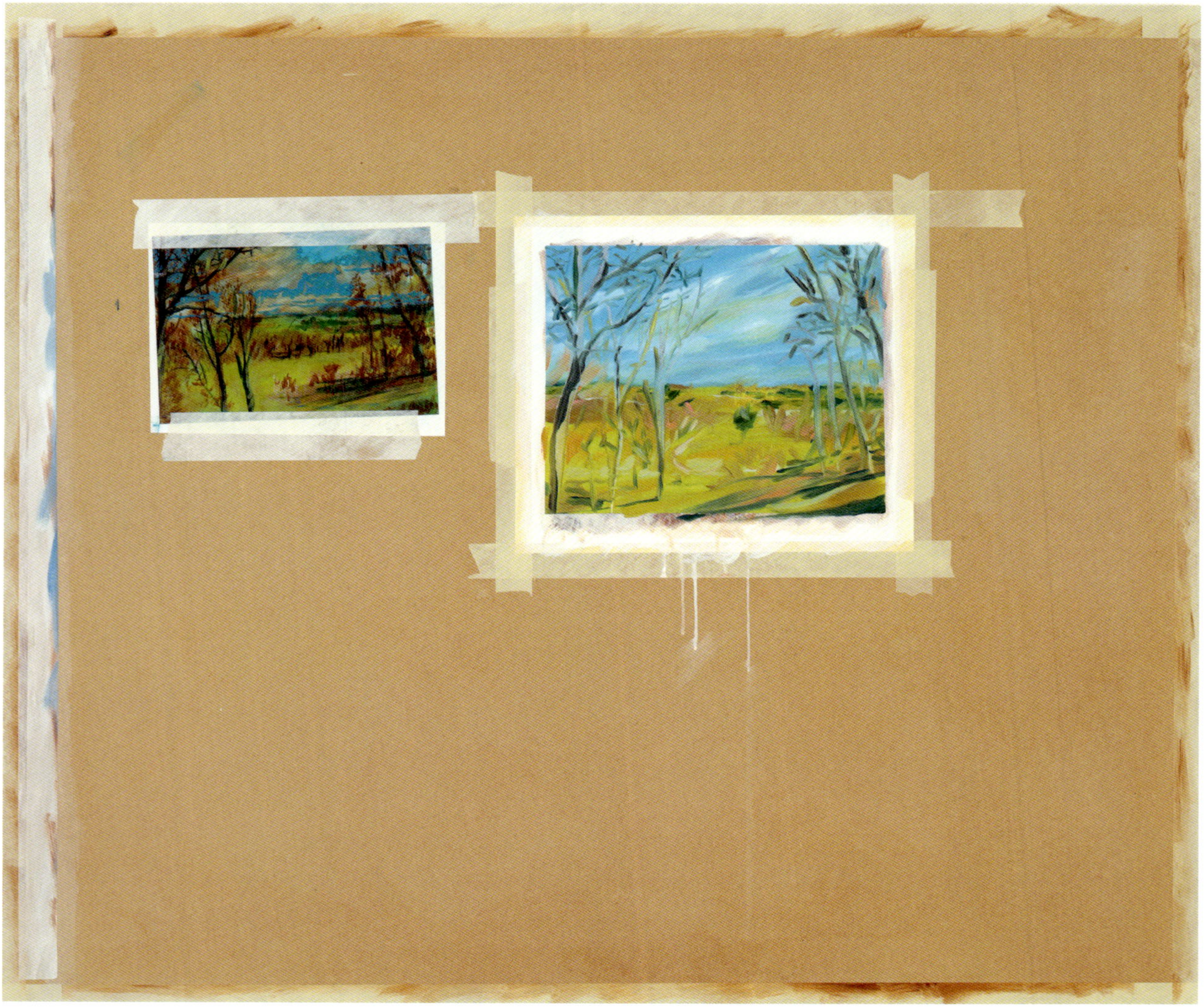

Duet 2022 Oil and acrylic on MDF 100 × 120 cm

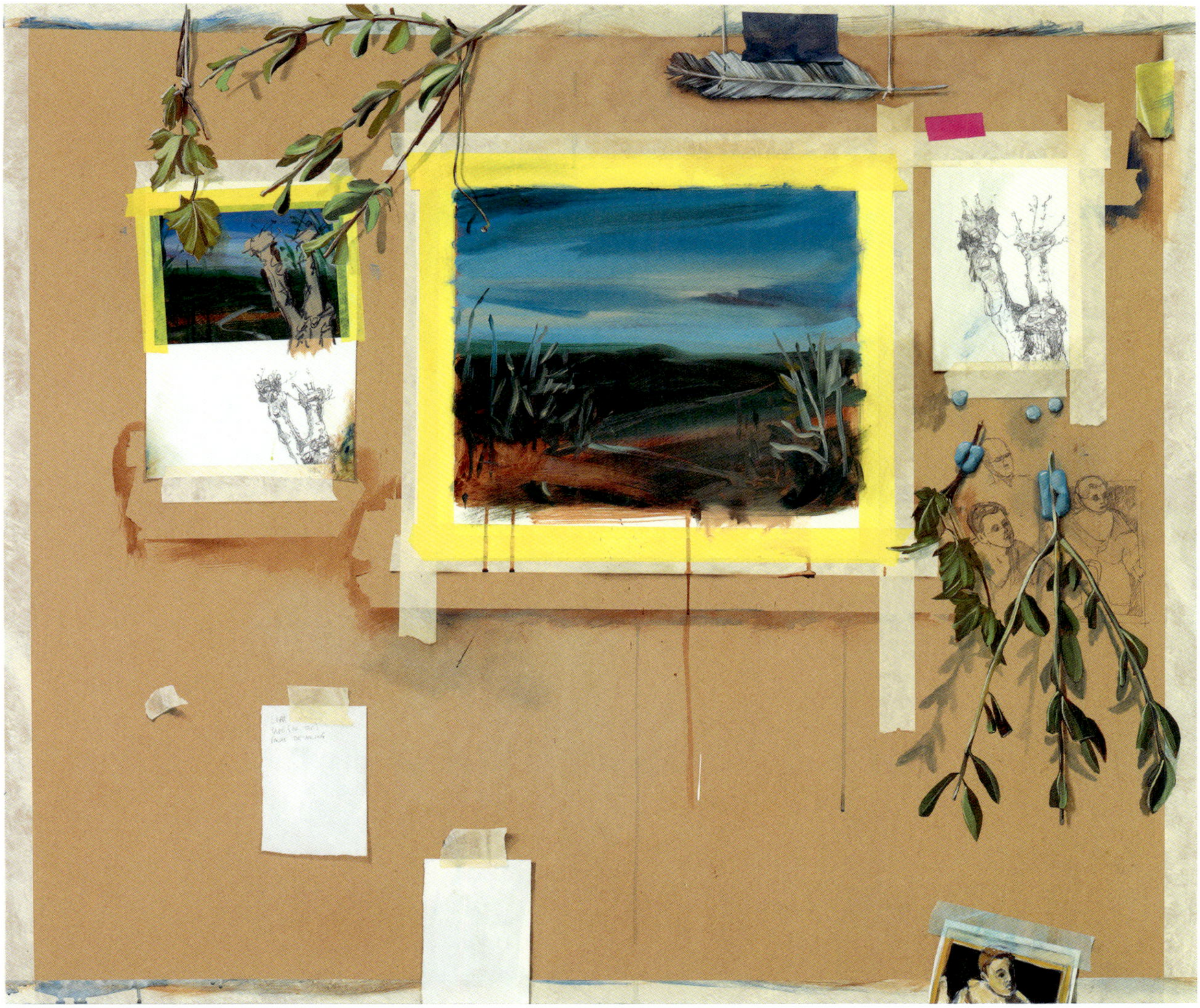

Improvisation 2021 Oil and acrylic on MDF 100 × 120 cm

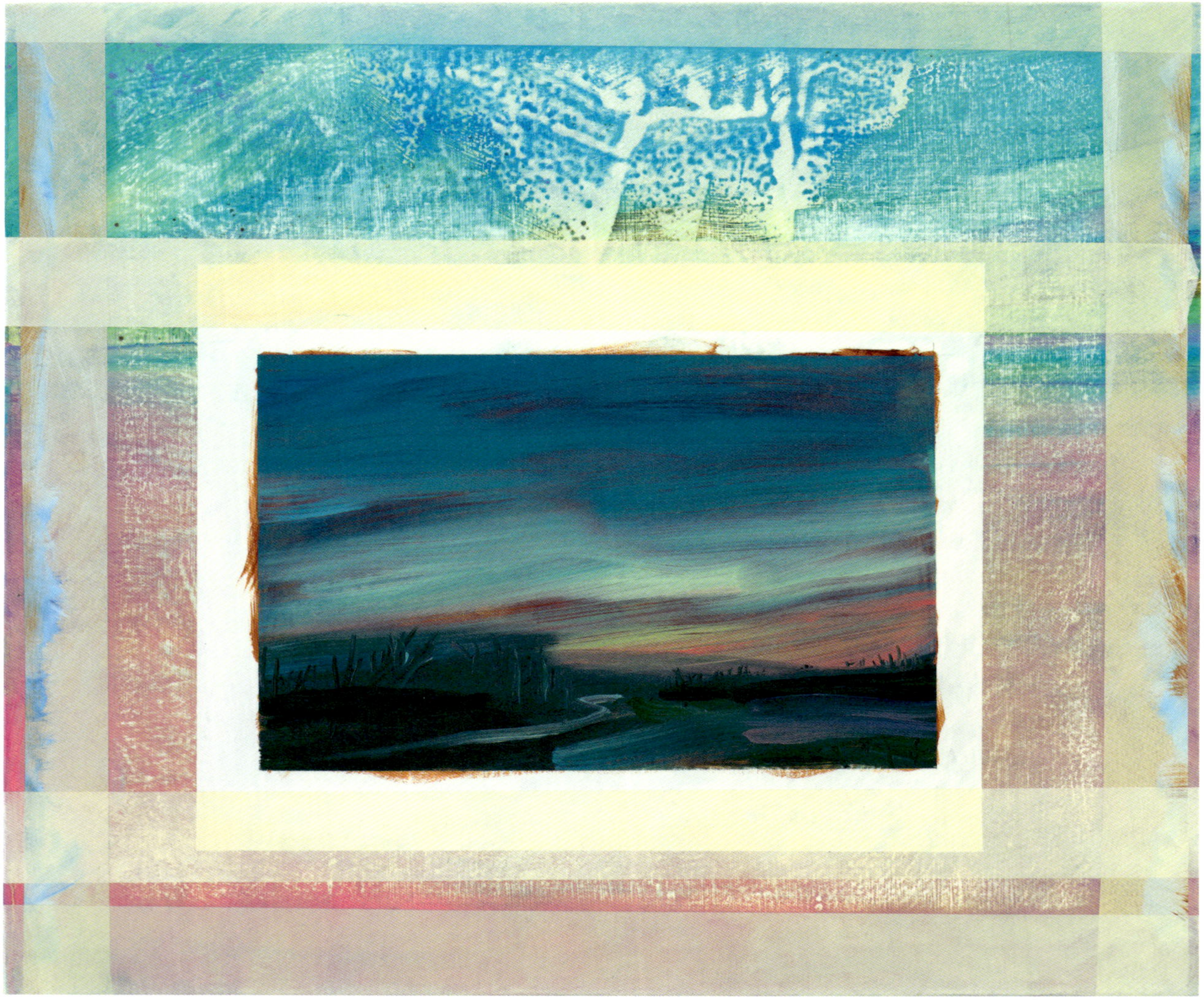

Pink Dawn Rising 2021 Oil, acrylic and gesso on canvas 54 × 65 cm

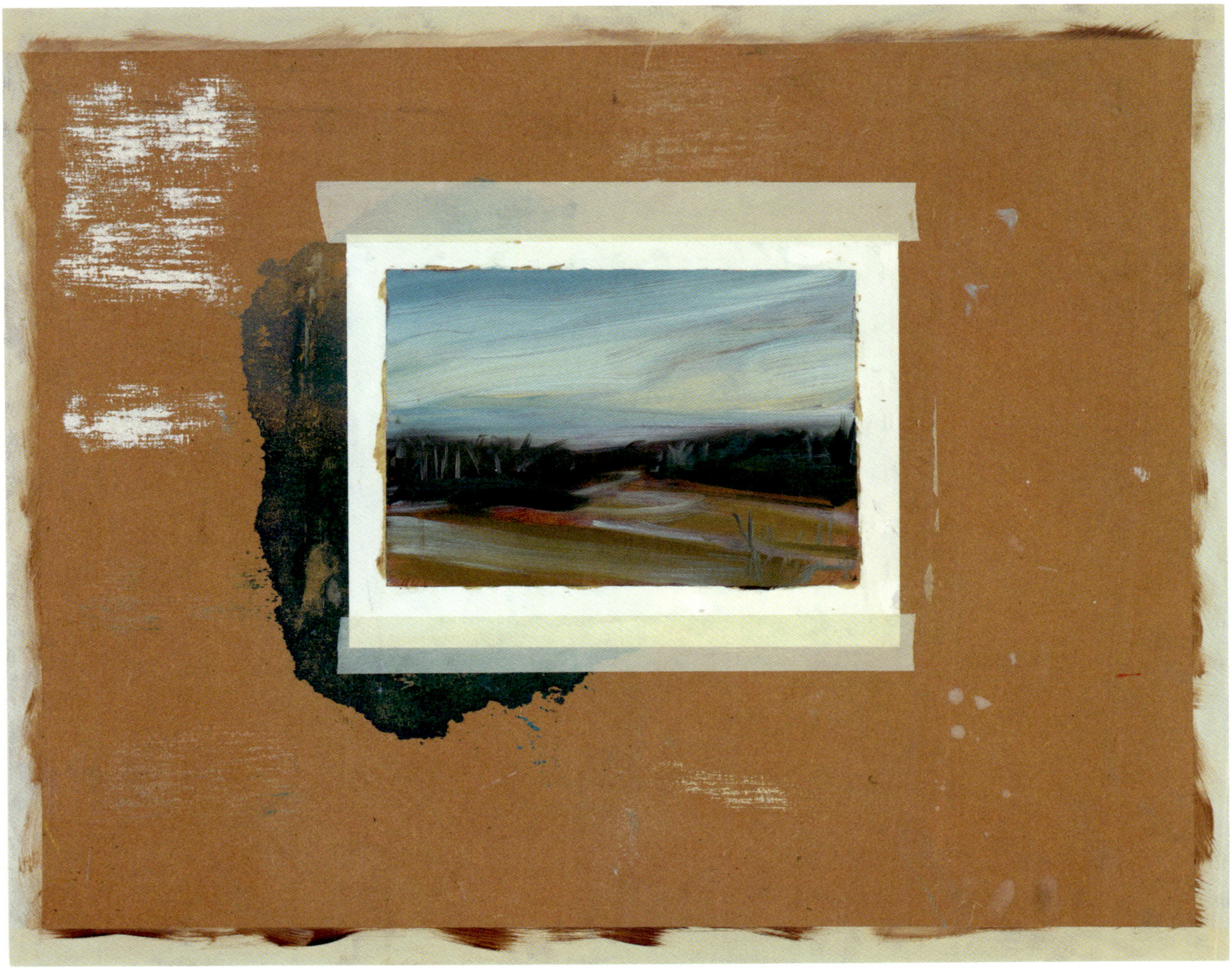

A New Beginning 2021 Oil and acrylic on MDF 59 × 76 cm

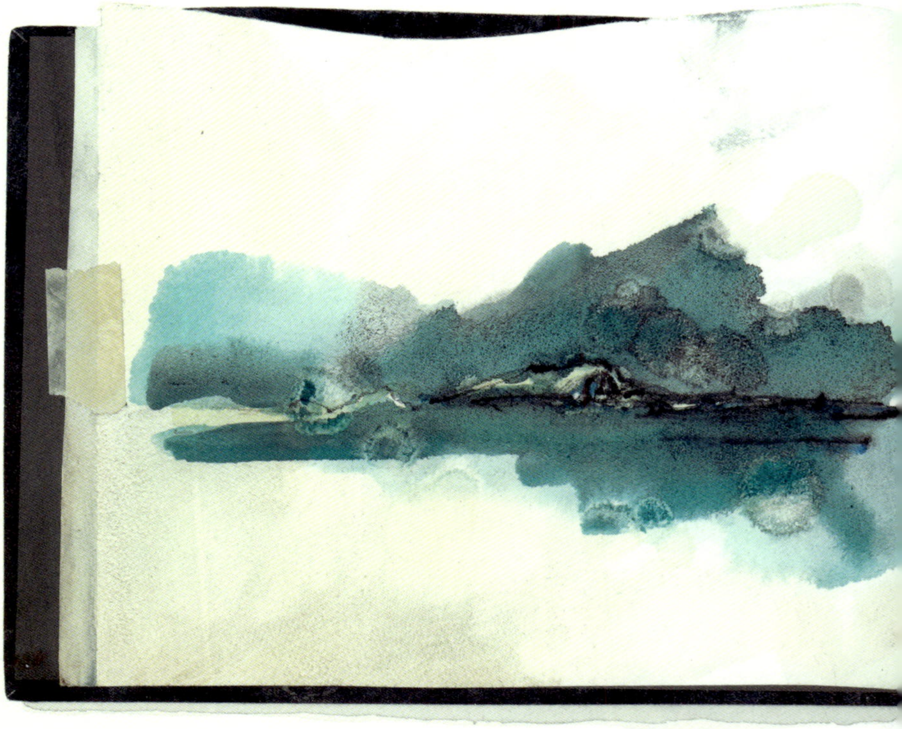

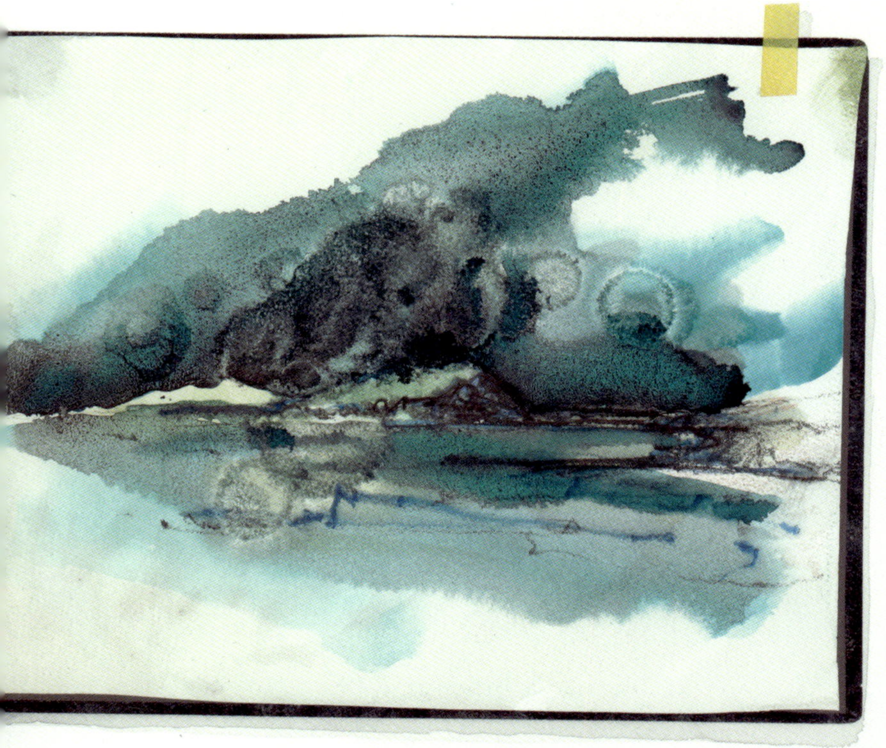

The Invisible in Terms of the Visible 2022
Oil and acrylic on paper
58 × 77 cm

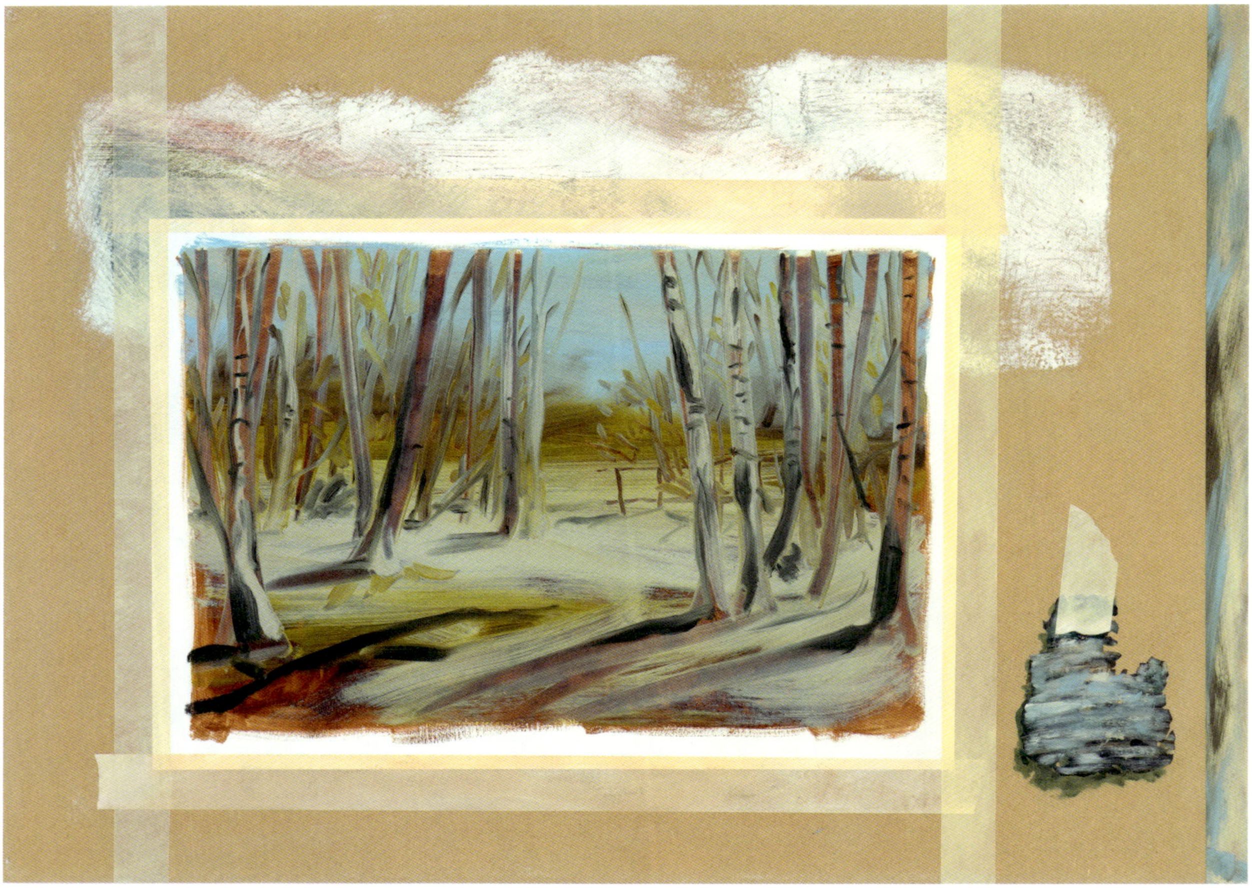

Harmony 2021 Oil and acrylic on MDF 59.5 × 83.5 cm

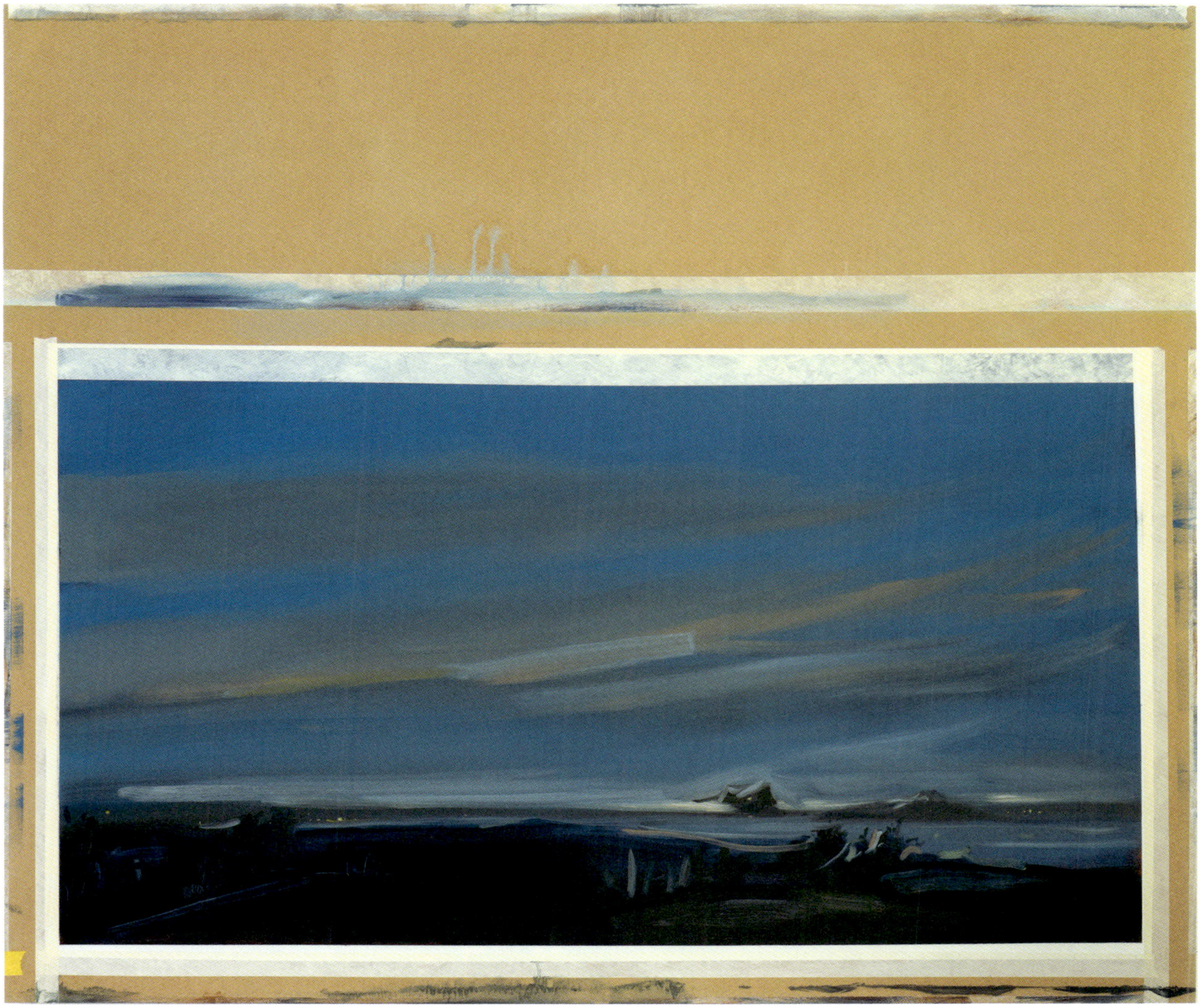

Nocturne 2022 Oil and acrylic on MDF 100 × 120 cm

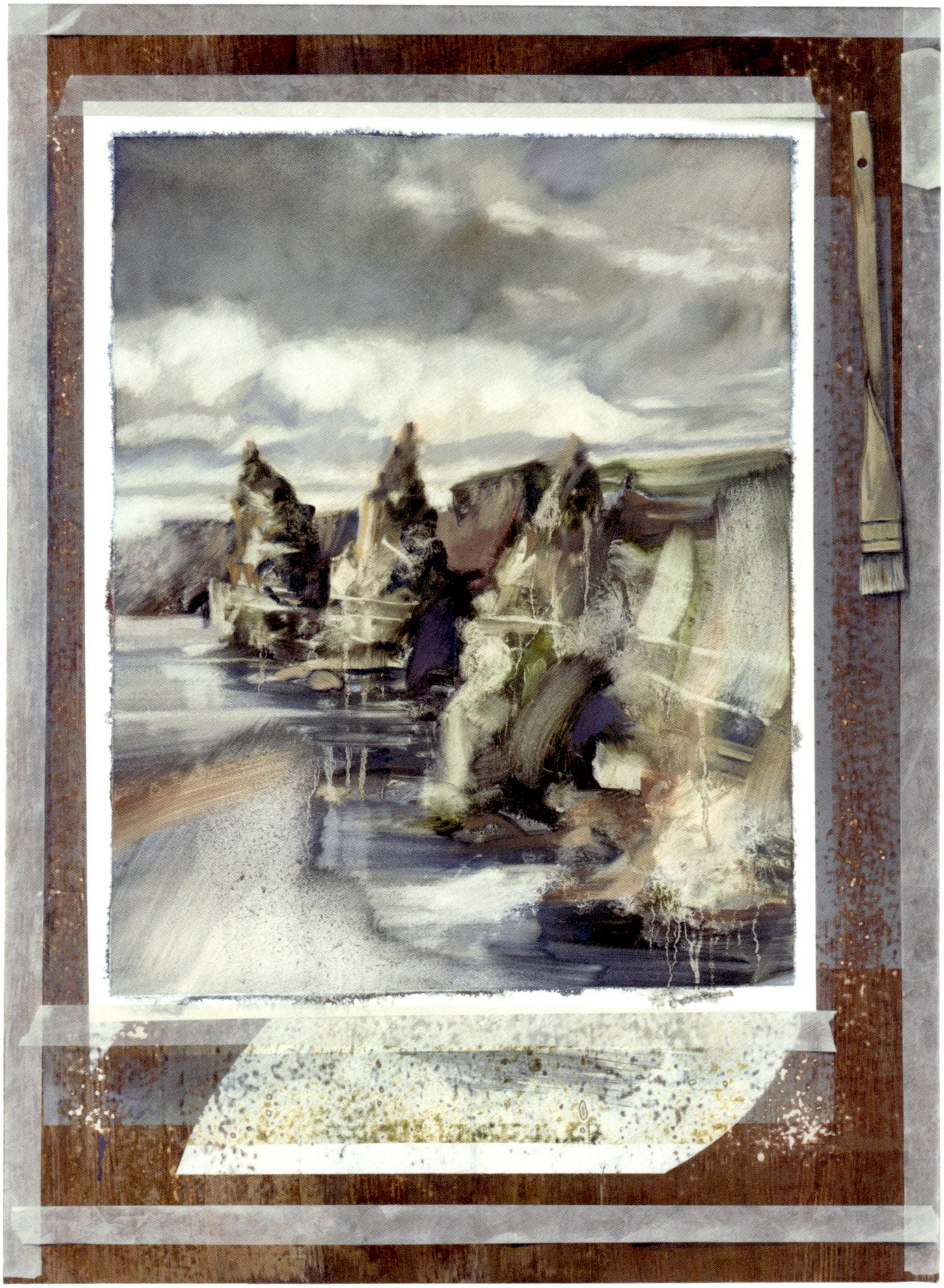

A Sacred Theory of Stupendous Forces 2022 Oil and acrylic on canvas 76 × 56 cm

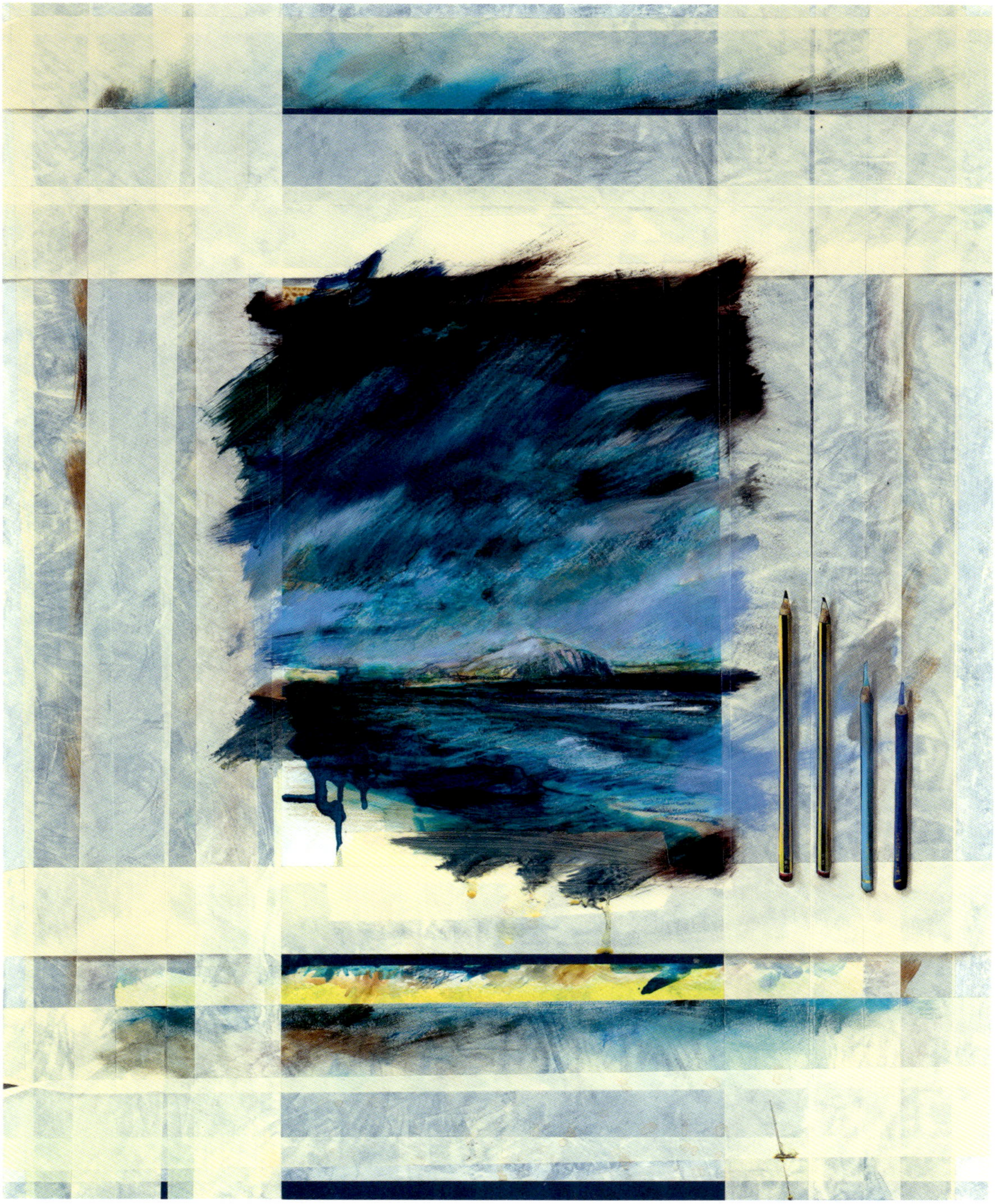

Craigleith After the Storm 2022 Oil and acrylic on wood 50 × 40 cm

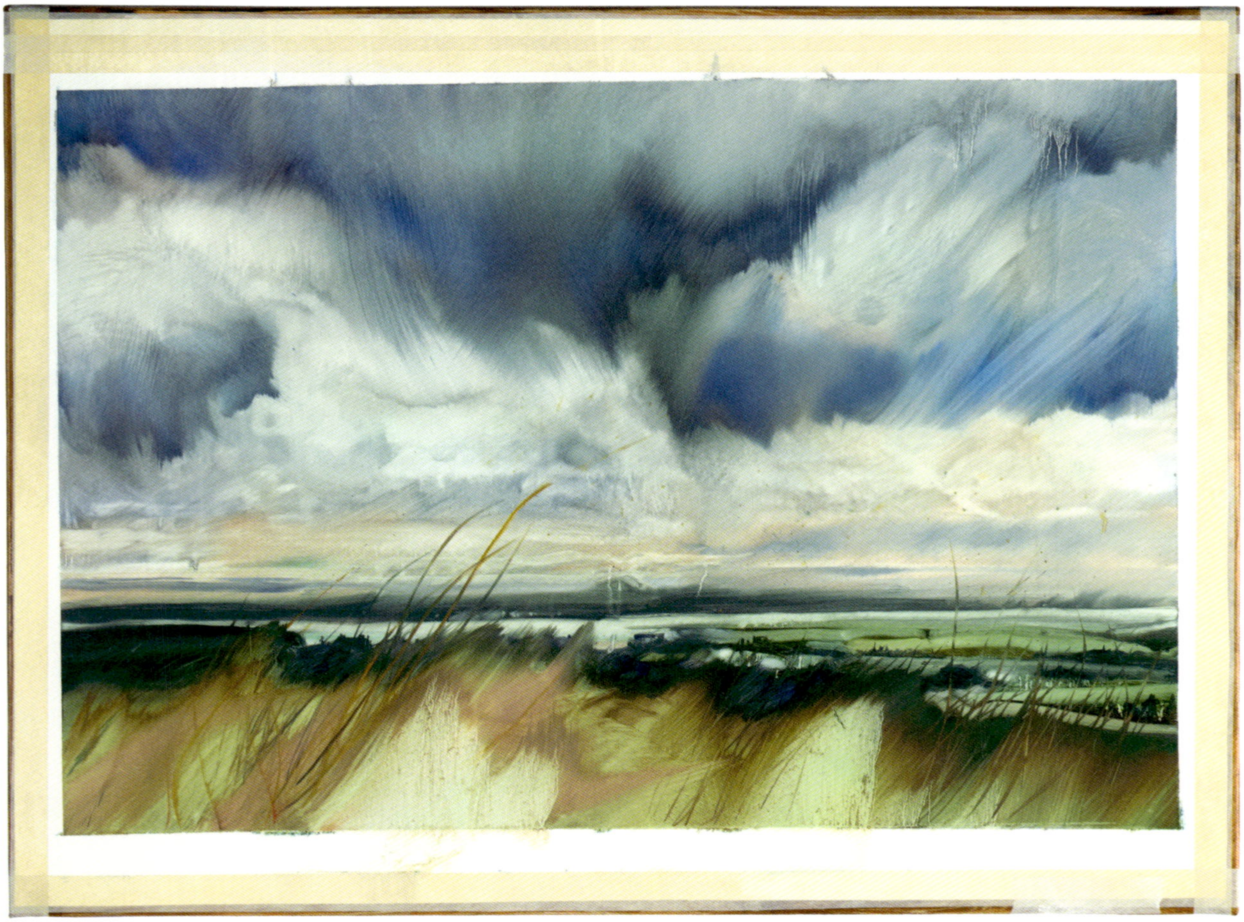

Look to Windward, Dunnet Head 2023 Oil and acrylic on canvas 56 × 76 cm

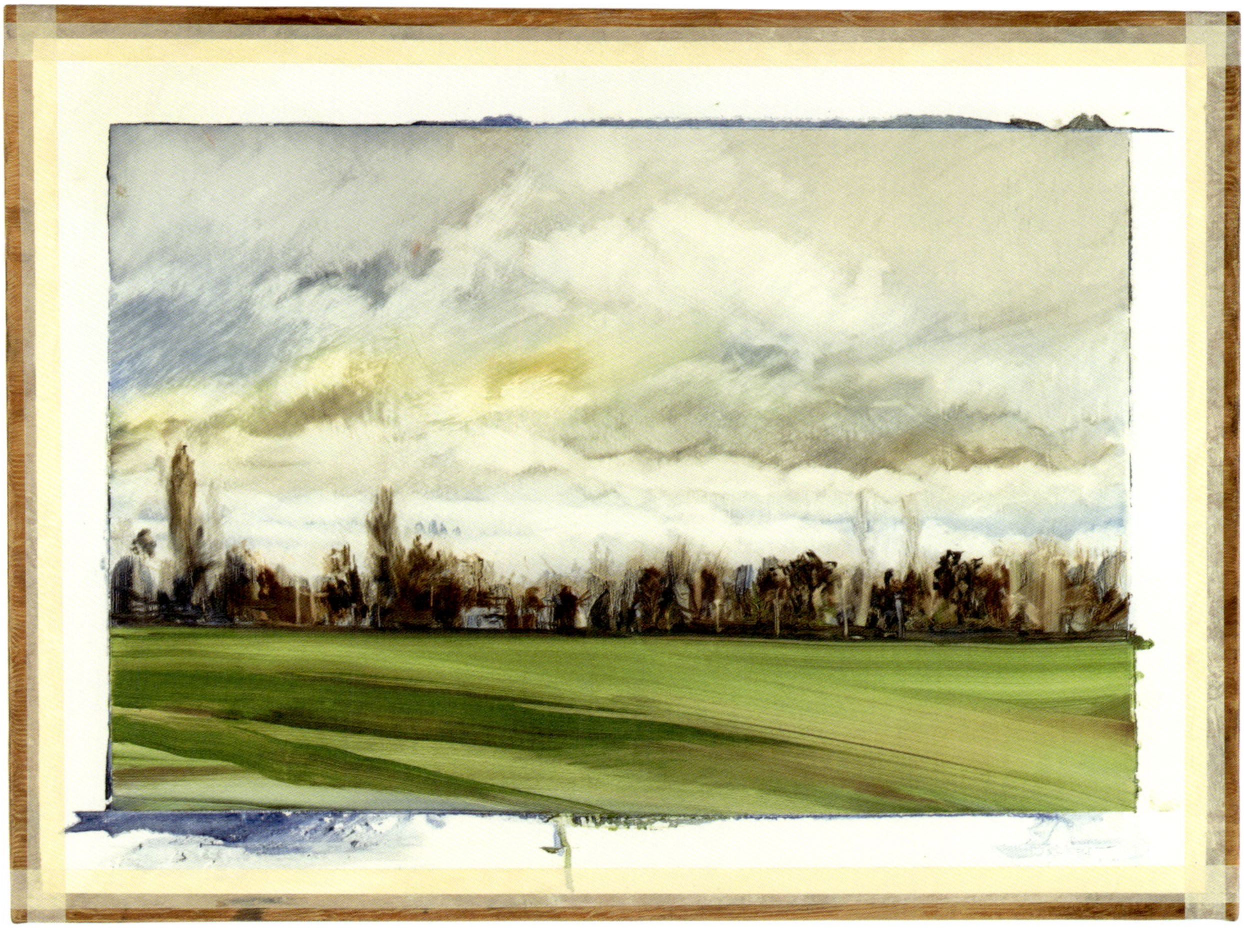

Tooting Common, January Sky 2023 Oil and acrylic on canvas 56 × 76 cm

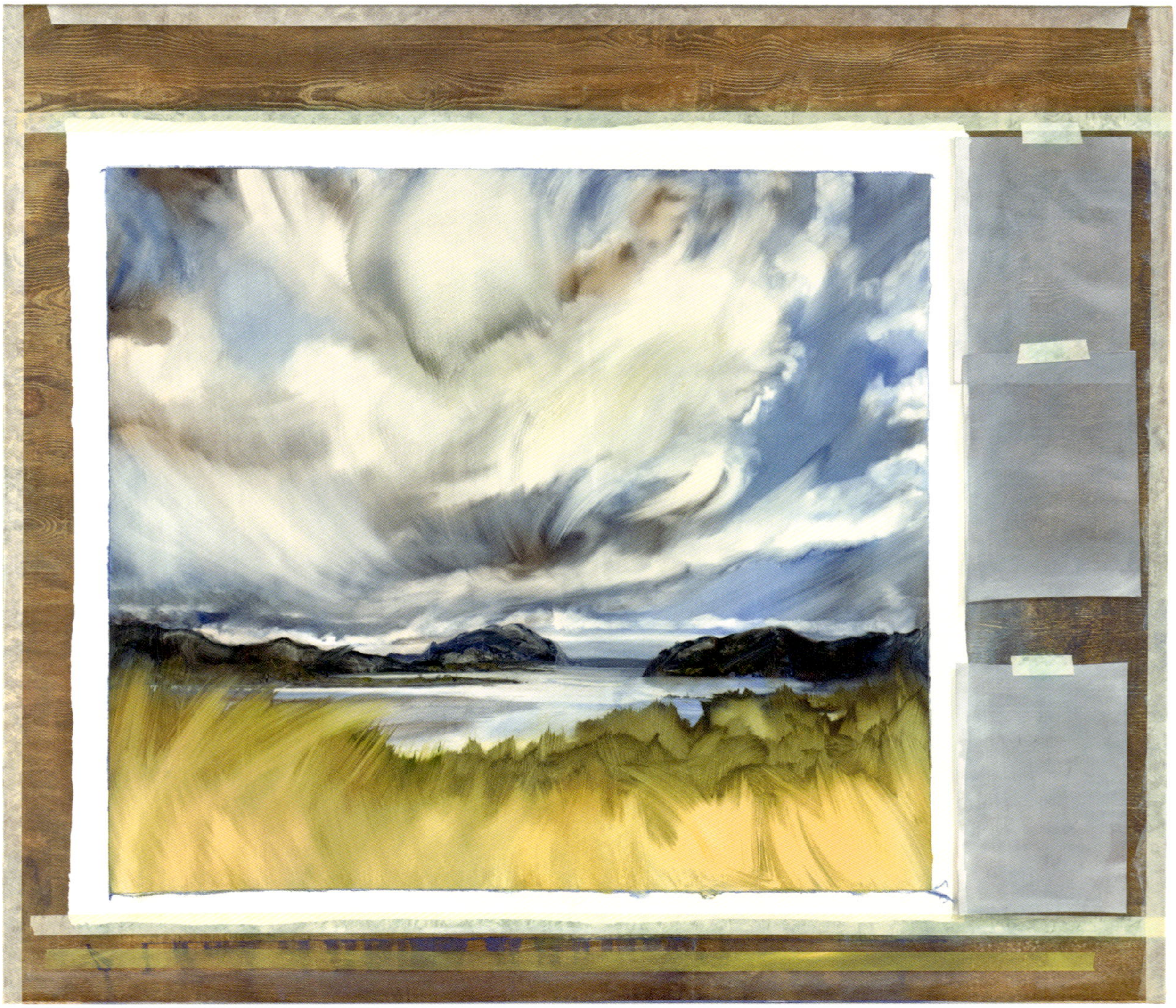

Above As Below, Bowglass 2023 Oil and acrylic on canvas 120 × 140 cm

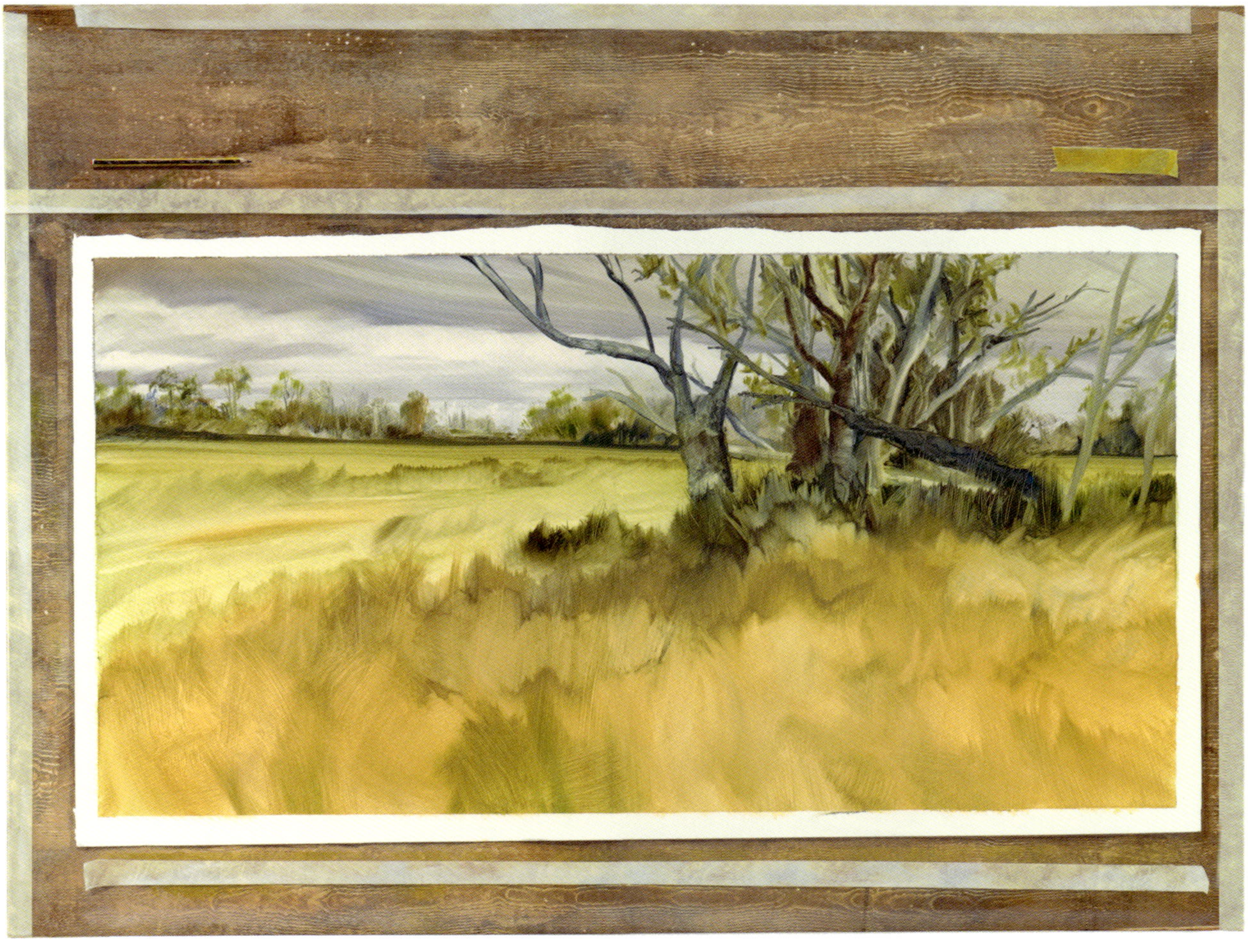

A Rustle Through the Grass, Richmond Park 2023 Oil and acrylic on canvas 90 × 120 cm

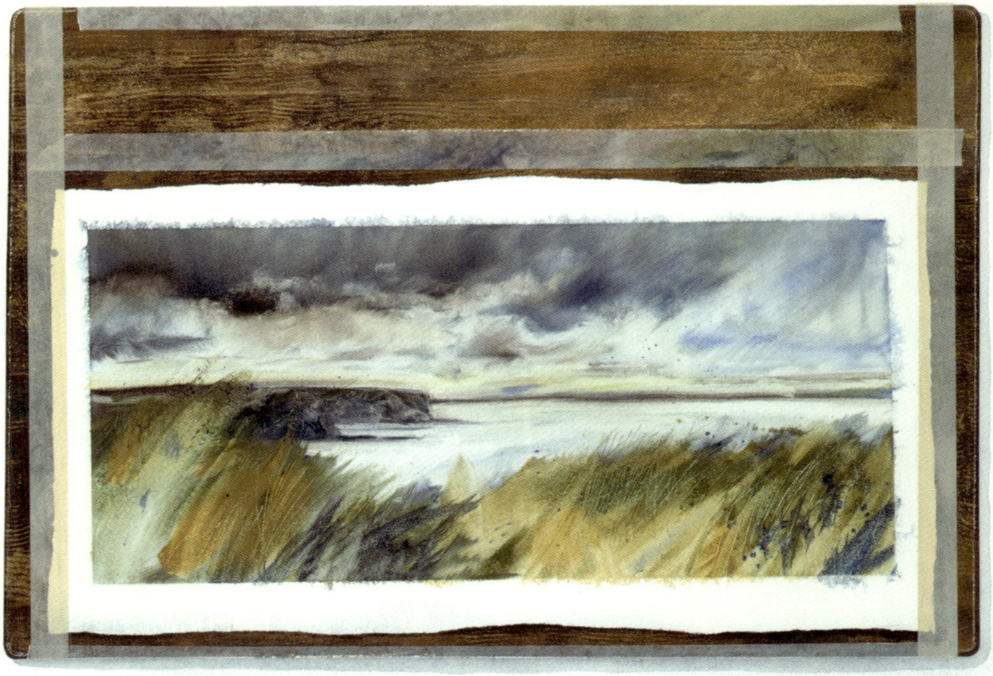

A Certain Exchange Between Salt and Pigment 2022 Oil and acrylic on paper 58 × 77 cm

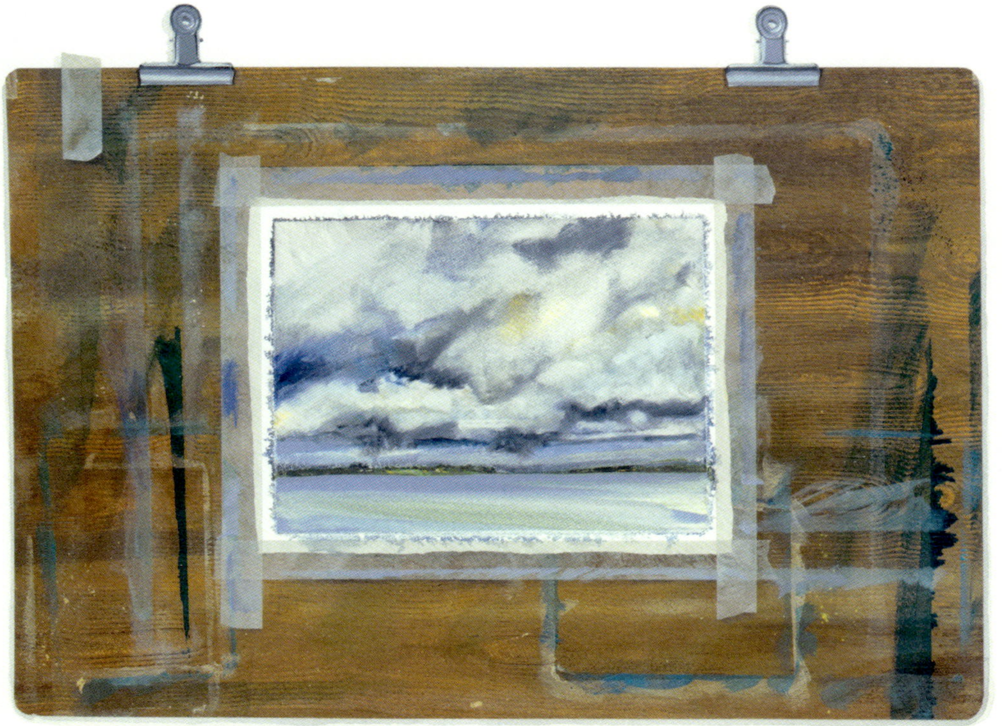

The Very Act of Things Unseen 2022 Oil and acrylic on paper 58 × 77 cm

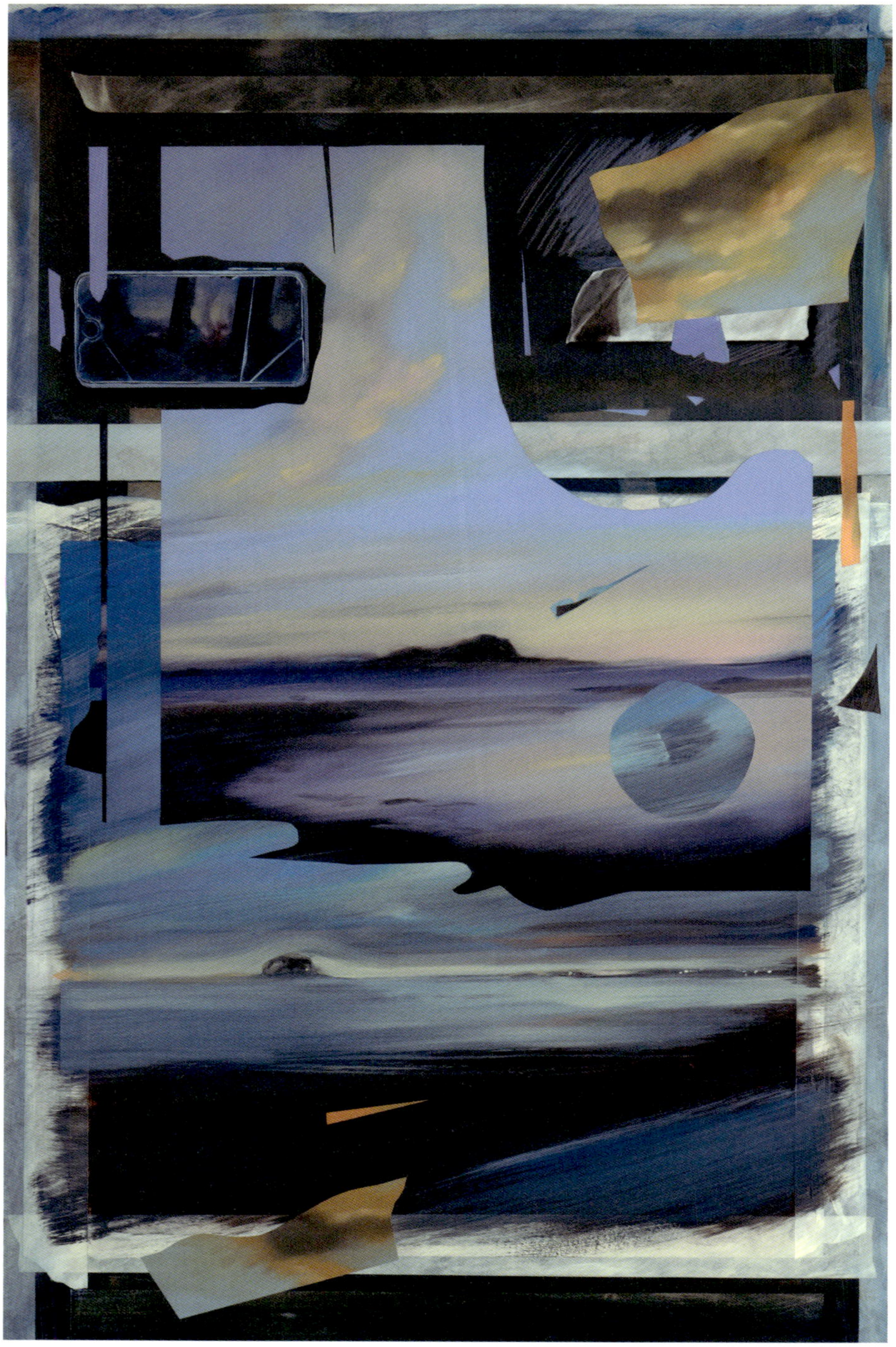

Astonishment in the Terrain of the Familiar 2022 Oil on panel 90 × 60 cm

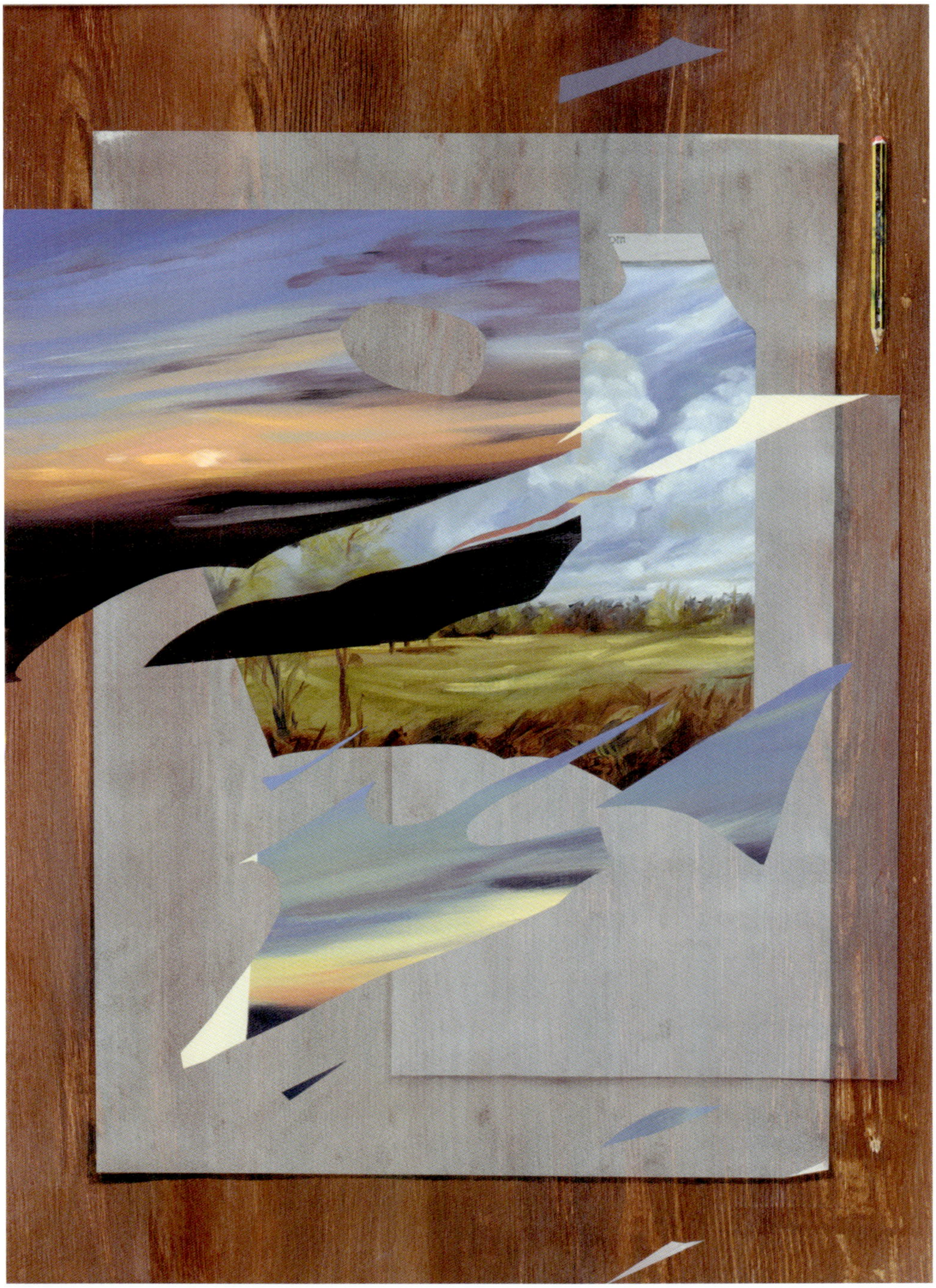

For Going Out Was Really Going In 2022 Oil and acrylic on canvas 76 × 56 cm

Artist's Acknowledgements

I would like to thank Howard and Roberta Ahmanson who funded this book through Fieldstead and Company, not only for their financial support and generosity of ideas but also their friendship and fellowship over many years; to Vivienne Roberts, of Aleph Contemporary, who first suggested this book; to Herman Lelie and Stefania Bonelli whose tireless work in designing this book, attention to detail and enthusiasm for working lunches have made the whole process a joy; Matt Price of Anomie Publishing for his steady hand and advice; Jorella Andrews and Julia Lucero for their words and generosity to sit with the work to really see it. I am part of a monthly crit group with artists Kieran Dodds, Anna Freeman Bentley, Craig Jefferson and Cully whose friendship and critique have been invaluable; to Sally Redway for our weekly conversations. Thank you my friends. My greatest thanks go to my wife Anna whose love and patience have supported me through this project and the paintings it represents. Some of our experiences are shared through these paintings. Anna, I love living these stories with you.

Alastair Gordon
Quodlibet

Edited by Alastair Gordon Studio
Designed and produced by Herman Lelie
Layouts by Stefania Bonelli
Copy-editing by Anna McNay
Proofreading by William Lambie
Repro by DPM, London
Printed and bound by EBS, Verona

Photography by Anna Arca, Martin Sturgess and Alastair Gordon Studio

Works replicated in montages include: p. 53: Elizabeth Peyton, Donald Judd; p. 54: William Gillies, Elizabeth Blackadder; p. 105: Henry Raeburn, *The Reverend Robert Walker Skating on Duddingston Loch*, 1795, oil on canvas, 76.2 × 63.5 cm. National Galleries of Scotland, Edinburgh.
Images reproduced with permission. All efforts were made to source copyright approvals.

Published in 2023 by Anomie Publishing, London
www.anomie-publishing.com

A catalogue record for this book is available from the British Library

ISBN: 978-1-910221-48-8

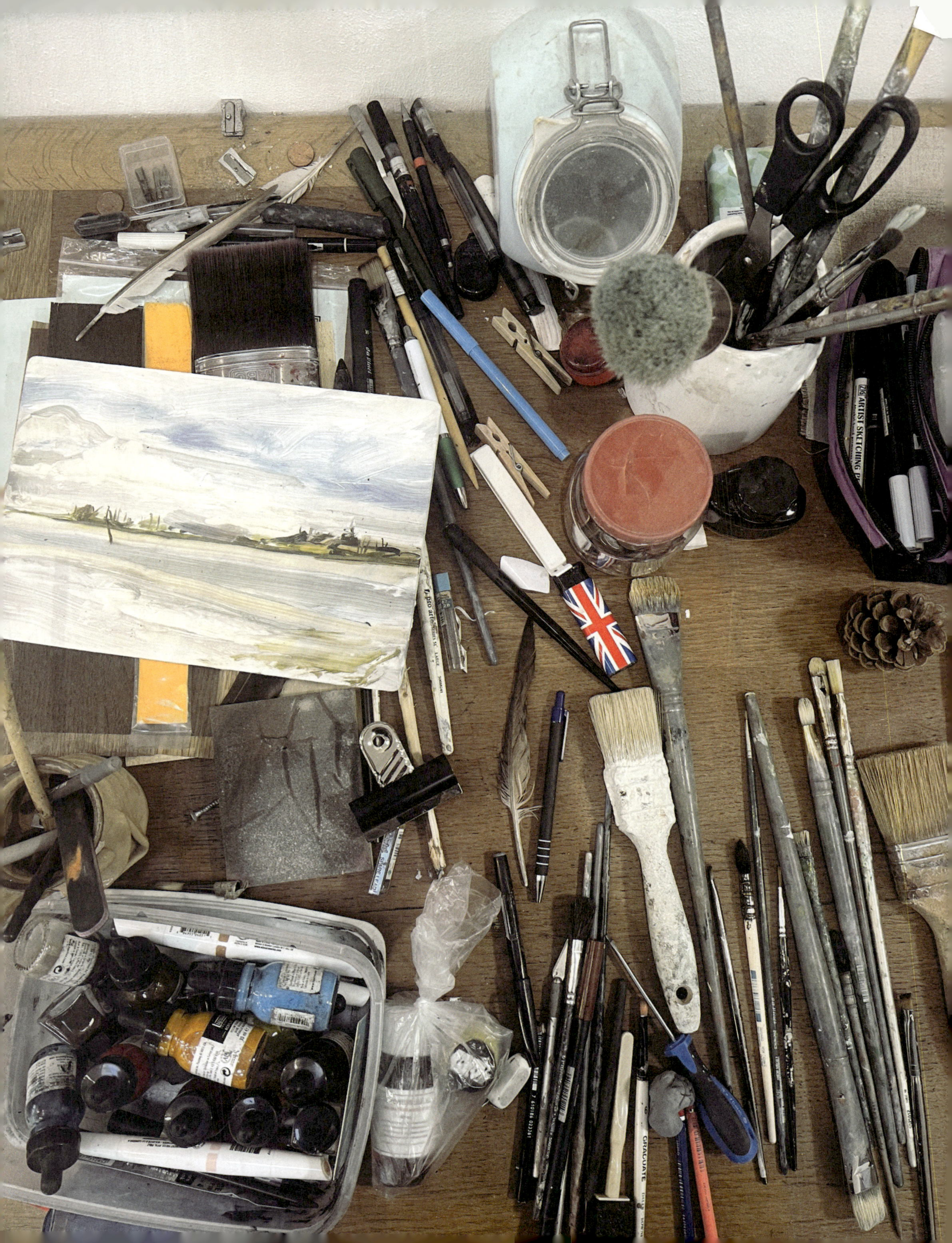
ARTIST SKETCHING
pro arte
GRADUATE